From Fact to Fiction

FROM FACT TO FICTION

Journalism & Imaginative Writing in America

Shelley Fisher Fishkin

Oxford University Press
New York   Oxford

Oxford University Press

Oxford   New York   Toronto
Delhi   Bombay   Calcutta   Madras   Karachi
Petaling Jaya   Singapore   Hong Kong   Tokyo
Nairobi   Dar es Salaam   Cape Town
Melbourne   Auckland

and associated companies in
Beirut   Berlin   Ibadan   Nicosia

First published in 1985 by Johns Hopkins Unversity Press,
701 West 40th Street, Baltimore, Maryland 21211

First issued as an Oxford University Press paperback, 1988

Oxford is a registered trademark of Oxford University Press

Library of Congress Cataloging in Publication Data

Fishkin, Shelley Fisher.
   From fact to fiction.

Revision of thesis (Ph. D.)—Yale University.
   Bibliography: p.
   Includes index.
   1. American fiction—History and criticism.
2. Journalism and literature—United States.
3. Journalism—United States—History.   4. Whitman,
Walt, 1819–1892—Criticism and interpretation.
I. Title.
PS374.J68F5 1985   813'.009   84–27765
ISBN 0-8018-2546-6 (alk. paper)
ISBN 0-19-520638-X (PPBK.)

2   4   6   8   10   9   7   5   3   1

Printed in the United States of America

To my father,
Milton Fisher,
and to the memory
of my mother,
Renée B. Fisher

The poets are thus liberating gods.
The ancient British bards had for
the title of their order, "Those who
are free throughout the world."
They are free, and they make free.
—Ralph Waldo Emerson,
"The Poet"

CONTENTS

PHOTOGRAPHS

ACKNOWLEDGMENTS

This book began as a Ph.D. thesis in American Studies at Yale, where it was nurtured by my advisor R. W. B. Lewis, whose fine insights and invaluable criticism were essential to this project's inception and completion. John Hersey and the late Charles Davis, both members of my doctoral-dissertation committee, supported my work with useful suggestions and warm enthusiasm; I am grateful to both for their help.

Scholars from literature, history, journalism, sociology, and a myriad of other fields, as well as practicing novelists and journalists, have offered valued encouragement and advice. I have benefited, at one stage or another of my work on this project, from suggestions and comments, from Harold Bloom, Warren Susman, Charles Feidelson, Michael Cooke, Michael Roemer, A. Bartlett Giamatti, William Ferris, Daniel Aaron, Mark Rose, the late Howard Sayre Weaver, Richard Leonard, William R. Taylor, Buchi Emecheta, Stanley Elkin, Linda Peterson, Marion Poynter, Eugene Patterson, Max Kampelman, Michael Harrington, Roy Peter Clark, Joanne Braxton, Leslie Rado, Henry Louis Gates, Jr., Michael Schudson, Ken Goldstein, Marty Linsky, David Eason, Jon Rieder, Joseph B. Treaster, Amy Kaplan, Alan Trachtenberg, and William Stott.

A number of journalists I have brought to Yale as Poynter Fellows have helped to focus my attention on critical issues surrounding the role of the media: John Chancellor, I. F. Stone, Ben Bradlee, Oriana Fallaci, Peter Davis, Fred Freed, Jeff Greenfield, Norman Mailer, Harold Evans, William A. Henry III, Robert Scheer, Steven R. Weisman, Christopher Lehmann-Haupt, Penny Lernoux, Erwin Knoll, John Gross, Jack Beatty, R. W. Apple, Jr., Jonathan Schell, Mercedes Lynn de Uriarte, Susan Stamberg, Richard Pollak, and Leon Wieseltier. I would like to thank the Aspen Institute Program on Communications and Society for having sponsored my participation in a conference on "The News Media and the Democratic Process," where I benefited from discussions with Michael Rice, Catherine Gay, Adolpho Critto, and others.

Many of the ideas in this book took shape during the three years in which I taught a seminar on "The Journalist as Novelist" in American Studies at Yale. I am grateful to all of my students for the questions and comments that helped focus my thoughts on the intersections between journalism and fiction.

I would like to thank the staffs of the Beinecke Rare Book Library at Yale, the Sterling Memorial Library at Yale, the University of Pennsylvania Library, the Library of Congress, the New York Public Library, the Kennedy Library, and the Mark Twain Memorial, as well as George Burg, executive assistant to the president of the *Kansas City Star* and *Kansas City Times*, and Sidney Goldberg, vice president and executive editor of United Feature Syndicate, for graciously providing me with material that made my research enjoyable and rewarding.

I am grateful to Eric Halpern, my editor at Johns Hopkins, for all of his expert guidance.

I am indebted to Richard Nelson and David Colesworthy of the Institution for Social and Policy Studies at Yale for having enabled me to complete this project in such a supportive and congenial environment, and to Beverly Apothaker and Janice Feldstein for their painstaking preparation of this manuscript.

I am grateful to Carol Plaine Fisher, Fanny Fishkin, David Fishkin, and the late Yetta Breger for their untiring enthusiasm and unwavering support, and to my sons Joseph and Robert, for having sustained me so richly throughout the work of writing this book. I would like to thank Flora Gibson for all her understanding and patient help; she enabled me to bring this project to fruition.

My father, Milton Fisher, has helped shape this book with outstanding critical insights, valuable editorial suggestions, and unending encouragement and support. My mother, the late Renée B. Fisher, nurtured in me the love of literature, language, and life that sparked my initial interest in this project and sustained it to its end.

I am immensely grateful to my husband, Jim Fishkin, for his advice and encouragement all along the way. He provided a combination of insight, judgment, enthusiasm, and warm support which destined this project to be both completable and enjoyable.

INTRODUCTION

Walt Whitman spent twenty-five years as a journalist before he published his first book of poems. Mark Twain was a journalist for twenty years before the publication of his first novel. The ranks of America's greatest imaginative writers overflow with men and women who served apprenticeships as reporters of fact. The list of great poets or dramatists or novelists whose careers began in journalism includes not only Walt Whitman, Mark Twain, Theodore Dreiser, Ernest Hemingway, and John Dos Passos, but also John Greenleaf Whittier, William Dean Howells, Stephen Crane, Ambrose Bierce, Jack London, Frank Norris, Upton Sinclair, Willa Cather, James Farrell, Katherine Anne Porter, John Steinbeck, Richard Wright, Eugene O'Neill, Robert Frost, Eudora Welty, James Agee, James Weldon Johnson, Sinclair Lewis, Carl Sandburg, John Hersey, and countless others.

The pattern itself, of course, is not unique to America. In the nineteenth century, Dickens in Britain or Zola in France comes to mind; in the twentieth century, the list would include Britain's George Orwell, Argentina's Gabriel Garcia Marquez, Peru's Mario Vargas Llosa, and Nigeria's Buchi Emecheta. But if the phenomenon is not uniquely American the frequency with which it has occurred in this country is. It is surprising, therefore, that it has received so little attention.

Critics and scholars of American literature have paid a price for this neglect. By glossing over the continuities between the journalism and fiction of these great writers they have missed an important aspect of American literary history and biography. By failing to focus on the *dis*continuities between their journalism and their fiction they have lost an opportunity to gain special insight into the limits and potential of different narrative forms. This book hopes to redress some of that neglect by exploring the continuities and discontinuities in the journalism and fiction of five great American writers.

Walt Whitman, Mark Twain, Theodore Dreiser, Ernest Hemingway, and John Dos Passos all worked as journalists in their youths—in New York during the heyday of the penny press in the 1840s; on the Comstock lode and in California in the 1860s; in Chicago, St. Louis, Pittsburgh, and New York in the 1890s; in Kansas City in 1918 and in Europe during the twenties and thirties; in Spain and Boston in the 1920s. Each of them was lucky enough to seek his first job as a writer at a time of expansion and opportunity in American journalism. The social, economic, technological, and demographic changes that helped give birth to the penny press in the East in the 1830s and 1840s, and to the Western Press in the 1850s and 1860s created hundreds of new newspapers and a host of new jobs that young men like Whitman and Twain were delighted to fill. Changes in the role of advertising helped give rise to thick Sunday supplements, expanded daily papers, and new mass circulation ten-cent magazines in the 1890s, creating opportunities for Theodore Dreiser that might not have been there had he come of age a decade earlier. William Rockhill Nelson's innovation of giving *Kansas City Star* subscribers an unprecedented thirteen papers a week for ten cents was an acclaimed success by the time Ernest Hemingway graduated from high school in 1918; the *Star*'s single-minded focus on nothing but the news (no gimmicks, no comics, no giveaways) and its expanded production schedule created openings for bright young reporters like Hemingway. John Dos Passos started his career as a freelance writer at a time when serious journals were multiplying profusely. Within months of graduating from college in 1916, for example, he sold his first article to a two-year-old weekly called the *New Republic*. The *Seven Arts*, begun in 1916, and the *Liberator*, begun in 1918, were two other new journals interested in what Dos Passos had to contribute in the 1920s. Two publications founded several years later, the *New Masses* (1926) and the *Daily Worker* (1924), would assign him to cover the story that would eventually inspire *U.S.A.*

This early apprenticeship in journalism exposed each writer to a vast range of experience that would ultimately form the core of his greatest imaginative works. It forced him to become a precise observer, nurtured in him a respect for fact, and taught him lessons about style that would shape his greatest literary creations. It taught him to be mistrustful of rhetoric, abstractions, hypocrisy, and cant; it taught him to be suspicious of secondhand accounts and to insist on seeing with his own eyes. It was as journalists that Whitman, Twain, Dreiser, Hemingway, and Dos Passos first discovered the importance, as Emerson once put it, of "fronting the fact, not dealing with it at secondhand, through the perceptions of somebody else."[1] (Journalism, of course, was not the only important influence on these writers' development. Their parents, families, and friends, the books they read, the operas and plays they attended, etc., are not explored here since they have received ample attention elsewhere, forming the core of many biographical and critical studies. Their education and experience as journalists, however, have received only casual attention.)[2]

The celebration of concrete, commonplace American realities, so central to Whitman's poetry, stems from his early work on the *New York*

Aurora, as do his earliest direct addresses to his reader. The respect for fact that runs through every page of *Adventures of Huckleberry Finn*, the structure of the book, the vernacular hero's dialect, and the moral concerns that are at the book's core, are rooted in Twain's early journalism, as is his skepticism of books as a source of truth or a guide for action. The turgid and expansive quality of Dreiser's prose can be traced to lessons he learned as a journalist in the 1890s, as can his insight into the dynamics of American society and the distorted images of it presented in newspapers and fiction. Hemingway acquired the terse and concrete style for which he is famous from his apprenticeship a generation later on the *Kansas City Star;* his respect for fact and suspicion of fiction are similarly rooted in his early experiences as a journalist. John Dos Passos first explored in nonfiction the subjects and strategies that would be central to his greatest work as an artist; it was as a journalist that he first became aware of the limitations of conventional nonfiction narrative to move people to reexamine their present and their past.

These apprenticeships in journalism help to explain not only the roots of the particular subjects, styles, and strategies that characterize the work of these authors, but also the contours of what one might consider a distinctively American aesthetic. What is American about American literature? The question has challenged critics for decades. Two qualities mentioned time and time again as being distinctively American might be best understood in the context of these writers' early experiences as journalists: (1) what Philip Rahv called "the cult of experience in American writing,"[3] and (2) what F. O. Matthiessen called "the frequent American need to begin all over again from scratch."[4]

In 1940 Philip Rahv suggested that the "basic theme and unifying principle" of American writing since Whitman was "the urge toward and immersion in experience." In his essay on "The Cult of Experience in American Writing," Rahv contrasts the " 'instinctive disregard of actual fact' " that characterized the literature of early America with "the primacy of American experience" that one finds in Whitman, and in poetry and fiction after Whitman.[5] Cleanth Brooks and Robert Penn Warren have reiterated this theme, citing the premium writers such as Hemingway placed upon "experience as such," as opposed to, say, ideas or ideologies or the shaping of values.[6] Yet nowhere in this recognition of "the urge toward and immersion in experience" is it noted that an astonishing proportion of major American writers since Whitman learned their craft as reporters of fact, that their first jobs required them to immerse themselves in the world around them and report what they saw, heard, and felt. No doubt there are many reasons why a "cult of experience" has dominated American letters since Whitman; but surely the rich apprenticeships these writers served as journalists should be counted among them.

Critics have often noted the tendency of American writers to improvise, to write as if no one had ever written a work of fiction before them, to continually "begin all over again from scratch," as F. O. Matthiessen put it.[7] R. W. B. Lewis observed that American "writers who even forgot that there was anything to remember have found themselves remote alike from their predecessors and their contemporaries."[8] From the nineteenth century on, this attitude often puzzled Europeans who saw their own artists comfortably entrenched within clearly identifiable traditions. Stephen Crane, a journalist before he turned to fiction, complained that Englishmen were forever exasperating him with questions like "from what French realist [he] shall steal [his] next book." Crane could not convince his inquisitor that his art was fueled not by the work of other artists but by facts he had personally witnessed (and documented in the daily press). "I told a seemingly sane man at Mrs. Garnett's that I got my artistic education on the Bowery, and he said, 'Oh really? So they have a school of fine arts there?' "[9]

Oblivious, by choice or by chance, to literary forebears and available cultural traditions, American writers have continually struggled to wrest art from the raw material of life as if no one had ever done so before. Writers who started out as journalists learned the lessons of what to look for, how to find it, and how to write about it largely on their own— with small assists from their peers in the newsroom. If they read poetry or fiction, the eccentric hodgepodge of popular favorites and classics they were likely to encounter had little to do with the kind of writing that paid their bills. When they first set out to write poems or novels themselves their crude notions of what "art" should look and feel like led them to produce, nearly without exception, uninspired verse and conventional stories—bad stuff that tried to fulfill the "demands" of the form as they saw it. Posterity would not miss much by being deprived of Whitman's early trite verse and maudlin temperance tales, young Twain's cliché-ridden doggerel and amusing but shallow light fiction, Dreiser's first (and only) disastrous comic opera, Hemingway's early heavy-handed short stories, or Dos Passos's first affected poems and effete fictional narratives. Each came to abandon these formulas in favor of a looser, freer, more eclectic approach that embraced whatever they chose to bring along from their careers as journalists. From Whitman through Dos Passos, people and subjects that had never before appeared in a work of imaginative literature in this country began to populate the American literary scene; styles that might have been at home in the nation's newspapers began to push their way into works of art. These writers succeeded as writers of fiction only when they returned, in new and creative ways, to material and approaches they had first come to know as documenters of fact. The result was a set of books that were brilliant, fresh, original, and distinctively American. The weird, wild, one-of-a-kind, Rube Goldberg-like literary structures they made—such as *Leaves of Grass* or *Adventures of Huckleberry Finn* or *U.S.A.*—work, despite their apparent violation of the laws of literary mechanics. There are, no doubt, many reasons why our writers are so cheerfully indifferent to their literary predecessors and peers. Their experiences as journalists, however, should be on the list: it was as journalists that they acquired the skills, the confidence, and the raw material they needed to "start all over again from scratch" and make it work. For that is, indeed, just what they did.

Why did these writers leave journalism? Each, of course, had his own reason for making the move to poetry or fiction. Some common themes, however, crop up again and again: censorship, boredom, and, most important of all, a sense that conventional journalism could engage a reader's mind and emotions in only very limited ways.

Whitman, Twain, Dreiser, Hemingway, and Dos Passos each encountered one or another variety of censorship during his career as a journalist. The subjects involved—slavery, prostitution, racism, economic inequality, and exploitation, the Spanish civil war, political persecution—would come up again in their fiction, where they would explore them with greater freedom. (It is an interesting footnote to literary history that these writers sometimes came up against censorship again after they turned to fiction—but for different reasons. No one objected to Dreiser's depicting in fiction the economic inequalities and exploitation that as a young journalist in Pittsburgh he had been instructed to ignore; his relatively open treatment of sex, however, resulted in the banning of *An American Tragedy* in Boston. Seventy years after Twain published *Adventures of Huckleberry Finn* his candid portrait of white America's racism—a subject his San Francisco newspaper editors had refused to touch for fear of alienating their racist subscribers—still drew censure, but on different grounds. Civil rights groups objected to his use of the word "nigger," and for many years the novel was banned from the curriculum in New York City schools.)

The task of covering "acreage," as Twain once put it, of filling the pages of a newspaper day after day, took its toll on the writers who worked on dailies. "San Francisco is a city of startling events," Twain wrote with undisguised disdain in the *Enterprise* in 1865. "Happy is the man whose destiny it is to gather them up and record them in a daily newspaper. . . . How dangerously exciting must be the employment of writing them up for the daily papers!"[10] "After having been hard at work from nine or ten in the morning until eleven at night scraping material together," he recalled some forty years later, "I took the pen and spread this muck out in words and phrases and made it cover as much acreage as I could. It was fearful drudgery, soulless drudgery, and almost destitute of interest."[11] On slow days, when nothing much was going on, Whitman found himself writing tongue-in-cheek editorials about how to concoct tongue-in-cheek editorials out of nothing. Dreiser was driven to distraction by dull and meaningless assignments; he quit newspaper work soon after being sent to cover extraterrestrial manifestations near Elizabeth, New Jersey. Hemingway found writing for newspapers boring and unsatisfying after Gertrude Stein began igniting his interest in more creative endeavors. "I am going to chuck journalism, I think," he wrote Stein in 1923, "You ruined me as a journalist last winter. Have been no good since."[12]

While censorship and boredom probably played a role in the decision of each of these writers to leave journalism, even more important were his rising doubts about the ability of conventional journalism to do justice to the complexities of the world he encountered.

These writers appreciated the role of the press in a democracy—educating, informing, unmasking hypocrisy and fraud, providing citizens with the facts on which they could base their participation in the polity. They understood that the power of the press was rooted in the trust it inspired in its readers, who believed what they read in the papers to be true. They viewed this trust as both a blessing and a burden—and a frequent source of discomfort, as well. For the limits of conventional journalism as they knew it—the subjects that were excluded, the superficial, formulaic treatment of subjects that *were* discussed, the lack of connection to any time but the present, the extravagant claims to authoritativeness, the failure to challenge the reader to think for himself—were apparent to them as well.[13] It was as poets and novelists that they both spotlighted and transcended those limitations, writing texts designed to engage the reader's mind and emotions in ways their journalism never could.

Where the formulaic newspaper story allowed the reader to distance himself from the people about whom he read, the poem or novel encouraged emotional intimacy with them. While the journalism was designed to appear "understandable in itself," as Walter Benjamin once put it,[14] the fiction focused on the complexity and opacity of experience, raising more questions than it answered. While the journalism implicitly reaffirmed the reader's familiar habits of thought and categories for understanding the world, the imaginative writing challenged those habits and categories and urged him to try on unfamiliar perspectives. The conventional nonfiction narratives they wrote as journalists were designed to be taken at face value by passive readers who would trust what they read; the self-effacing, open-ended, fiction-blasting fictions they wrote as poets or novelists were designed to create active readers capable of questioning everything they read and of constructing new patterns of meaning on their own.[15] While the journalist could hope, at best, to shape the reader's view of a specific phenomenon or event, the imaginative writer aspired to nothing less than transforming the reader's way of seeing.

When Whitman, Twain, Dreiser, Hemingway, and Dos Passos grew impatient with the limits of conventional journalism they turned to fiction. The move made sense. Liberated from what Douglass Cater once called the "straitjacket of straight reporting," these writers produced the masterworks of fiction that help to define the American literary tradition. When Tom Wolfe and other writers grew impatient with the limits of conventional journalism in the 1960s their goal was the same as that which propelled these writers from fact to fiction: they wanted, as Wolfe put it, "to excite the reader both intellectually and emotionally"[16] in ways that conventional journalism could not. But unlike these earlier writers, they saw no need to turn away from the world of fact. They still wanted "to write accurate non-fiction," Wolfe asserted, but they wanted to do so using "techniques usually associated with novels and short stories."[17] In the 1980s, we are witness to another phenomenon in which reporters borrow not only the techniques of the fiction writer but also his prerogatives, presenting their own inventions as fact within the format of conventional journalism. In our final chapter we will briefly explore some recent efforts to "have it all"—to appropriate the novelist's tricks-of-the-trade without forfeiting the journalist's special claim on the reader's trust. Recent public dismay at fabrications by Janet Cooke in the *Washington Post*, by Michael Daly in the

New York Daily News, by Christopher Jones in the *New York Times*, and by Alastair Reid in the *New Yorker* suggest that the marriage of fact and fiction hailed in the sixties may be on the rocks: the time has come to redraw those elusive boundaries that separate the world of the journalist from the world of the imaginative writer.

2

WALT
WHITMAN

Walt Whitman as a young journalist in
New York City in the early 1840s.

Photo credit: Brown Brothers

Twelve-year-old Walt Whitman got his first job in a newspaper office in 1831 on the eve of a revolution in American journalism. That revolution was destined to change forever the nature of newspapers in America. Through its influence on Whitman, it changed the shape of American literature as well.

Before the 1830s newspapers in America had consisted solely of party organs and commercial advertisers priced above the means of the average citizen. During the 1830s a combination of technological and demographic developments gave birth to a new, cheap, and different kind of newspaper. The "penny press," born in the 1830s, catered to the increasingly literate masses of the country's growing urban centers. While the earlier papers had offered a fare of advertising, shipping notices, and political editorials, the penny press was responsible, as Michael Schudson has put it, for having "invented the modern concept of the 'news.'"[1] It was during this decade that newspapers in America first began to concentrate on reporting "facts"; and facts close to home began to receive more emphasis than any others.

For the first time thousands of Americans began to see scenes from everyday life in print. For the first time in this country young men found jobs as reporters, and were sent roaming about the city streets, police stations, and courthouses to report events they witnessed. As these young men began to compete with one another for the timeliness, liveliness, and accuracy of their reports, their employers vied among themselves for the attention and loyalty of the citizen who, for a penny or two, could purchase one of a dozen papers hawked on the street on his way home from work. While the penny papers were generally ignored by American intellectuals, they did not escape the notice of Alexis de Tocqueville. "The inhabitants of the United States," he wrote, "have, then, at present, properly speaking, no literature. The only authors whom I acknowledge as American are the journalists. They indeed are not great writers, but they speak the language of their countrymen and make themselves heard."[2]

Those who migrated to the city from the village in the 1830s lost the institution of the village gossip and the sense of knowing, through the grapevine, what was going on around them. Benjamin H. Day was the first American entrepreneur to cash in on that most basic and universal of human qualities, curiosity. Day's *New York Sun*, founded in 1833, promised "to lay before the public, at a price within the means of every one, all the news of the day"[3] and at the same time afford an advantageous medium for advertising. For a penny a day, porters, draymen, carpenters, barbers, signpainters, mechanics, butchers, tailors, and milk-men could read about everything "from the gold mines of Georgia to the gold vaults of the Bank . . . from Alabama squatters to psalm-singing Puritans . . . from Cincinnati pork to Brussels lace."[4]

Two years after Day founded the *Sun* James Gordon Bennett founded the *New York Herald* and expanded Day's original formula by adding political essays, commercial and financial news, tidbits from abroad, and editorials on a wide range of subjects. He also urged a new role for the newspaper, one which would be accepted by Whitman when he capped his own journalistic career with an important editorial post. In an early *Herald* editorial, Bennett asked,

> What is to prevent a daily newspaper from being made the greatest
> organ of social life? Books have had their day—the theatres have had
> their day—the temple of religion has had its day. A newspaper can
> be made to take the lead of all these in the great movements of hu-
> man thought and human civilization. A newspaper can send more
> souls to Heaven, and save more from Hell, than all the churches or
> chapels in New York—besides making money at the same time.[5]

As Bennett saw it, newspapers could carve a unique niche for themselves as shapers of popular thought. His dream of influence and respectability would be shared by fellow editors throughout the century that followed.

The revolution of the penny press made it possible for a young man like Whitman to earn a living by walking through the city streets and capturing for his readers what he saw. Before that, no subsidy for such walks had been available; the penny press gave Whitman a profession to which he was temperamentally well-suited. What began as a job, however, would soon be transformed into a calling. And American letters would never be the same.

Whitman's first job was at the *Long Island Patriot*, a Tammany-supported weekly where he was taught how to sort fonts, dampen paper, ink type, and pull impressions. By 1835, at sixteen, after having worked in several printing shops, he had become a full-fledged journeyman printer. His appetite whetted by the "sentimental bits" he had written for the *Patriot*, and by the "piece or two" he had contributed to the *New York Mirror*,[6] Whitman bought a used hand press and case of types for fifty dollars in 1839 and started his own weekly newspaper in Huntington, Long Island. The venture was short-lived due to financial problems and Whitman's own restlessness.

In 1841, near his twenty-second birthday, Whitman set out to try his luck as a newspaper man in New York City. By now New York boasted scores of new and independent dailies. The great newspaper war fought between Bennett's *Herald* and Greeley's *Tribune* fueled the fires of rivalry among all the papers in the city as hawkers on every busy street-corner competed for the patronage of the thousands of working people streaming by. Whitman's first real break came in 1842 when the editor of a twopenny paper for which he had freelanced was discharged for having printed libelous charges of graft against the city.

On March 28, 1842, the publishers of the *New York Aurora*, the fourth largest twopenny daily in New York City, announced the appointment of "Mr. Walter Whitman, favorably known as a bold, energetic and original writer," as their leading editor.[7] Whitman seems to have had the job for several weeks before this announcement; he would hold it officially for a little over a month. Whitman's pieces in the *Aurora*, some of his earliest extant journalism, have received virtually no critical attention, even from biographers as sensitive and skilled as Justin Kaplan and Paul Zweig.[8] But the brevity of this chapter in Whitman's life and the neglect it has suffered among critics should not belittle its significance. It was at the *Aurora* that Whitman first explored the material and method that he would later combine to produce the book which launched him as a poet.

"Without vanity," Whitman wrote in his editorial columns, "we can say that the *Aurora* is by far the best newspaper in town."[9] Aimed at the same public that bought the *Herald*, the *Tribune*, and the *Sun*, the *Aurora* bore a great physical resemblance to its competitors. But from its start in 1841 it devoted more columns than any other daily to the social life of the city. During the month that Whitman was at its helm, it also paid more attention than any other paper to the sights and sounds of everyday life in New York—to what Whitman called in an editorial about his paper, "pictures of life as it is."[10]

In the two weeks between March 14 and March 28, 1842, for example, Bennett's *Herald* carried a generous number of stories on local stabbings, murders, political debates, lectures, and letters from England; Greeley's *Tribune* supplemented these items with book reviews, concert notes, letters from China, and news from Mexico. There was nothing in either paper, however, like the city "walks" to which the reader of the *Aurora* was treated. It was in these pieces that Whitman first stumbled upon subjects, styles, stances, and strategies to which he would later return in *Leaves of Grass*.

An excerpt from one of these pieces, "Life in a New York Market," will illustrate these points. While an article titled "New York Market" published in Greeley's *Tribune* that day was filled with the prices of cotton and flour, the "Market" piece that appeared in Whitman's *Aurora* was dense with vivid concrete detail:

One Saturday night, not long since, a fantasy popped into our brain that we would like to take a stroll of observation through *a market*. Accordingly, sallying forth, we proceeded to put our wishes into execution. A short distance brought us to that large, dirty looking structure in Grand Street, where much store of meats, vegetables, et cetera, is daily dispensed to the sojourners of that section of our city.

We entered. What an array of rich, red sirloins, luscious steaks, delicate and tender joints, muttons, livers, and all the long list of various flesh stuffs, burst upon our eyes! There they hung, tempting, seductive—capable of begetting ecstasies in the mouth of an epicure—or curses in the throat of a Grahamite. By the powers of cookery! The condition of the republic is not so grievous after all; we cannot be on the verge of despair, when such spectacles as these may be witnessed in the land!

How the crowd rolls along! There comes a journeyman mason (we know him by his *limy* dress) and his wife—she bearing a little white basket on her arm. With what an independent air the mason looks around upon the fleshy wares; the secret of the matter is, that he has his past week's wages in his pocket, and therefore puts he on that devil-may-care countenance. So marvellous an influence hath money in making a man feel valiant and as good as his neighbor.

Notice that prim, red cheeked damsel, for whom is being weighed a small pork steak. She is maid of all work of an elderly couple, who have sent her to purvey for their morrow's dinner. How the young fellow who serves her, at the same time casts saucy, lovable glances at her pretty face; and she is nothing loth, but pleased enough at the chance of a little coquetry. . . .

With slow and languid steps moves along a white faced thin bodied, sickly looking middle aged man. He is dressed in a shabby suit, and no doubt will look long and watchfully before he spends the two cent pieces to which his outlay is limited. . . .

The fat, jolly featured woman is the keeper of a boarding house for mechanics, and every one else who chooses to take up with good solid accommodations, for a moderate price. She is foraging for her Sunday dinner. What is it to be? She has piece after piece taken down from its hook, but none seem to suit her. She passes on.

A heterogeneous mass, indeed, are they who compose the bustling crowd that fills up the passage way. Widows with sons, boys of twelve or fourteen, to walk with them for company; wives, whose husbands are left at home to "take care of the children"; servant women; cooks; . . . careful housewives of grades high and low; men with the look of a foreign clime; all sorts and sizes, kinds and ages, and descriptions, all wending, and pricing, and examining and purchasing.[11]

Nearly all of the subjects of Whitman's article—the people mentioned and the ideas explored—will find their way into the 1855 *Leaves of Grass*, and particularly into "Song of Myself." The mason, the wife, the young maid, and the sickly man will all reappear (as will the omnibus drivers, butchers, auctioneers, fashionable ladies, and firemen mentioned in other articles he wrote for the *Aurora*). And the two major themes seen in this market walk will be central to "Song of Myself": (1) the wonder of the "heterogeneous mass" (a variant on the "many in one" theme that would later be so important to him), the diversity of forms that make up life, of people who make up a crowd, a market, or a nation, and (2) the joys of "sallying forth" (as Whitman puts it here), into the market (and into life), the exhilaration he feels at being able to witness "such spectacles," at absorbing the dense richness of the world he documents.

These themes are developed by techniques that prefigure the style that will distinguish "Song of Myself." While vague and abstract phrases often intrude ("independent air," "the mouth of an epicure") they are counterweighted by a number of vivid and concrete images (the mason's wife's "little white basket," the maid's "small pork steak," the sickly man's "shabby suit"). Straining to evoke the scene before him in all its color and solidity, Whitman records the kind of specific concrete details which will later form the core of his poetry. One also sees the early use of the catalog technique to create the lush density of the world he documents (note, for example, his handling of the butcher's display). In another piece in the *Aurora* ("New York Boarding Houses") Whitman uses catalogs again to communicate the "many in one" or "unity within diversity" theme that so fascinated him: "It will perhaps surprise many persons to hear, but it is no less true, that half the inhabitants of the city hire accommodations at these [boardinghouses]. Married men and single men; old women and pretty girls; milliners and masons; cobblers, colonels, and counterjumpers; tailors and teachers; lieutenants, loafers, ladies, lackbrains and lawyers, printers and parsons, 'black spirits and white, blue spirits and gray'—all 'go out to board.'"[12] (This passage also represents the first occasion when Whitman recognized the resonance that alliteration and parallel stress lent to his theme of "unity in diversity.")

The stance that suits Whitman in his city sketches is that of a fascinated spectator moving in and out of the bustling scene before him, probing surfaces, charting depths, and setting in print the world he witnesses. As he walks, brushing shoulders with the flow of life he watches, or as he sits on a balcony and sees and hears from afar the world of the street, one recognizes the poet who would later characterize himself as "both in and out of the game, and watching and wondering at it."[13] Not content with surface pictures of a "red cheeked damsel" and a mason's "limy dress," Whitman probes pockets and polite exchanges for motives and meaning. As he projects his imagination behind the surface of the scene he witnesses, the reporter resembles the poet who in 1855 will write, "I force the surfaces and the depths also."

While the editorial "we" that narrates these articles will give way to the less pretentious "I" in "Song of Myself," the stance—the intently observant writer moving through the world, absorbing what he sees, recording it, filling out silhouettes, penetrating surfaces, making original connections, linking parts to wholes, casting forth in a new form the spectacle he saw—is, in large part, the same stance that will dominate "Song of Myself."

The strategies Whitman uses in the *Aurora* for involving the reader foreshadow techniques that will be central to his first great poem. He often addresses the reader as "you," injecting him into descriptive scenes with playful brashness. "Be careful, as you pass," he warns the reader of a story about the city a little before sunrise, "lest you get a sousing from some of those Irish servant women, scrubbing the marble stoops, and dashing pails of water upon the flagging of the side walks."[14] In another piece Whitman tries to lure his reader into the scene he paints with a direct invitation: "Reader, let us take a lounge together. Be'st thou gentle lady, or busy merchant, or indolent idler, or workingman, or student—it will do thee no harm. Nor, if high bred dame, needest thou stare at our familiarity; we only ask thee to lock arms with us—in imagination."[15] This request is, indeed, the same one Whitman will make of his reader in "Song of Myself."[16]

Whitman's willingness to let his reader in on the process by which his articles evolve can also be seen in the occasional humorous pieces Whitman wrote for the *Aurora* about writing. In one such piece ("How to Write a Leader") he shows his reader how he used his imagination to concoct an editorial on a day when nothing had happened. He begins the piece saying "Yesterday was dull, stupid, misty, cold, wet and disagreeable in every respect. We dawdled through the early hours, those between breakfast and dinner time—and the period of present writing can call to mind no occasion worthy of being noted down in this article, (which we intend, before we get through, to make very interesting and very amusing)."[17] He then proceeds to write a leader about writing a leader about the weather, showing the reader how (1) "an observant French writer," (2) some imaginary common fellows named "Higgins and Snugs," and (3) "one Whitman" of the *Aurora* might parlay the "dull, stupid, misty, cold, wet" weather into (respectively) a portentous novel, a banal conversation, or an amusing editorial. Whitman's strategy of sharing with the reader ways in which an imagination may "use" the weather may be seen as a precursor of section 6 of "Song of Myself," where Whitman shares with the reader the ways in which an imagination may "use" the grass.

Whitman's journalism for the *Aurora* was filled with the clichés, the posturing, the moralizing, and the political vituperation that characterized the large New York papers of his day. (Some of these qualities, indeed, occasionally would creep into *Leaves of Grass*, as well.)[18] In often rather undistinguished ways Whitman covered the requisite rallies and rows, fights and fires. But on occasion, Whitman's reports differ significantly from those of his competitors. His report of a city fire at Christie, Broome, and Delancey Streets on March 31, 1842, is a case in point.

The account of the fire in Bennett's *Herald* was briefer than that which appeared in Greeley's *Tribune* or Whitman's *Aurora*.[19] It was a dry, straightforward account of how the fire began and spread, and a list of some of the buildings destroyed and some of the people deprived of shelter. The article in Greeley's *Tribune* was substantially longer, with a fuller description of the origins and course of the blaze, a more complete account of the property destroyed (listing dollar value as well as street and number), and a more detailed list of the two thousand people who were injured or left homeless. It noted that many of the unfortunate people who had lived in the gutted buildings had "lost all of their furniture and the few household goods which years of frugal industry had enabled them to accumulate."[20] But this comment (along with a brief reference to the dreadful plight of a mother who had had to abandon her children to save herself) was all the article told the reader about how the victims of the blaze might have felt about their suffering and loss. It also lacked any description of how the scene looked. In short, ninety percent of the article consisted of names, addresses, and an account of how the fire spread.

Unlike the accounts in the *Herald* and the *Tribune*, the account of the fire that Whitman wrote for the *Aurora*, while longer than any story run by the competition, contains not a single address, name, or statement of property value. It does, however, give the reader something that neither of the other stories do: a sense of being there.

Whitman gives the reader the sensation of being at his side as he approaches the scene of the fire, leading him along the same route he himself had to travel to get there.

> For several blocks before arriving there, our passage was impeded by squads of people hurrying to and fro with rapid and eager pace. Women carrying small bundles—men with heated and sweaty faces— little children, many of them weeping and sobbing— met us every rod or two.[21]

As he etches with painstaking care a series of vividly concrete details, the reader's sense of immediacy is heightened:

> Puddles of water and frequent lengths of hose-pipe endangered the pedestrian's safety; and the hubbub, the trumpets of the engine foreman, the crackling of the flames, the lamentations of those who were made homeless by the conflagration—all sounded louder and louder as we approached, and at last grew to one continued and deafening din.

At its most successful, he makes the reader feel as if he were watching the fire himself.

For names of victims left homeless Whitman's report substitutes vivid images ("women carrying bundles—men with heated and sweaty faces"); for specific addresses of buildings destroyed Whitman substitutes a picture of the scene of destruction:

. . . we beheld a space of several acres, all covered with smouldering
ruins, mortar, red hot embers, piles of smoking half burnt walls—
a sight to make a man's heart sick and keep him awake at night when
lying in his bed.

Whitman concludes his account of the fire with a description of the
way the victims look and with extended empathetic musings on the
way they must feel:

The most pitiful thing in the whole affair was the sight of shiver-
ing women, their eyes red with tears, and many of them dashing
wildly through the crowd, in search, no doubt, of some member of
their family, who, for what they knew, might be buried 'neath the
smoking ruins nearby. Of all the sorrowful spectacles in God's world,
perhaps no one is more sorrowful than such as this!
And those crumbled ashes! What comforts were entombed there—
what memories of affection and companionship, and brotherhood—
what fruition—fell down as the walls and the floors fell down, and
were crushed as they were crushed!
On the minds of hundreds there, no doubt, these and similar reflections forced themselves. We saw it in the sombre countenances of
the spectators—their fixed look; and heard it in their conversation one
to another. And so, elbowing and pushing our way for many rods
through the crowd, we at last made it out to get once more where
the air was less hot and stifling, and the press of people less intense.

By the end of the piece, when Whitman says "we at last made it out
to get once more where the air was less hot and stifling," the reader
feels himself included in that "we," ready as Whitman was to leave that
hot and stifling scene for fresh air.
While the fire described in the *Herald* and the *Tribune* was unmistak-
ably a particular fire on a particular night in New York, Whitman's fire
seemed to take on certain almost generic properties common to every
city fire. Indeed, Whitman recognized this fact when he inserted large
chunks of his description unchanged into an article he wrote four years
later for the *Brooklyn Eagle* about a completely different fire! [22] (This
was not the last time Whitman would return to his *Aurora* fire story. He
would visit the scene again in section 26 of "Song of Myself.")
The differences among Whitman's approach to this story and those of

his competitors reveal something about Whitman's sense of what is important. His colleagues' view of "the facts"—who, what, where, when, why—differs markedly from his. For them the "who" means names, the "what" means figures of property damage and numbers left homeless, and the "when and why" mean a fire marshal's explanation of the principles of combustion. For Whitman the "who" means staring hard at faces and movements and trying to fathom from these images a sense of the pain, the pathos, the dread, the frustration, and the bewilderment that lay behind them. For Whitman "what" means the visual and aural images of flames and firemen, of cracked glass and crushed dreams. For Whitman "where" is simply "Broome and Delancey Streets" and "when" is simply the hour, between seven and eight o'clock, that Whitman visited the scene of the fire.

The facts, for Whitman, rather than being statements extracted from fire marshals, police officials, building appraisers, hospital staffs, and the like, are all that he was able to see, hear, feel, and imagine; they are his expression of what it felt like to be at the scene of the blaze. His account is closer to the kinds of eyewitness reports made famous a century later by Edward R. Murrow for CBS Radio News than to the reports of Whitman's contemporaries.

In "Life in a New York Market," "Scenes of Last Night," and some seventeen other pieces he wrote for the *Aurora*, Whitman managed to extricate himself from the conventions of the journalism of his day and explore new modes of reporting.

On the day when Greeley's *Tribune* was filled with articles about a coming election and prospects for decentralizing the eighth ward, for example, Whitman's *Aurora* ran an extraordinary piece called "Dreams," in which he tried to imagine what various inhabitants of the city might be experiencing at any given hour late at night; it is, in many ways, a rehearsal for his 1855 poem, "The Sleepers." It was also in the *Aurora*, in a highly unusual article called "The Ocean," that Whitman first explored images and emotions that he would return to in poems such as "Out of the Cradle Endlessly Rocking" (1859) and "As I Ebb'd with the Ocean of Life" (1860).[23] When his colleagues mapped the surface of city life, Whitman tried to chart its depths. While his colleagues usually treated their readers as passive consumers of the news, Whitman asked his reader to "lock arms with us in imagination" and aided him by a variety of creative strategies. While his colleagues pushed the abstract (Fourierism and Associationism), Whitman pushed the concrete (mutton chops and marbles). While they camped out in well-trodden courthouses and legislatures, Whitman struck out for new journalistic territory—synagogues and beaches.[24] The revolution of the penny press led all of the mass newspapers to focus more on the lives of common people, but Whitman's colleagues often emphasized the less common aspects of those lives; while they focused on the sensational (murderers and madmen), Whitman focused on the ordinary (milkmen and maids).

Yet for all their admirable qualities these unconventional pieces were the exception rather than the rule in Whitman's career as a journalist, and even in his career at the *Aurora*. The nineteen or so highly distinctive pieces he wrote for the *Aurora* were outnumbered three to one by some sixty-five conventional ones. For example, Whitman wrote twenty-one articles for the *Aurora* about attempts by a local bishop to divert part of the city's public-school funds to parochial schools; the issue played a key role in the local election of 1842, and Whitman's vituperative diatribes against "Plots of the Jesuits" were as routine as any that appeared in the New York press. The ratio of memorable to forgettable was even lower for Whitman's work on the *Brooklyn Eagle*, the *New Orleans Crescent*, and other papers for which he wrote.

But even his most conventional journalism played an important role in molding the poet that emerged in 1855. The attitudes and facts he assimilated served to enlarge his intellectual awareness and moral sympathy. These attitudes and facts, different, but recognizable, would reappear in 1855 as the themes and subjects of "Song of Myself."

The most important attitude Whitman acquired during his career as a journalist was his respect for the project of seeing and thinking for oneself, a goal which would be central to his achievement in 1855. Whitman's experience as a journalist made him aware of how unexamined conventions, narrow perspectives, misleading appearances, and all varieties of the counterfeit could interfere with the accurate perception and interpretation of one's world. Whitman felt that it was an editor's job to cultivate "a sharp eye, to discriminate the good from the immense mass of unreal stuff floating on all sides of him," and that he should be relied upon to be able to distinguish the real from a "counterfeit presentment of the real."[25] The poet who would later urge his reader to "re-examine all you have been told at school or church or in any book"[26] first commented on the importance of seeing and thinking for oneself in the *Aurora*, the *Eagle*, and the *Crescent*.

In a number of rather conventional editorials in the *Aurora* Whitman urged his reader to learn to step as far as he could beyond convention. Convention is responsible, he noted, for such absurdities as "the large triangle which people call Chatham *Square.*"[27] "We are free to confess, for ourself," Whitman wrote elsewhere, "that we have no reference for the statute book, any further than it jibes with our notions of truth and justice."[28] It is convention that lets what society *calls* justice be taken for justice itself. In these editorials Whitman urges his readers to question the labels society attaches to life. He doesn't want his reader to see a triangle as a square just because everyone calls it one, or to fail to question an unjust law just because it is on the statute books. He urges his reader to question the authority of these conventions, and to be wary of the ways in which they could blind him to a more clear-sighted view of his world.

In the *Brooklyn Eagle* he often pointed out the ways in which unpleasant realities were frequently masked by empty abstractions. He concludes an editorial attacking England's oppression of Ireland, for example, with the observation:

Human flesh and sinews, and their own good soil, sacrificed, that
a few pampered strangers may retain *their* serene arrangements—and
that the "government" may preserve its dignity? *DIGNITY!* quotha!
while groaning men, and pale women, and dying children, attest
the damnable selfishness of the fiction!"[29]

And in the *New Orleans Crescent* he subjected the rhetoric of poetry and romance to the same scrutiny to which he had earlier subjected the rhetoric of politics. "In poetry and romance these rivers are talked of as though they were cleanly streams," he observed, as he traveled down the Ohio, "but it is astonishing what a difference is made by the simple fact that they are always and altogether excessively murky—mud, indeed, being the prevailing character both afloat and ashore . . . there is no romance in a mass of yellowish brown liquid."[30]

At this point in his life Whitman was wont to assert flatly the superiority of fact to fiction or romance. It was a theme which would permeate every edition of *Leaves of Grass*, from 1855 on. He commented in the *New York Post*, for example, that drama interested him less than fields, water, trees, and people, and that his conversations with "the originals I see all around me" were "more refreshing than a comedy at any of the New York theatres."[31] He turned a geography text into a scrapbook of facts that interested him,[32] and even asked to be put on the list of people to whom the federal government sent "statistics" and "census facts."[33] The young editor put all of these facts to good use, marshaling them to condemn such practices as capital punishment, the slave trade and flogging in the schools, and to support such reforms as the establishment of playgrounds, free schools, cheap postage and free art exhibitions. His far-flung interests as an editor led him to share with his reader facts about health, medicine, science, sanitation, transportation, economics, and grand opera, as well.

The world of contemporary realities out of which he made his newspapers was the same world out of which he would make his poems, not only in 1855 but throughout his career. Sometimes he would sing lyrical hymns to that world, as in "Crossing Brooklyn Ferry" (1856), where he draws the reader's attention to "The glories strung like beads on my smallest sights and hearings, on the walk in the street and the passage over the river," or in "Sparkles from the Wheel" (1871), where he evokes a street scene like those he often painted in the *Aurora*. [34] Other times he tackled his theme with bravura:

> Away with old romance!
> Away with novels, plots and plays of foreign courts,
> Away with love-verses sugar'd in rhyme, the
>   intrigues, amours of idlers, . . .
> I raise a voice for far superber themes for poets
>   and for art,
> To exalt the present and the real. [35]

Long after Whitman had ceased writing journalism himself, his poems were filled with the same events that filled the daily newspapers. His 1865 poem "A Year of Meteors," for example, includes references to the 1859 hanging of the abolitionist John Brown, the 1860 electoral contest between Lincoln and Douglas, the 1860 visit to New York by the prince of Wales, and the 1860 arrival in New York of a famous British iron steamship. [36] As he would put it in "A Backward Glance O'er Travel'd Roads" in 1888, "the true use for the imaginative faculty of modern times is to give ultimate vivification to facts, to science, and to common lives, endowing them with the glows and glories and final illustriousness which belongs to every real thing, and to real things only." [37]

Despite his propensity to get lost, on occasion, in his own rhetoric, Whitman the journalist returned, with the inevitability of an organist's pedal point, to the theme that "Our Newspapers should never hestitate boldly to exhibit to the public gaze the *facts* . . ." [38] It was an idea which had animated the penny press from the beginning. As Dan Schiller has observed, from its start the penny press was committed to lifting "restrictions that barred the public from information" and to making generally available "cheap, value-free information" or "objective fact."[39] In an 1847 editorial on "The Sewing-Women of Brooklyn and New York," Whitman wrote: "It is difficult to say, at present, what particular means must be fixed on to obviate the dangers to which we have alluded; but once open the eyes of men to the fact of the intimate connection between poor pay for women, and crime among women, and the greatest difficulty is overcome."[40] In Whitman's view of things, reform of unjust conditions would follow exposure of "the facts" just as surely as day follows night. While his exuberant confidence may seem naïve, his faith in the value of disseminating "the facts" to the public was widely shared by his fellow editors and reporters.

As a reporter and editor during this period Whitman found himself documenting contemporary social history that his colleagues seemed content to ignore. The "many long dumb voices" would later find their way into "Song of Myself," where he could write,

> Through me many long dumb voices,
> Voices of the interminable generations of slaves
> Voices of prostitutes and of deformed persons,
> Voices of the diseased and despairing,
> And of thieves and dwarfs, . . .
> And of the rights of them the others are down upon . . .[41]

He deplored in his editorials the evils of the slave trade, of capital punishment, of police brutality toward prostitutes and children of the poor, the low wages of garment workers, the flogging of children in the public schools, the long hours of store clerks, prison conditions, and the hostility of many Americans toward foreigners. His compassion for the poor, the forgotten, the outcast, the suffering, and the oppressed resonated with greater force with each new instance of injustice and oppression he exposed. This compassion would play a central role in his achievement as a poet not only in "Song of Myself," but in such later poems as "You Felons on Trial in Courts" (1860) and "To a Common Prostitute" (1860).[42]

There were limits, however, to Whitman's freedom as a journalist to evoke compassion for "them the others are down upon." He was called upon occasionally to retract some of the force with which he had pressed his case. Referring to an article he had written the previous day in the *Aurora* about the mass arrest of prostitutes, he wrote, "The language we used in our article of yesterday, denouncing the kidnapping of women in Broadway, by the police authorities, was not intended to apply to [the police] as citizens . . . The whole proceeding was villainous—wrong—but perhaps we may have used rather hard words in denouncing it."[43] Presumably, direct or indirect pressure from the owners helps to explain this curious softening of the previous day's "hard words" by such a proud and doggedly tenacious editor. But forced retraction represents a minor limit on journalistic freedom compared with the ultimate incursion on that freedom: firing. Whitman's habit of exposing disagreeable facts and championing unpopular causes contributed to his being fired from the *Aurora*, the *Eagle*, and the *Crescent*.

While the precise cause of Whitman's dismissal from the *Aurora* is clouded in some ambiguity, a journalist who had worked beside him during this period commented, "though affable and unassuming in personal intercourse, [Whitman] was occasionally so trenchant with his pen that the proprietors had, now and then, to broadly hint that some restraint would be desirable."[44]

Whitman's "trenchant pen" similarly incited the displeasure of the owners of the *Eagle* when he began to write editorials that ran counter to the position of the local party bosses regarding the Wilmot Proviso. Whitman claims to have been the first New York editor to endorse the move to prohibit the extension of slavery into the new territory. His publisher sided with the Anti-Wilmot Proviso Democrats. Whitman seems to have been discharged from the paper shortly after refuting point by point a well-known anti-Free-Soil document which his publisher was known to support.[45]

After leaving the *Aurora*, Whitman worked on some ten different newspapers before assuming the editorship of the *Brooklyn Daily Eagle* four years later in 1846. These papers included the *Evening Tattler*, which specialized in crime reporting, two political sheets, the *New York Statesman* and the *Democrat*, the *Sun*, where he covered the police stations and the coroner's office, and a motley assortment of other publications including the *Sunday Times*, the *Plebeian*, and the *New Mirror*. When his two-year stint at the *Eagle* ended, Whitman accepted the offer (made during a chance meeting in a theater lobby) to be the first editor of a newspaper about to come out in New Orleans, the *Crescent*. His post in New Orleans lasted two months before the paper's proprietors decided Whitman's Free-Soil political views would probably be an embarrassment to them in the coming presidential elections.[46] The following year he became the editor of the *Freeman*, a Free-Soil newspaper in Brooklyn plagued throughout its short life by natural and political disasters (first its office burned to the ground the day after its first issue appeared in September 1848; then the Free-Soil candidate lost the next presidential election and the paper expired shortly thereafter). Whitman wrote a few human-interest sketches for the *New York Evening Post* and the *Brooklyn Daily Advertiser* in 1850 and 1851, but in general, between 1849 and 1855, he ceased to be employed as a full-time journalist. While the frequency with which he changed jobs made it impossible for Whitman to achieve the security and stature he would have liked to have had as a journalist, it exposed him to many styles, formats, editorial voices, political perspectives, and varieties of experience, all of which were an asset to him in his later career as a writer.

The limits Whitman felt as a journalist came from many sources. His publishers censored his moral and political sympathy.[47] The discipline of deadlines cut short his walks.[48] The expectations of his public constrained the subjects, style, stance, and strategies of what he wrote.[49] A lecture by Emerson which he attended on March 5, 1842, while working on the *Aurora* may have planted some further doubts in his mind about the kind of truth he could hope to capture in his newspaper work. "In poetry you may tell the Truth, but in Prose you must not," Emerson said (according to Horace Greeley's account of the lecture in the *Tribune*), "Out of this love of music men will hear it; and those truths which are of highest import, which, if in a newspaper would be rejected are received and loved in poetry."[50] "The lecture," Whitman wrote in the *Aurora*, "was one of the richest and most beautiful compositions, both for its matter and style, we have ever heard anywhere, at any time."[51]

As attractive as the idea of being a poet may have seemed to Whitman in 1842, he was still a long way from the realization of that goal. Indeed, while Whitman found Emerson's theoretical musings on poetry intriguing, the verse he was actually writing at the time had much more in common with the banal, formulaic doggerel that had become a familiar staple in the columns of the penny press than with the work of the great poets Whitman claimed, in later years, to have admired in his youth (Shakespeare, Homer, etc.). While he was paid small sums for some of the early poems that made it into print, it was the journalism that paid his bills. The twenty-five poems Whitman published between 1838 and 1850, mainly in New York and Long Island newspapers,[52] are, in general, simply awful.

In place of the "pictures of life as it is" that had characterized his early reporting, Whitman's early poems feature the saccharine, sodden, abstract and sentimental musings standard in popular graveyard verse: "But where, O Nature, where shall be the soul's abiding place?"[53] Instead of the spontaneous concrete detail that had made his "city walks" and editorials often fresh and surprising, they are filled with stale cliché: "O, Death! a black pierceless pall hangs 'round thee, and the future state."[54] The vague, mawkish, and didactic verse is burdened by archaic and pretentious "literary"-sounding forms of speech ("tis said," "n'er," "o'er,"), pompous diction ("dark oblivion's tide," "days of yore"), and exotic subjects (a descendant of the royal family of Castile, a young Inca girl) about which Whitman clearly knew very little.[55]

It is hard to believe that the same poet who gushes "O, beauteous is the earth! and fair / The splendors of Creation are"[56] will one day produce one of the most original and concrete hymns to the "splendors of Creation" in the English language. At the same time that he was breaking new ground as a journalist, Whitman was sloshing through well-trodden slush as an artist. The verse Whitman wrote during his early years as a journalist bears almost no relation to the works which catapulted him to the ranks of America's greatest poets. His success as a poet came only when he stopped trying to be "artistic" and circled back to the subjects, style, stance, and strategies he had first developed as editor of the *New York Aurora*.

During his early years as a journalist Whitman's literary endeavors included, in addition to banal verse, some melodramatic and moralistic short stories and short novels which he published in periodicals such as the *Democratic Review*. In many of these pieces Whitman claimed that the tales he told were narratives of fact. "Death in the School-Room," the first story he published (1841), which exemplified the evils of corporal punishment, was subtitled "(A Fact)."[57] "Bervance: or, Father and Son," a story that came out the same year, began with the author's comment that "Almost incredible as it may seem, there is more truth than fiction in the following story."[58] Whitman began his temperance novel "Franklin Evans" (1842) by saying

I would ask your belief when I assert that, what you are going to read is not a work of fiction, as the term is used. I narrate occurrences that have had a far more substantial existence, than in my fancy.[59]

And in a series of sentimental pieces he wrote in 1845 and titled, "Some Fact-Romances," Whitman wrote, "They literally came to pass, as now told."[60] But his claims for the "truthfulness" of the narratives simply reflected conventions current among popular fiction writers of his day who, like Whitman, were apt to subtitle their stories "A Tale of Truth," or "Founded on Fact."[61] Despite his protestations to the contrary, however, Whitman's tales, like most of the sentimental and didactic popular fiction of his contemporaries, were, in general, rooted more in the author's fancy than in fact. Some of the scenes he depicted in these tales—the country schoolroom, for example—were undoubtedly familiar to him. On the whole, however, Whitman's claim that something "literally came to pass, as now told," indicates that the story one is about to read will honor not the journalist's concern with "pictures of life as it is," but rather the popular novelist's concern with hackneyed conventions of propriety.

The tales shamelessly imitated the atmosphere of Poe and Hawthorne and the themes and styles of Cooper, Scott, and others. While the stories reflected anxieties about separation, death, and identity that were clearly of great concern to Whitman at the time, they explored these subjects in melodramatic and imitative ways; Whitman's early fiction, like his early verse, is wholly undistinguished. In light of these early artistic failures, the poetry that burst upon the world in 1855 appears all the more extraordinary.

In place of the vague and trite musings that had weighted down all of his earlier poetry, the volume Whitman published in 1855 boasted vivid images as concrete as they were original. The archaic forms of speech and pompous diction of his previous poems gave way to sharp, clear, contemporary language. The conventional meters and rhyming patterns were replaced by an unconventional free verse punctuated idiosyncratically and sometimes not punctuated at all. Spanish princesses and Inca daughters were banished from this work; ordinary folks—sign painters and omnibus drivers—took their places. The sermonizing of temperance tales and didactic poems was replaced here by a kind of sympathy that rendered the poet loath to pass judgment on a "sinner" and eager to feel each wretch's private pain. While the earlier poet had trained his pompous oratory on a sedentary listener, the author of *Song of Myself* audaciously pushed his reader out the front door and refused to address him anywhere but in the open air. All of these innovations had their roots in Whitman's early journalism—a fact which diminishes neither the mystery nor the magic of the poem into which they blossomed in 1855, but one which deserves closer attention. While our discussion will focus primarily on the long poem he would later call "Song of Myself," it has bearing on Whitman's project as a poet for the rest of his life.

The subjects that are central to the poem—the vast range of people that appear and the sympathetic manner in which they are presented, the contemporary and historical events that are discussed, the scenes from everyday life that are evoked—are drawn directly from Whitman's journalism, as are the themes that dominate the poem—the importance of the world of fact, the superiority of fact to fiction, and the importance of seeing and thinking for oneself.

A metaphor that was central to the penny press's presentation of itself would be central to the poet's presentation of himself in *Leaves of Grass*. The poet who judged "not as a judge judges but as the sun falling around a helpless thing,"[62] who wanted his poem to be available to everyone, had much in common with the founding father of the penny press, Benjamin Day, who coined, as his motto for the first penny paper, the *New York Sun*, "It shines for ALL."[63] And it is in familiar tones that Whitman voices his belief, in his preface to *Leaves of Grass*, in "the superiority of genuineness over all fiction and romance." One is not surprised to hear him proclaim, "The United States themselves are essentially the greatest poem . . . As soon as histories are properly told there is no more need of romances."[64] Much as he had urged the editor to be "in general information . . . complete, particularly with that relating to his own country,"[65] in this preface Whitman urges the poet to absorb and express in his poem all the social, political, psychological, and physical realities that comprise America:

> To him enter the essences of the real things and the past and present events— . . . the perpetual coming of immigrants—the wharfhem'd cities and superior marine—the unsurveyed interior—the loghouses and clearings and wild animals and hunters and trappers . . . the free commerce—the fisheries and whaling and gold— . . . the Yankee swap— the New York fireman and the target excursion—the southern plantation life—the character of the northeast and of the northwest and southwest—slavery and the tremulous spreading of hands to

protect it, and the stern opposition to it which shall never cease till it ceases or the speaking of tongues and the moving of lips cease.[66]

As Whitman accepts his own challenge and tries to make his poem dense with American realities the words he chooses often coalesce into a cacophony of vernacular concreteness. His language is in many ways a lexicon of contemporary social history, including, as it does, implicit identification of a way of life. As a "pavingman" leaning on his "two-handed rammer" or a "fare-collector . . . jingling . . . loose change" stroll naturally across the page, it takes effort to remember that they were not always invited to poets' banquets. The common people whose lives Whitman chronicled in the penny press for two decades were just now for the first time finding their way into a major American poem. In his preface Whitman calls those lives "unrhymed poetry" (p. 6).

While the influence of Whitman's experience as a journalist pervades every line of the 1855 "Song of Myself," certain sections of the poem have more of a journalistic feel about them than others; section 8, for example, reads as if it were transcribed directly from the reporter's note-book: "The suicide sprawls on the bloody floor of the bedroom. It is so . . . I witnessed the corpse . . . there the pistol had fallen" (p. 31).

Passages most laden with vividly concrete visual images are often those sections most closely related to earlier newspaper articles. Take section 12, a scene painted with stunning clarity and confidence, and one related to a profile of blacksmiths Whitman had sketched for the *Aurora*:

Blacksmiths with grimed and hairy chests environ the anvil,
Each has his main sledge . . . they are all out . . .
　　there is a great heat in the fire.
From the cinder-strewed threshold I follow
　　Their movements,
The lithe sheer of their waists plays
　　even with their massive arms,
Overhand the hammers roll—overhand so slow—
　　overhand so sure,
They do not hasten, each man hits his place.
(P. 35)

Much of the poem's aural imagery, too—"the blab of the pave," the "sluff of bootsoles," the "clank of shod horses on the granite floor," the "recitative of fish pedlars and fruit pedlars"—reflects the journalist's practice at recording the subtle timbres of complex but familiar sounds.

But while Whitman's journalism is interesting, the 1855 "Song of Myself" is astonishing. The journalist's observations here become infused with a new sense of radiance and wonder. His sympathies resonate more profoundly and inclusively than ever before. Familiar characters appear fresh and new. Scenes which in the journalism reflected their time are here made to reflect all time. Surfaces the journalist explored with concentration and precision here give way to unsuspected depths and corridors of mystery. Familiar diverse, discrete, and apparently random particulars, linked by subtle reiterated patterns, here unite in a vibrant shimmering and seemingly all-inclusive whole.

This puzzling transformation of journalist into poet has been attributed by some to a sexual awakening or a mystical experience. The murkiness of the evidence cited, however, makes all of these accounts unsatisfactory. Clearly, the many limits Whitman encountered as a journalist (political and moral censorship, limits of form, style, and subject, etc.), as well as his long-standing interest in verse, helped propel him along the road to being a poet. But the roots of this transformation will undoubtedly remain as opaque as they are complex; the origins of poetic inspiration simply *are* that way. But while we may never know what went on in Whitman, we do know what went on in his work. The brilliance of Whitman's greatest poems stems from the ways in which the poet transformed fact into art. It is this effort to which we will now turn.

Whitman spent his years as a journalist absorbing the world around him and then reflecting that world, in all its richness and fullness, in articles, editorials, and sketches. His project as a poet is largely the same, but with a key difference: it is the triadic relationship of the writer, his world, and his work, rather than the world alone, which is his main concern. "Song of Myself" is a celebration of self and world and the process by which the two interact and, in a paradoxical sense, create each other. The poem is a lesson in how each writer might celebrate the miracle of being, himself.

As the journalist's pen transcribed the woes of "many long dumb voices" and projected them onto the public's consciousness, concrete and suffering slaves, prostitutes, and criminals would suddenly come to life for readers for whom they had not previously existed. The poet of "Song of Myself" carried this view of the writer's role farther than he ever had as a journalist, and farther than he would in any later poem, as well. As poet absorbs real persons and events which exist independently of himself and then casts them forth in a poem, we see these familiar persons and events as if for the first time. While the poet's sustenance is drawn from the world which surrounds him, in an important sense the beings he evokes owe their existence to the poet who has made them come alive. The world the poet creates is equal in fullness and significance to the one he absorbs.

The self that is celebrated in the poem is defined by this ongoing process of absorption and creation, of taking in and casting forth, of "to me" and "through me." "Song of Myself" begins with the "I" of the poem celebrating the mystery of its own identity, and, by a series of patterned inductive leaps, the mystery of all identity, of being itself. The mystery of being is envisioned in the poem as a process as perpetual and mysterious as the movement of the tides. The self for the poet is no more contained in any fixed shape than the sea is contained in the navigator's chart; rather, any one identity is but a phase in an ongoing, ever to be renewed, process of merging with the world and retreating into the soul, of ebbing and flowing, of receiving and creating, accepting and offering, giving and getting, acting and being acted upon, touching and being touched. Like the tides, the self is seen as constantly flowing out toward a shore of all that is not itself, casting up forms of itself, and ebbing away from the shore, absorbing multiform shapes it did not bring. All forms of life—a leaf of grass absorbing sustenance from the graves it covers, for example, and projecting the sights and smells and textures from which the poet will make a poem—participate in this ongoing process.

A process in which the journalist constantly engages is elevated by the poet to the central subject of the poem. The poem celebrates the poet's realization that the activity of "sallying forth" into the rich, dense "heterogeneous mass" of all that is not himself, absorbing it and casting it forth as a world of words of his own creation—the project, indeed, that fascinated him as a journalist and drew him to journalism in the first place—is nothing less than the project of being fully alive; it celebrates his exhilaration at discovering that the activity that intrigued him most was, at its root, emblematic of the laws underlying existence itself.

The journalist's range of interests may be broad, but the poet's concerns are more far-flung and diverse. "If my poem is not everything," the poet wrote, "then it is nothing" (p. 41). Whitman presents a vast panorama of occupations and locations, of activities and scenes, linked by apparently random conjunctions; most of Whitman's catalogs are, however, far from random, although they are structured and designed to deny the existence of any plan or structure. As seemingly random particulars are linked by subtly reiterated patterns of ebb-and-flow and many-in-one (which we will explore further) the illusion of all-inclusiveness is inductively established. The ultimate openness of "Song of Myself" invites the reader to complete the uncompleted (and by definition uncompletable) project the poet had begun, of getting "everything" in.

While Whitman the journalist expressed a lively interest in the world of fact, Whitman the poet is positively intoxicated by it. The morning glory is more of a miracle for the poet than "the metaphysics of books," and the simplest of human actions—the poet walking up his stoop—fills him with awe (p. 50). Each leaf of grass is "no less than the journey-work of stars" (p. 55) in the poet's vision, and the leaves, we are told in the poem, are "limitless" (p. 29). How might the poet begin to encompass such vast material? The answer, for Whitman, lies in focusing on the *process* by which the world is absorbed and projected by the poet; it is the process by which a poem and a poet come into being. It is the process by which facts become "vivified" through art.

Whitman the poet is convinced, even more than was Whitman the journalist, of the importance of enabling each individual to encounter the world of fact for himself. "You shall no longer take things at second or third hand," he tells his reader, "you shall listen to all sides and filter them from yourself" (p. 26). Whitman had come to believe that only when facts and events are seen as if for the first time, in as fresh and unmediated a manner as possible, do they radiate (as he would later put it) with "the glows and glories and final illustriousness which belong to every real thing."[67] It was the poet's good fortune, Whitman felt, to be able to watch "every real thing" come alive and glow with meaning, to be able to see the world freshly, to be able to detach the familiar from the realm of the commonplace and make it new. His central project in "Song of Myself" is communicating the nature of this vision to his reader.

His journeys into the possible begin and end on the plane of the actual: the final goal of his act of creation is to enable the reader to see the world around him with his own newly opened eyes. Whitman teaches this lesson in two ways: (1) by showing the reader how the poetic imagination first absorbs and then "vivifies" the world of fact, and (2) by exhorting the reader to embark on an analogous project of his own. The poet wants the reader to see not *what* the poet saw, but *as* the poet saw—freshly, as if for the first time. The project of seeing freshly implies an openness to all the facts, and an unwillingness to impose any artificial structurings upon them. The artist who would espouse the goal of seeing freshly must select and structure the facts he wishes to treat in a manner which condemns the very processes of selection and structure. Since his final goal is to direct the reader's attention to life rather than art, he must take on the complex task of creating a work of art which features its own incompleteness. In the 1855 "Song of Myself" Whitman grapples with these problems with a large measure of success.

From his earliest days on the *Aurora*, and throughout his career as a journalist, wherever he turned Whitman seemed to encounter a theme which bound his world together as a kind of elemental glue: unity within diversity. A city street, a boardinghouse, a nation were all emblems for Whitman of a phenomenon that intrigued and exhilarated him: the "many in one."[68] Whitman the journalist often used catalogs to explore this theme, as when he urged Americans of diverse occupations to raise a united voice as "workingmen" in the fight against the extension of slavery.

> We call upon every mechanic of the North, East and West—upon the carpenter, in his rolled up sleeves, the mason with his trowel, the stonecutter with his brawny chest, the blacksmith with his sooty face, the brown fisted ship-builder, whose clinking strokes rattle so merrily in our dock yards—upon shoemakers and cartmen, and drivers, and paviers, and porters and millwrights, and furriers, and ropemakers, and coach and cabinet makers—upon the honest sawyer and mortarman—to speak in a voice whose great reverberations shall tell to all quarters that the *workingmen* of the free United States and their business, are not willing to be put on the level of Negro slaves.[69]

The union of interests Whitman evoked in this paragraph is not established by the passage itself; the "voice" with "great reverberations" emanates not from the workingmen but from the journalist who hands them their lines. These cardboard workmen remain one-dimensional in the editorial, political counters Whitman would move into the Free-Soil camp, joined rhetorically but not organically by a journalist trying to project an ideology rather than a vision.

In "Song of Myself," however, these familiar workmen are seen in a new light; animated by the poet's vision, they breathe new life. Pictured, not merely listed, they become both themselves, and emblems of being. Here they do "speak in a voice whose great reverberations" ring throughout the poem; the voice speaks not against a particular policy but, rather, against all that degrades and diminishes the fullness of human existence. As the poet's art choreographs (rather than calls for) the unity of "many into one," they become emblems of the self whose celebration brought into being not only them, but the entire astonishing poem.

Nearly half of the workmen named in this paragraph appear in "Song of Myself," some reappearing as many as three times. While most are scattered throughout the poem, seven appear in the catalog in section 15. Compare the journalistic and poetic treatments of three in particular: the "carpenter," the "mason," and the "pavier." An initial comparison of the two catalogs reveals that the workmen in the editorial are static ("the carpenter, in his rolled up sleeves," "the mason with his trowel," "paviers"), while those in the poem are seen doing their customary activity ("the carpenter dresses his plank," "the masons are calling for mortar," "the pavingman leans on his twohanded rammer") (SOM, pp. 37, 38, 39). Through a series of subtle and almost subliminal patterns, these activities become emblematic of the process by which the poet makes a poem.

In the editorial the "carpenter in his rolled up sleeves" is a conventional image. The carpenter who appears at the start of section 15 may at first appear equally familiar; on closer look one sees that he is indeed a very different person:

> The pure contralto sings in the organloft,
> The carpenter dresses his plank . . . the tongue of
>   his foreplane whistles its wild ascending lisp.
> (P. 37)

The carpenter and contralto are linked by more than proximity and alliteration. As the "tongue" of the carpenter's foreplane "whistles its wild ascending lisp," one cannot help but associate its sound with the sound of the "pure contralto" singing in the organloft. The timbres may be different, but the vibrations are shown to have something in common. Activities which seem to be distinct and separate are shown, by the fresh and original images and by artful juxtaposition, to be really one and the same.

A lover of opera and a journeyman carpenter himself, Whitman knew these tones well. The carpenter's "wild ascending lisp" will reverberate in the poet's "barbaric yawp over the roofs of the world" (p. 85); its very timbre will vibrate in lines such as: "with the twirl of my tongue I encompass worlds and volumes of worlds" (p. 50), or "I rise ecstatic through all . . . The whirling and whirling is elemental with me" (p. 68). Images of carpentry will reappear in the poem as descriptions of both the poet, who is "well-entreatied, braced in the beams" (p. 27) and the process of creation, whose "kelson," we are told, is "love" (p. 29).

The pure contralto's tones will also find themselves echoed as images of the poem ("it is a grand-opera . . . this indeed is music!") and of the poet himself:

My own voice orotund sweeping and final
Come my children.
Come my boys and girls, and my women and household
    intimates,
Now the performer launches his nerve . . . he has
    passed his prelude on the reeds within.
(P. 73)

Rough carpenter and refined contralto join in singing in their own distinctive ways, as the poet, "stuffed with the stuff that is coarse and stuffed with the stuff that is fine," (p. 40), unites them in a song of his own.

In the editorial, the "mason with his trowel" is as conventional and unnotable an image as the "carpenter in his rolled up sleeves." In section 15 of "Song of Myself," the mason appears as follows:

The floormen are laying the floor—the tinners are tin-
    ning the roof, the masons are calling for mortar.
(P. 39)

What at first glance might appear to be random activities proves to have a subtle and important cohesion. The three activities are really one—the building of a house—and the scene evoked by the poet casts the three activities in a new light.

From laying a floor, tinning a roof, and calling for mortar, a house will result. The mason, as he binds together the farthest parts of the house and turns them into one unified structure, has much in common with the poet who asks, "Shall I make my list of things in the house and skip the house that supports them?" (p. 46) Like the mason, the poet binds together the farthest parts; a unifier of opposites, he plays marches for the victors and for the slain and joins living and dead, body and soul, now and eternity. It is the enigma of how one can be many and many can be one that has given rise to the central preoccupation of both the poet and the poem.

For the poem's occasion, in short, is the poet's celebration of the temporary unification (and potential for unification) of "I"—physical, social, entangled in a web of quotidian exchanges and obligations—and "me-myself," or the "soul"—invisible, intangible, mysterious, timeless. The poem itself, echoing its narrator's celebration, weaves in and out of the mystery of "the many in one" as it binds together diverse parts into a cohesive whole.

The "paviers" in the editorial reappear as the "pavingman" in section 15.

> The pavingman leans on his twohanded rammer—the
>   reporter's lead flies swiftly over the notebook—
>   the signpainter is lettering with red and gold.
> (P. 38)

By replacing the term "pavier" with the invented term "pavingman," Whitman focuses greater attention on both the activity involved and its object. The core of the new word—"paving"—is both the participle of the verb and the end result of the activity. The new term, a statement of the basic activity, leaves Whitman free to focus on that activity—the workman leaning on "his twohanded rammer." Our visualization of the pavingman's activity as involving a heavy, focused implement helps us connect it with the other implements in the line: the swift and light reporter's lead, and (implicitly) the careful brush of the signpainter.

Heavy and light, swift and slow, are united in one line as pavingman, reporter, and signpainter are seen to be engaged in the same activity—an activity, not surprisingly, in which the poet engages as well. Pavingman, reporter, signpainter, and poet organize reality in lines; they structure reality with forms made by men, they project "form and union and plan" on rough and unformed material, and they make possible communication (in all senses of the term), whether their medium be asphalt, lead, paint, or typography. Builder of paths and roads (primarily "between reality and [men's] souls"), reporter of facts ("I witnessed the corpse . . . there the pistol had fallen"), and painter of signs ("my signs are a rain-proof coat and good shoes and a staff cut from the woods"),[70] the poet recognizes the unity underlying these disparate activities and binds them together in his poem.

As carpenter, mason, and pavier are detached from familiar contexts and made to radiate far beyond the sphere they normally inhabit, we see them, in an important sense, as if for the first time. And as the poet infuses them with new associations and meaning, so they infuse the poet with new associations and meaning as well. As we see the carpenter, mason, and pavier, respectively, as singer of songs, unifier of the highest and lowest parts, indicator of the path between reality and the soul, so we see the poet as carpenter, mason, and pavier.

The catalog in section 15, as these typical examples show, is far from the structureless chaos it has often been considered. It is a subtle, inductively built statement of the miracle of how a man may absorb many forms, cast out many forms, and still be one. The closing lines of the catalog eloquently summarize this statement:

> And these one and all tend inward to me, and I tend
>   outward to them,
> And such as it is to be one of these more or less I
>   am.[71]

Section 15 is a living and flowing enactment of the ways in which one may absorb reality and project one's forms upon it. It is this mysterious process of absorption and projection, of inhaling and exhaling, which is the central study of the poem.

> The respiration and inspiration . . .
> The sniff of green leaves and dry leaves, and of the
>   shore and dark colored sea-rocks and of hay in the
>   barn,
> The sound of the belched words of my voice . . . words
>   loosed to the eddies of the wind.
> (P. 25)

Somewhere between the inhaling of the smell of green leaves and the exhaling of "words loosed to the eddies of the wind" (p. 25), a poet and a poem are born. The poet, "both in and out of the game" (p. 28), "caresser of life wherever moving. . . . backward as well as forward sluing" (p. 35), "partaker of influx and efflux" (p. 46), is identified closely

with the omnipresent inward and outward movement which defines
both the poem and how it came to be.

There are similar patterns in section 8, where nearly all of the subjects
have been dealt with in Whitman's journalism, a fact that may account
for its particularly reportorial tone. In the newspaper articles Whitman's
concern was limited by the particular events at hand; here, as in section
15, the real characters and scenes are woven into a pattern which binds
them together, shows them in a new light, allows them to radiate beyond
themselves, and tells us something of the process by which one makes a
poem.

> The little one sleeps in its cradle.
> I lift the gauze and look a long time, and silently
>   brush away flies with my hand.
>
> The youngster and the redfaced girl turn aside up
>   the bushy hill.
> I peeringly view them from the top.
>
> The suicide sprawls on the bloody floor of the
>   bedroom,
> It is so . . . I witnessed the corpse . . .
>   there the pistol had fallen.
> The blab of the pave . . . the tires of carts and
>   sluff of boot-soles and talk of the promenaders,
> The heavy omnibus, the driver with his interrogating
>   thumb, the clank of the shod horses on the granite
>   floor,
> The carnival of sleighs, the clinking and snorted
>   jokes and pelts of snowballs;
> The hurrahs for popular favorites . . . the fury of
>   roused mobs,
> The flap of the curtained litter—the sick man inside,
>   borne to the hospitals,
> The meeting of enemies, the sudden oath, the blows
>   and fall,
> The excited crowd—the policeman with his star quickly
>   working his passage to the center of the crowd;
> The impassive stones that receive and return so many
>   echoes,

> The souls moving along . . . are they invisible
>   while the least atom of the stones is visible?
> What groans of overfed or half-starved who fall on the
>   flags sunstruck or in fits,
> What exclamations of women taken suddenly, who hurry
>   home and give birth to babes,
>
> What living and buried speech is always vibrating
>   here . . . what howls restrained by decorum,
> Arrests of criminals, slights, adulterous offers
>   made, acceptances, rejections with convex lips,
> I mind them or the resonance of them . . . I
>   come again and again.
> (Pp. 31–32)

As we watch the poet "lift the gauze and look a long time, and silent-ly brush away flies," "peeringly view . . . from the top," and "[wit-ness]," we see him moving from participatory sympathy (through voyeurism) to objective detachment—variant stances of the poet who earlier characterized himself as "both in and out of the game, and watching and wondering at it" (p. 28). It is this mixture of sympathy and objective detachment, the ability to merge with the lives of others and to extricate oneself from the merge, that characterizes the poet's relation to the world he reports.

The world the poet moves in and out of is a world of opposites united— rough and refined, small and large, heavy and light, loved and hated, passive and violent, visible and invisible, overfed and half-starved, living and buried. The poet unites these opposites by more than proximity; as the opposing images are juxtaposed to each other, they reveal that they oppose each other only on one level, and that in the larger scheme of things they are really one. The blab of the pave is as much the product of the refined talk of the promenaders as it is of the rough tires of carts and sluff of boot-soles; the small carts and large omnibus are just parts of the overall din, and only the timbre of clinking versus clanking dif-ferentiates the part played by the heavy omnibus and the light sleigh in the reverberating echo chamber of the poem. Mob energy has largely the same chemistry whether roused in fury or in adulation. And the sick man passively borne to the hospital and the enemy felled with a violent blow will meet the same end, as will the overfed or the half-starved.

Like the "impassive stones that receive and return so many echoes" (p. 32) the poet receives the diverse images of city life and returns them somehow altered, freshly perceived. The penultimate line of the section summarizes this inward/outward movement as the poet evokes images of action, withdrawal from action, offer, acceptance, and casting off. Throughout "Song of Myself" the processes of inhaling and exhaling, ebbing and flowing, absorbing and projecting, receiving and creating, recur as an ever-present pedal point, uniting the diverse particulars in the poem and explaining the process by which the poet unites them. Through a series of subtle patterns, as we have mentioned, they are made to radiate beyond the seemingly random particulars they describe to include all of creation, to encompass anything that is.

Following Emerson's edict that the form should come from the facts, Whitman's goal, in "Song of Myself," is to make a man-made structure as fluid, open, and ongoing as the "form and union and plan" (p. 85) that characterize the universe. In its consciously crafted lack of finality, this "form and union and plan" point up the inability of any less open structure to include as much. The poem leaves the reader not with a finished product but with a lesson in the process of how one becomes an original perceiver and creator, of how one learns to see and think for oneself. In the 1855 "Song of Myself" Whitman treats his reader not as a passive consumer but as a cocreator of the world the poet explores, as a practitioner of what Emerson had called "creative reading."[72] Whitman had been thinking about this subject for at least ten years before he published "Song of Myself," although this poem was his first extended effort to deal with it as a writer. In an article titled "Thoughts on Reading" that he had torn out of an issue of the *American Whig Review* in 1845, he had underscored the sentence, "An author enriches us, not so much by giving us his ideas, as by unfolding in us the same powers that originated them."[73] And in a review of his own book that Whitman published anonymously soon after the 1855 *Leaves of Grass* appeared, he emphasized the importance of the book's special effect on its reader, inviting (perhaps more directly than any other American writer) the kind of analysis that characterizes current reader-response criticism: "Every sentence and every passage [of this poet] . . . ," he wrote, "exudes an impalpable something which sticks to him that reads and pervades and provokes him to tread the half-invisible road where the poet, like an apparition, is striding fearlessly before."[74]

One of Whitman's most central concerns in the 1855 "Song of Myself" is to transform his reader from a passive consumer of the text into a producer of the text himself. In his preface to the 1855 *Leaves of Grass* Whitman announces his intention of furthering this end by using a paradoxically "anti-structure" structure:

> What I experience or portray shall go from my composition without a shred of my composition. You shall stand by my side and look in the mirror with me.
> (P. 13)

And on the second page of "Song of Myself" Whitman writes,

> Stop this day and night with me and you shall possess
>   the origin of all poems . . .
> You shall no longer take things at second or third
>   hand . . . nor look through the eyes of the
>   dead . . . nor feed on the spectres in books,
> You shall not look through my eyes either, nor take
>   things from me,
> You shall listen to all sides and filter them
>   from yourself.
> (P. 26)

"All I mark as my own you shall offset it with your own" (p. 43), Whitman asserts in section 20 of "Song of Myself." It is in the closing pages of the poem, however, that Whitman elaborates most fully on this mandate to the reader:

> Nor I, nor any one else can travel that road for
>   you,
> You must travel it for yourself . . .
>
> You are also asking me questions, and I hear you;
> I answer that I cannot answer . . . you must
>   find out for yourself.
>
> Sit awhile wayfarer,
> Here are biscuits to eat and here is milk to
>   drink.
>
> But as soon as you sleep and renew yourself in sweet

clothes I will certainly kiss you with my good-
bye kiss and open the gate for your egress hence.

Long enough have you dreamed contemptible dreams,
Now I wash the gum from your eyes,
You must habit yourself to the dazzle of the
light and of every moment of your life.

Long have you timidly waded, holding a plank by
the shore,
Now I will you to be a bold swimmer,
To jump off in the midst of the sea, and rise again
and nod to me and shout, and laughingly dash with
your hair.

I am the teacher of athletes,
He that by me spreads a wider breast than my own
proves the width of my own,
He most honors my style who learns under it to
destroy the teacher.
(Pp. 80–81)

The poet would push his reader away from the poem into life; he is
most satisfied if he succeeds in simply "washing the gum" from his
reader's eyes, thus enabling him to be dazzled by the brilliance of "every
moment of [his] life." The poet's goal is to teach his reader to absorb
the world around him in a manner that will allow its unfiltered radiance
to shine through; he wants to help his reader learn to project that world
in forms of his own crafting.

Whitman leads the reader through several object lessons in how one
goes about being an original perceiver and creator. The most memorable
of these lessons takes place in section 6 of the poem, which begins with
the question, "What is the grass?"

A child said, What is the grass? fetching it to me
with full hands;
How could I answer the child? . . . I do not know
what it is any more than he.
I guess it must be the flag of my disposition, out
of hopeful green stuff woven.

Or I guess it is the handkerchief of the Lord,
A scented gift and remembrancer designedly
    dropped,
Bearing the owner's name some way in the corners,
    that we may see and remark, and say Whose?
Or I guess the grass is itself a child . . . the
    produced babe of the vegetation.

Or I guess it is a uniform hieroglyphic,
And it means, sprouting alike in broad zones and
    narrow zones,
Growing among black folks as among white,
Kanuck, Tuckahoe, Congressman, Cuff, I give them
    the same, I receive them the same.

And now it seems to be the beautiful uncut hair
    of graves.

Tenderly will I use you curling grass . . .
(Pp. 29–30)

The subject of the child's inquiry is clearly rooted in the world of fact; grass exists as a concrete entity and may be fetched with full hands. And yet, when the poet is asked to define it, to contain it in a string of words, all he can do is "guess"—project hypothetical identities out of his imagination—which is precisely what he would have the reader learn to do.

First, the poet suggests, the grass is the poet's own banner unfurled. And like the poet, who is not "contained between my hat and boots," the grass may not be contained within one metaphorical identity. The grass becomes a sign of God; and as the grass changes from a sign of the poet to a sign of the Lord, so the man who begins "Song of Myself" will transform himself, eventually, into a divinity. But this definition, too, is revised. The grass is seen as something natural, new, growing, posing (like the child who fetches it) wonderful questions that have no answers. "The produced babe of the vegetation" suggests the fertility of the imagination that allows the imagery of the poem itself to flow. Yet this image, too, is transformed into another possibility. The grass is seen as a "uniform hieroglyphic," as a mysterious, untranslatable sign that somehow unifies all space, that binds together all that is, as God binds the world together, and as the poet binds the world of the poem together. And finally, the grass is seen as a unifier of time, joining the living and the dead. Like the poet who makes his poems from both the living and the dead, the grass is a link between the two worlds. "Tenderly will I use you curling grass." Whitman is explicit in summarizing his lesson.

The images of the grass are revised as quickly as the images of the poet himself will be in the poem; the poet "tenderly uses" the grass as a means of exploring the creative process. These explorations are not the comments of a randomly wandering "innocent eye"; they are the comments of an experienced eye seeing freshly, sensing the brilliant possible transformations which nature may undergo when shaped by an imagination unfettered by rigid or static ways of viewing the world. As the poet's imagination "guesses" out loud, highlighting the whimsical and seemingly off-the-cuff nature of the images it produces, it invites the reader to participate in the guessing game. By playing out a few of the infinite metamorphoses the grass may undergo when appropriated by the imagination, Whitman shows the reader what it means to see and structure reality for oneself.

Just as the poet "uses" the grass to help his reader understand the nature by which the poem and poet come to be, he also "uses" scenes he had first explored in a very different way as a journalist. In section 34 of the poem, for example, Whitman returns to a scene he had described in a *Brooklyn Eagle* editorial urging that the United States declare war on Mexico. In the *Eagle* he had written,

> We have dammed up our memory of what has passed in the South years ago—of the devilish massacres of some of our bravest and noblest sons, children not of the South alone, but of the North and West—massacres, not only in defiance of ordinary humanity, but in violation of all the rules of war. Who has read the sickening story of those brutal wholesale murders so useless for any purpose except gratifying the cowardly appetite of a nation of braves, willing to shoot down men by the hundred in cold blood—without panting for the day when the prayer of that blood should be listened to—when the vengeance of a retributive God should be meted out to those who so ruthlessly and needlessly slaughter in His image?[75]

Nine years after he wrote the editorial, Whitman the poet "uses" this scene in a new way: it becomes another occasion for him to teach his reader something of the "origin of all poems."

"Hear now the tale of a jetblack sunrise," the poet writes in section 34, "Hear of the murder in cold blood of four hundred and twelve young men" (SOM, p. 64). The journalist had laid his cards on the table at the start: he would tell the story of a "devilish massacre." The details he assembles are there to make a point: war is justified. The more conventional the language, the more easily the reader may be persuaded. Thus we receive such conventional adjectives and adverbs as "bravest and noblest," "sickening," "brutal," "cowardly," "ruthlessly," and "needlessly," and such familiar abstractions as "in defiance of ordinary humanity" and "in violation of all the rules of war." The poet opens more obliquely. In place of the abstract generalizations, we see concrete dramas enacted. We watch the soldiers as they "received writing and seal, gave up their arms, and marched back prisoners of war" (p. 64). We then watch them as they are commanded to kneel and as they are shot, bayoneted, battered, and burned. The difference in the ways in which the two pieces use the word "massacre" is instructive. In the journalism the word is linked with a subjective judgment in the phrase, "devilish massacre." In the poem, there is merely objective comment:

> The second Sunday morning they were brought out in squads
>   and massacred . . . it was beautiful early summer,
> The work commenced about five o'clock and was over by eight.
> (P. 64)

No judging voice is allowed to enter between the reader and the scene; in the absence of a structuring filter, the reader views the scene in all its brittle horror. The only obvious intrusion of a consciousness other than that of the reader comes at the beginning and end of the segment, when the meaning of the unifying images is revealed:

> Hear now the tale of a jetblack sunrise,
> Hear now of the murder in cold blood of four hundred
>   and twelve young men. . . .

> At eleven o'clock began the burning of the bodies;
> And that is the tale of the murder of the four hundred
>   and twelve young men,
> And that was a jetblack sunrise.
> (Pp. 64, 65)

48

Section 34 is indeed a "jetblack sunrise" sent out by the poet himself.

> Dazzling and tremendous how quick the sunrise would kill me,
> If I could not now and always send sunrise out of me.

> We also ascend dazzling and tremendous as the sun.
> With the twirl of my tongue I encompass worlds and volumes of
>   worlds.
> (P. 50)

As the brilliantly oxymoronic central image unites and illuminates the facts the poet relates, it also reminds us of the project which is the subject of the poem.

Throughout the poem Whitman offers the reader other models of the kind of imaginative participation in life he might develop. When he tells the reader, "Now I will you to be a bold swimmer" (p. 81), in the closing section of the poem, associations with a different, earlier swimmer are triggered: the "twenty-ninth" bather, splashing, dancing, laughing in the water while staying "stock still in [her] room" (sec. 11) (p. 34). In section 9 of the poem Whitman spells out this process in greater detail.

First the poet sets the scene:

> The big doors of the country barn stand open
>   and ready,
> The dried grass of the harvest-time loads the slow-
>   drawn wagon,
> The clear light plays on the brown gray and green
>   intertinged,
> The armfuls are packed to the sagging now.
> (P. 32)

The scene now visualized, seen clearly from an external perspective, the poet moves into it, as a participant:

> I am there . . . I help . . . I came stretched
>   atop of the load,
> I felt its soft joints . . . one leg reclined on
>   the other,

> I jump from the crossbeams, and seize the clover
>   and timothy,
> And roll head over heels and tangle my hair full
>   of wisps.
> (P. 32)

First the poet sees the load of grass as both a unified whole and a collection of separate wisps, sensing carefully its weight, its color, and its texture. After vividly visualizing the scene in all its concrete detail, the poet walks into it and imprints upon it his presence, making it glow with immediacy and freshness. As he outlines this process step by step for the reader, Whitman shows the reader how to join him on this journey.

Whitman constantly draws the reader into the poem by asking questions, unanswerable ones, in particular. The questions are of the kind that may be answered only hypothetically, the kind best suited to being answered, perhaps, in poems: "What is man anyhow? What am I? and What are you?" (p. 43), Whitman asks, "To be in any form, what is that?" (p. 53). "You are also asking questions, and I hear you," Whitman tells his reader near the end of the poem, "I answer that I cannot answer . . . you must find out for yourself" (p. 80). Throughout the poem Whitman himself has responded to questions such as those mentioned above with evasiveness and ingenuity; as he does so, he provides a model for ways in which the reader might project his own "guesses" onto the world.

Leaves of Grass was not to be presented, however, as a "lesson"; Whitman preferred to write a book which "sets down bars to a good lesson."[76] The 1855 volume was to be taken more as the presence of a human being than as the product of an author's toil. No author's name appeared on the cover or title page. While a portrait of Whitman stared out from the frontispiece, one had to turn the page in order to find the name of Walter Whitman in small print in the copyright notice. The "presence" who invites his reader to join him on a journey of perception and creation, who guides his reader's imagination, but who leaves him free to inject his own thoughts into the ellipsis, to round out the poet's imaginings with his own, tells his reader at the close of "Song of Myself,"

> Failing to fetch me at first keep encouraged,
> Missing me one place search another,
> I stop some where waiting for you
> (P. 86)

The reader must carry on from where the poet left off.

While "Song of Myself" makes use of much of the material and method that characterized Whitman's early journalism, the poem also charts vast new territory of its own. While the journalist usually moved in a world of seemingly clear and certain answers presented in simple straightforward narrative from a single perspective, the artist moves in a world of ambiguous and doubt-laden questions explored from multiple viewpoints in complex and self-reflexive vortexes.

Whitman has created a work of art which impels the reader away from art; he has constructed a structure that condemns selection and structure and points up its own incompleteness. "There is a humiliating lesson one learns," Whitman would later write in "Specimen Days": "Nature seems to look on all fixed-up poetry and art as something almost impertinent." [77] While his first major work includes the riddle and the untying of the riddle, the mystery of being and how we come to know it, the poem and how a poem is made, it is, nevertheless, open-ended enough to acknowledge its own insufficiency. Its form purports to be as fluid and open and ongoing as nature itself. And it implies that any form that is less open will be inferior. [78]

"A great poem is no finish to a man or woman, but rather a beginning," Whitman wrote in his preface to the 1855 *Leaves of Grass.* "Has anyone fancied he could sit at last under some due authority and rest satisfied with explanations and realize and be content and full? To no such terminus does the great poet bring . . . he brings neither cessation or sheltered fatness and ease. The touch of him tells in action. Whom he takes with firm grasp into live regions previously unattained . . . thenceforward is no rest. . . ." [79]

3

MARK TWAIN

Mark Twain as a young reporter on the *Territorial Enterprise*, covering the Nevada Territorial Legislature in Carson City, Nevada, 1863.

Photo credit: Mark Twain Memorial, Hartford, Conn.

Like Walt Whitman, Mark Twain was introduced to newspaper work at age twelve. But the world of journalism in which he flourished for the next twenty years was separated from the world of journalism that had nurtured Whitman by much more than the continent and the decades that physically and temporally divided them.

The world of journalism in which Twain rose to prominence in the 1850s and 1860s was as much the product of demographic and technological changes as the world of Eastern journalism in the 1830s and 1840s had been. Much as the brisk growth of the East Coast's urban population in the 1830s and 1840s had created a profitable market for the new penny press, the tidal wave of emigration West that began with the gold rush of 1849 and continued throughout the 1850s and 1860s created a lucrative market for newspapers catering to the interests of the West's new citizens.

The technological changes that had helped give birth to the penny press in the 1830s (the invention of the two-cylinder printing press and processes for producing cheap newsprint) had their counterpart in technological changes that fueled the growth of the Western press in the 1850s and 1860s. High-speed rotary presses, 50,000 miles of telegraph wire, 30,000 miles of railroad, and propeller-powered ships all made it possible for the editor of a Western paper to offer news as "timely" as the reports his colleagues in the East could present. The demand for news skyrocketed, quickly outstripping the supply. Hundreds of new papers were born west of the Mississippi in the 1850s alone, as ambitious entrepreneurs tried to reap the benefits of this expanding and profitable market. Among them were five papers which would help shape Twain's literary apprenticeship.[1]

There were changes in style and content as well, which would have direct impact on Twain. The 1850s brought a great increase in the use of letters from correspondents in far-off places. While from the start the penny press had published letters from European correspondents, by the 1850s many daily papers were posting correspondents in Washington, D.C., and were running, with great frequency, letters from correspondents across the United States and from other continents as well—particularly South America and Africa. The great increase in domestic and foreign travel made possible by the thousands of new miles of railroad and by propeller-powered ships made distant places more interesting to newspaper readers in the 1850s. Twain himself sent special reports from the West, from the nation's capital, from the Sandwich Islands, South America, Africa, and Europe. Indeed, newspaper readers were so familiar with the letters of special correspondents as a genre during this period that they delighted in parodies of the form. Twain's first extended pieces of journalism were, indeed, a series of satires on such letters which he wrote for the *Keokuk* (Iowa) *Saturday Post* in 1856.

By the 1850s the formula of "entertainment, sensation, and humorous miscellany" developed originally by the urban penny papers had filtered down into the country pressrooms as well, and had shaped all the new papers of the West, large and small. [2] Indeed, as the expanding wire services became a primary source of "hard" news, the country editor's role involved, to a greater and greater extent, the development of amusing and readable anecdotes, local tidbits, and clever editorial vituperation. Melodrama, mudslinging satire, sentiment, dialect, diatribe, and downright buffoonery were by now expected modes of discourse in an institution patronized by people wishing to be entertained as well as informed. The papers of New Orleans and St. Louis overflowed with familiar comic narratives. Wilbur Storey's *Chicago Times*, founded in 1861, became known for its boisterous irreverence, and for its pun-filled alliterative headlines. [3] In Nevada, tall tales, fantasy, and humorous diatribe livened up reports of the most commonplace events. [4] Twain would work on small papers and large ones—weeklies, dailies, and monthlies—and he would learn the art of entertaining readers better than any of his editors had learned it. He was proud of the inventiveness that earned him a reputation for puncturing "unto death the heavy-sides of brainless fact that in its narrowness becomes falsehood." [5]

During the 1860s two opposing trends in journalism developed, both of which shaped Twain's own career: the push toward greater accuracy and the push toward greater extravagance and fabrication. The Civil War raised the standards of fullness and accuracy among journalists. People demanded facts, and they wanted them straight, correct, and complete. These standards persisted after the war, and flowed into other areas of reporting as well. Twain learned to report clearly and thoroughly during the 1860s (although he himself did not cover the war); he could lay out the bare, unvarnished facts with the best of them.

But alongside this demand for straight, clear factual reporting, the late 1860s and 1870s also saw a rise in the manufactured story: newspaper stunts and journalistic hoaxes sometimes meant to be taken straight by the readers, sometimes patently transparent and designed solely to amuse. [6] The most famous of the newspaper stunts was probably Henry Stanley's search for the missing Dr. Livingstone, which ended with the dramatic confrontation between the two men in Africa, all of which was plotted and stage-managed by James Gordon Bennett for the titillation of the *New York Herald*'s readers.

Twain proved himself as adept in the realm of fantasy as in the realm of fact. While he had neither the inclination nor the resources to stage elaborate stunts and then "report" on them for his readers, he proved to be a master of a close cousin of the "stunt," the journalistic "hoax." Physically less demanding but intellectually more challenging, the "hoax" involved manufacturing stories designed to "take in" even the most skeptical readers *up to a point*, only to blast them, in the end, with a refreshingly humbling sense of their own vulnerability to the narrator's skill and charm. For Twain, as we will show, those harmless hoaxes were very different in both kind and degree from the numerous not-so-harmless hoaxes perpetrated by the real-life charlatans who roamed the West trying to separate honest men from their life's savings. But Twain was not blind to what the two different enterprises had in common. He knew even then that there was often a close relation between one's ability to lie and one's ability to recognize someone else's lie. Helping his readers to unmask the lies that surrounded them was to be a major goal of Twain's work, both as a journalist and a novelist.

Newspapers in the 1850s and 1860s, particularly in the western states, were potpourris of different voices, styles, and forms. They included, alongside sentimental verse, searing sarcasm, and good-natured irreverence. Impressive arrays of accurately reported facts coexisted with outrageous tall tales, hoaxes, and outright lies. Stories of the local drunk appeared next to letters from the other side of the globe. Twain absorbed and produced all of these forms. And each of them would find its way into his fiction.

Twain's experience as a journalist during the twenty-five years preceding the 1873 publication of his first novel might conveniently be divided into four major phases: (1) early newspaper work, mainly in Hannibal, Missouri; New Orleans; and Keokuk, Iowa, 1847–59; (2) reporting and feature writing for Nevada and California newspapers, 1862–66; (3) traveling correspondence for California and New York newspapers, 1866–67; and (4) free-lance magazine writing, from 1866 throughout the rest of his career. There were, of course, other chapters of Twain's career as a journalist that do not fall neatly into one of these four categories, such as his stint as literary editor of the *Buffalo Express* from 1869 to 1871. But these four main phases have more than simply chronological significance. Each of them made a major contribution to

Twain's development as a writer; and each would leave a clearly recognizable imprint on the masterpiece that would appear in 1884, *Adventures of Huckleberry Finn.*

As an editorial assistant and printer's devil in Hannibal, Missouri, as a journalist and printer in St. Louis, New York, Keokuk, and Cincinnati, and as an occasional columnist in New Orleans from 1847 to 1859, Twain was introduced to the project of casting his world into print. Twain would return, in *Adventures of Huckleberry Finn*, to several of the subjects he had documented during his earliest newspaper days in Hannibal. He would, for example, incorporate aspects of a story he had written in 1852 about a fraudulent hoax of a road show that had passed through town into "The King's Cameleopard"; and aspects of an 1853 piece he had written about the town drunk would be incorporated into his characterization of Pap Finn.[7] But it was in the realm of style rather than content that Twain's early newspaper work had the greatest significance for his growth as a writer.

From his earliest days as a printer's devil Twain was put in intimate contact with the humorous forms of newspaper writing that were becoming increasingly popular in the nation's daily and weekly press. As he set into type skits, tall tales, anecdotes, and satires by well-known national humorists and by little-known local comics, Twain absorbed lessons in style and stance that would inform his finest literary creations. He wrote his first political satire for the *Hannibal Journal* in 1852.[8] (It is more memorable for effort than for effect.) His earliest published piece on the Mississippi River was a burlesque he published in 1859 in the *New Orleans Crescent*,[9] the same paper Walt Whitman had founded some ten years before. But it was in a series of three pieces Twain wrote for the *Keokuk Saturday Post* between November 1856 and April 1857 (his most sustained effort at newspaper humor thus far) that Twain first hit upon a voice which would eventually be transformed into that of Huck Finn.

The three pieces Twain published in the *Keokuk Post* under the pseudonym "Thomas Jefferson Snodgrass" were parodies of the letters from traveling correspondents that had begun to appear with regularity in the nation's papers. Twain's first parodies of a literary form were far from his last. As a journalist Twain would parody not only letters from traveling correspondents, but also stock prospectuses, political speeches, art criticism, romantic novels, travel guidebooks, Sunday school primers, and history textbooks.[10] Throughout these parodies Twain would extract great humor, sometimes broad, sometimes subtle, from a common human failing that would become a central concern in his fiction: literalness, or the tendency to accept without question the surface meaning of a text.

In these letters, Snodgrass came across as a wide-eyed, semiliterate rube with almost none of the endearing charm that would later characterize Huck Finn. But he *did* speak a variant of Pike County dialect, which is something none of his fellow correspondents did. For while both letters from traveling correspondents and humorous dialect stories (boxed off with comments from a narrator more cultured and educated than the hicks in the tale) were common in newspapers of the day, they were rarely combined. By merging the two forms to create an entertaining parody of the travel letter, Twain also brought about another original feat which would have lasting significance in his own career and in the shape of American fiction to come: he dispensed with the "box" and allowed an innocent, simple, sincere, and unrefined observer to tell his own story in his own words.

Some of Snodgrass's constructions were turns of phrase one could easily imagine coming out of the mouth of Huck Finn. Peanut boys "tearin around . . . indiscriminate like," fiddlers who "went at it," something which "warn't no use," and a lecture that was "uncommon severe"[11] are just a few of the Pike County expressions that would be at home in Twain's later novel. Snodgrass's mangled spellings—"Bimeby," "laffin," etc.—would, for the most part, be eliminated in Twain's later rendition of vernacular speech, as would Snodgrass's accurate characterization of his own "unsofisticated vision." But the style which Twain developed as he showed Snodgrass trying to summarize a Shakespearean tragedy he had seen, being victimized by deceivers more sophisticated than himself, and being generally perplexed by the pageant of life flowing by him was, by and large, the same style in which Huck Finn would later cruise through Shakespeare, shams, scams, and life itself.

A number of the subjects on which Twain wrote during the second phase of his career as a journalist, as a reporter and feature writer for Nevada and California newspapers from 1862 to 1866, would eventually find their way into *Adventures of Huckleberry Finn.* Architecture, drama, politics, education, steamboat disasters, shipwrecks, racial prejudice, and myriad forms of fraud, corruption, villainy, and humbug were all first explored in print by Twain during these years as a journalist in the West. His apprenticeship in the West taught him how to transcribe dialect, manipulate vocational jargon, and puncture verbal pomposity.[12] It taught him how to paint a vivid picture with the written word, how to communicate a visceral sensation, how to evoke a noxious smell.[13] It exposed him to a wide range of people, practices, and policies. As he would comment in later years, "Reporting is the best school in the world to get a knowledge of human beings, human nature, and human ways. Just think of the wide range of [a reporter's] acquaintanceship, his experience of life and society."[14]

Above all, Twain's apprenticeship in journalism educated his eye and ear to be suspicious—to probe surfaces and wallow in depths, to discriminate (as Whitman had put it, describing the task of the editor) "the good from the immense mass of unreal stuff floating on all sides of him."[15] As a fellow journalist rightly observed, it was as a reporter on the Comstock that Twain first acquired "that shrewd, graceless, good-humored way of looking at things as they in fact are—unbullied by authority, and indifferent to tradition."[16]

"I know from experience the proneness of journalists to lie," Twain wrote in the early 1870s, looking back on his own career as a journalist,

I once started a peculiar and picturesque fashion of lying myself on the Pacific coast, and it is not dead there to this day. Whenever I hear of a shower of blood and frogs combined, in California, or a sea serpent found in some desert there, or a cave frescoed with diamonds and emeralds (*always* found by an Injun who died before he could finish telling where it was), I say to myself I am the father of this child—I have got to answer for this lie.[17]

The credit Twain claims for this "picturesque fashion of lying" is itself a "stretcher," since the artful lie, or tall tale, was alive and well in the western states while Twain was still learning to compose type in Hannibal, Missouri, and often made its way into the columns of the local paper.[18] But Twain does deserve some credit for raising the standards. For while all of his fellow journalists lied, few of them were as good at it as Twain was. And few were taken as seriously.

Two weeks after he was hired as a "loculitems" reporter for the *Territorial Enterprise*, for example, Twain reported (with some subtle obfuscations) that a century-old stone mummy with a wooden leg had been found, sitting, winking, and thumbing his nose at his excavator.[19] The hoax was motivated, Twain claimed (although evidence indicates he may have been mainly having some fun), by his desire to deflate what he called "the growing evil" of the mania for digging up petrifactions.[20] Gullible newspaper editors across the country reprinted the story without comment, as did a London journal of chemistry, criticism, literature, and news. The facility with which Huck Finn would later spin outrageous lies about himself and Jim—the facility, indeed, which saved them both from detection and destruction—was first developed by Twain in the pages of the wild, unbridled newspapers of the West.

While Twain clearly enjoyed burlesque for its own sake, he recognized its power in the service of a larger cause. He realized (with the sense of ironic doubleness, perhaps, reflected both in his work and in the nom de plume he chose) that genuine fidelity to the world of fact might require blatant departures from that world. Treading the same road Whitman had before him—one which circled away from the facts in order to move the reader closer to them—Twain often burlesqued the facts of a case to highlight, emphasize, and dramatize the follies and deceptions they entailed.

There was no shortage of follies and deceptions to expose in "Washoe" or in San Francisco in the 1860s, where lying seems to have been a major industry. For every successful mining venture, there were a dozen horror stories of clever chicanery—and Twain himself was occasionally "taken in." While Twain was often rather silent about those fraudulent enterprises in which he himself had "bought feet," he generally relished the opportunity to expose in painstaking detail instances of humbug that came to his attention. It was a stance that he would find appealing throughout his career as a writer, both as a novelist, first in *The Gilded Age* and later in *Huckleberry Finn*, and as a short-story writer ("The Man that Corrupted Hadleyburg" is a good example). In Washoe and San Francisco, when he smelled a swindle he was quick to declare, both in theory and practice, the obligation of the journalist to ferret out the truth, to document the facts fully. He shared Whitman's view that the journalist's role is, in part, to help the reader discriminate "the real" from "the counterfeit."

In an 1863 article called "A Gorgeous Swindle" Twain took great delight in scrupulously identifying numerous discrepancies between the misleading generalities contained in Read and Co.'s prospectus and the concrete facts to which they allegedly referred:

The certificate of stock is a curiosity in the way of unblushing rascality. It does not state how many shares there are in the company, or what a share is represented by. It is a comprehensive arrangement—the company proposes to mine all over "Nevada Territory, adjoining California"! They are not partial to any particular mining district.

They are going to "carry on" a general "gold and silver mining business"! The untechnical, leather-headed thieves! The company is "TO BE" organized—at some indefinite period in the future—probably in time for the resurrection.[21]

Twain's own ready imagination allows him to relish with special gusto the specious touch of "art" with which the pamphlet concludes:

But the coolest, soothingest, the most refreshingest paragraph (to speak strongly) is that one which is stuck in at the bottom of the circular, with an air about it which mutely says, "it's of no consequence, and scarcely worth mentioning, but then it will do to fill out the page with." The paragraph reads as follows: "N.B.—Subscribers can receive their dividends, as they fall due, at Messrs. Read and Co.'s Banking House, No. 42 South Third Street, Philadelphia, or have them forwarded by express, of which all will be regularly notified!" We imagine we can see a denizen of some obscure western town walking with stately mien to the express office to get his regular monthly dividend; we imagine less fortunate people making way for him, and whispering together, "There goes old Thompson—owns ten shares in the People's Gold and Silver Mining Company—Lord! but he's rich!—he's going after his dividends now." And we imagine we see old Thompson and his regular dividends fail to connect. And finally, we imagine we see the envied Thompson jeered at by his same old neighbors as "the old fool who got taken in by the most palpable humbug of the century."[22]

Twain was shocked by this scheme to "cheat multitudes of the poorest classes of men in the States," a scheme which, he felt, "would go far toward destroying confidence in our mines and our citizens if permitted to succeed." Like Whitman, who asked that newspapers "never hesitate boldly to exhibit to public gaze the *facts* . . . ,"[23] Twain felt it was the responsibility of the journalist to bring the facts to light:

Now this swindle ought to be well ventilated by the newspapers—not that sound business men will ever be swindled by it, but the unsuspecting multitude, who yearn to grow suddenly rich will assuredly have their slender purses drained by it.[24]

Twain accomplished this "ventilation" by printing not only his own article, but the entire prospectus itself alongside it. His piece thus gave his reader an object lesson in how to approach a text suspiciously—a kind of lesson that would grow increasingly important to Twain, one which would, in fact, be central to *Adventures of Huckleberry Finn.*

Twain occasionally chastised fellow journalists (particularly on competing newspapers) for failing to keep in constant view their professional obligation to unmask lies and expose frauds. "Where did you get your notion of the duties of a journalist from?" he demanded of another local editor who claimed it was "the duty of citizens—to ferret out abuses and correct them. ... Any editor in the world will say it is YOUR duty to correct them," Twain wrote, "What are you paid for? What use are you to the community? What are you fit for as conductor of a newspaper, if you cannot do these things?"[25] Twain himself shouldered these responsibilities cheerfully; indeed, while his colleagues would go out of their way to ignore flagrant abuses of justice and power, Twain was most content when exposing harmful hypocrisy, flummery, stupidity, or sham. When he saw a gap between rhetoric and reality, his pen wedged its way in and broadened it into a gaping chasm which no member of the "unsuspecting multitude" could miss.

While Twain was as adept at telling the truth as he was at telling lies, he found much of the truth unrelievedly boring. "San Francisco is a city of startling events," he wrote with undisguised disdain in the *Enterprise* in 1865, in an article on "The Spirit of the Local Press":

Happy is the man whose destiny it is to gather them up and record them in a daily newspaper! That sense of conferring benefit, profit and innocent pleasure upon one's fellow-creatures which is so cheering, so calmly blissful to the plodding pilgrim here below, is his, every day in the year. When he gets up in the morning he can do as old Franklin did, and say, "This day, and all days, shall be unselfishly devoted to the good of my fellow-creatures—to the amelioration of their condition—to the conferring of happiness upon them—to the storing of their minds with wisdom which shall fit them for their struggle with the hard world, here, and for the enjoyment of a glad eternity hereafter. And thus striving, so shall I be blessed!" And when he goes home at night, he can exult and say: "Through the labors of these hands and this brain, which God hath given me, blessed and wise are my fellow-creatures this day!

"I have told them of the wonder of the swindling of the friend of Bain, the unknown Bain from Petaluma Creek, by the obscure

Catharine McCarthy, out of $300—and told it with entertaining verbosity in half a column.

"I have told them that Christmas is coming, and people go strangely about, buying things—I have said it in forty lines.

"I related how a vile burglar entered a house to rob, and actually went away again when he found he was discovered. I told it briefly, in thirty-five lines.

"In forty lines I told how a man swindled a Chinaman out of a couple of shirts, and for fear the matter might seem trivial, I made a pretense of only having mentioned it in order to base upon it a criticism upon a grave defect in our laws.

"I fulminated again, in a covert way, the singular conceit that Christmas is at hand, and said people were going about in the most unaccountable way buying stuff to eat, in the markets—52 lines . . . Much other wisdom I disseminated, and for these things let my reward come hereafter."

And his reward *will* come hereafter—and I am sorry enough to think of it. But such startling things do happen every day in this strange city!—and how dangerously exciting must be the employment of writing them up for the daily papers![26]

"After having been hard at work from nine or ten in the morning until eleven at night scraping material together," Twain recalled some forty years later, "I took the pen and spread this muck out in words and phrases and made it cover as much acreage as I could. It was fearful drudgery, soulless drudgery, and almost destitute of interest."[27]

Twain's criticisms of the "spirit of the local press" would turn up again in his novel *A Connecticut Yankee in King Arthur's Court,* published in 1889, when he has the book's narrator come across a "Court Circular" whose "startling events" must have harkened back to those Twain covered in San Francisco:

COURT CIRCULAR

On Monday, the King rode in the park.
   "   Tuesday   "   "   "
   "   Wendesday   "   "   "
   "   Thursday   "   "   "
   "   SaTurday   "   "   "
   "   Sunda5,   "   "   "

                                (*sic*)[28]

The narrator offers some advice on how a reporter should deal with the monotony of his "beat":

> The best way to manage—in fact, the only sensible way—is to disguise repetitiousness of fact under variety of form: skin your fact each time and lay on a new cuticle of words. It deceives the eye; you think it is a new fact; it gives you the idea that the court is carrying on like everything; this excites you, and you drain the whole column, with a good appetite, and perhaps never notice that it's a barrel of soup made out of a single bean.[29]

Despite his publishers' complaints that Twain tended to stray from the facts more often than they wished, there is evidence that his close adherence to the facts troubled them more than his free-wheeling departures from them. Twain was bearing witness to a San Francisco that no one else was recording, and the truth was often a pill too bitter for editors and publishers to swallow. Some of his most searing and trenchant criticisms of local hypocrisy and fraud were censored by omission: his papers simply refused to run them. Twain met his first instance of direct censorship with disbelief; he thought the absence of a piece in which he documented the police's outrageously hypocritical treatment of a Chinese man to be simply a mistake. He soon learned that his publishers cared more for not offending the paper's subscribers (who shared the police's prejudices) than for the truth. (He would return to this early encounter with censorship in *A Connecticut Yankee* when the narrator would warn the editors of the *Weekly Hosannah and Literary Volcano* that a certain passage might "give offense to the hermits, and perhaps lose us their advertising.") The racial prejudice he first covered in San Francisco—particularly the ways in which such prejudice distorted American ideals of justice and equality—was a subject which, with subtle transformations, would form the core of the novel he would publish in 1884.

As Twain's social criticism began to pervade more and more of his humor, the California papers to which he was a regular contributor began to stop printing his pieces. He struck back by getting his friend Joe Goodman to publish his columns in his old Nevada paper, the *Enterprise*. Virginia City, Nevada, was far enough away from San Francisco authorities to publish searing attacks on them with impunity—but not too far for Twain's growing stature as a social critic to reach the Coast. Twain would soon respond to the daily paper's censorship by writing up his criticisms for national monthly magazines in quasi-fictional forms that allowed him to dramatize as well as report the outrages that he witnessed in San Francisco.[30]

In 1867 Twain left for a trip around the world as a traveling correspondent for the *San Francisco Alta California*. His letters from abroad would be printed by Horace Greeley's *New York Tribune* and James Gordon Bennett's *New York Herald* as well, and would win him unprecedented fame. They would also provide him with the chance to experiment in print with the kind of ironic deflation and juxtaposition that would later play such a key role in *Adventures of Huckleberry Finn*. Most important, perhaps, they provided him with the opportunity to explore the project of creating a narrative comprised of a montage of multiple styles and modes—a project which would be central, as well, to his later novel. Twain's work as a traveling correspondent in 1867 acclimated him to the very form which he would choose, consciously or not, for *Huckleberry Finn*, a novel which is, at its core, an extended travel letter from a correspondent who has much in common with the correspondent who set sail on the *Quaker City*.

One of Twain's central projects in these letters (and in the volume in which they would be eventually collected with some revisions, *The Innocents Abroad*) is to help extricate the reader from the false, hackneyed, empty, or misleading images, attitudes, and perspectives that church legends, travel guidebooks, and certain stylized genres of fiction tended to export and promote. A healthy and established tradition of dissent from the romantic treatment of Europe had been in existence for some time before Twain set sail on the *Quaker City*, as Bernard DeVoto has observed.[31] The stance was not new; but the superiority with which Twain carried it off was. Not every text Twain unmasks is necessarily pernicious; rather, his repeated pattern of challenging images, symbols, and auras to jibe with the realities they purport to represent is designed to get the reader into the habit of being suspicious of *all* texts, both harmless and harmful ones.

By highlighting the deception entailed by the narrow focus of guidebooks, romantic novels, and church legends, Twain helps his reader avoid being victimized by these misleading texts. "I can almost tell, in set phrase what [my shipmates] will say when they see Tabor, Nazareth, Jericho and Jerusalem—*because I have seen the books they will smouch their ideas from*. These authors write pictures and frame rhapsodies, and lesser men follow and see with the author's eyes instead of their own . . . "[32] Like Whitman, Twain was disturbed by people's willingness, as Whitman had put it, to "take things at second or third hand," to "look through the eyes of the dead . . . [and] feed on the spectres in books."[33] In his chapter on Galilee he takes his readers (much as Whitman had) through an object lesson in how they might go about seeing with "their own" eyes.

First he quotes the lush, overblown, sentimental, and romantic descriptions of Galilee one finds in various travel books and juxtaposes them to a stark view of the scene as it actually is—"an unobtrusive basin of water, some mountainous desolation, and one tree." Then night falls and Twain takes a different tack: "when the day is done, even the most unimpressible must yield to the dreamy influences of this tranquil starlight. The old traditions of the place steal upon his memory . . ." Twain then shares with the reader his own shimmering poetic reverie inspired by Galilee "in the starlight."[34] His point is not that one must forswear the subtle shadows and sublime lights that the imagination can impart to a scene which, from a purely objective standpoint, is physically bare and unimpressive. It is that one cannot see the scene itself *or* the marvelous shadows and lights one's imagination can impart to it if one simply parrots uncritically the views others have recorded.

While not totally immune from the flaws it attributes to other texts, Twain's own narrative successfully challenges the authority of those texts as guides for the world they purport to describe.[35] By focusing solely on the elegant palace or cathedral, for example, the guidebook implicitly denies the reality of the slum down the road or the beggar at the gate. The opulence, grace, and beauty represented by the palace or cathedral, Twain points out again and again, through artful enlargement of context, are often bought by denying the basic human needs of the masses that live in its shadow. Twain's own text deflates the false pretenses of a culture which, on the one hand, aspires to be respected as the height of civilization but which at the same time systematically degrades the lives of its own citizens. Thus the opulence of Versailles is dimmed by the close proximity (geographically and within the text) of the degradation of the slum at Faubourg St. Antoine. The king's magnificent palace at Naples is put in perspective by the miserable vagabond on the curb in front. The Italy so often described by the guidebooks as "one vast museum" is characterized by Twain as "one vast museum of magnificence and misery."[36]

Twain deflates the language in which the culture is described in conventional texts not only by enlarging the context of the scene painted, but also by presenting it through the eyes of a narrator who seems oblivious to the import of the contradictory details he strings together. This narrator, who seems to accept unquestioningly the "accepted" view of things, seems always unaware of the ways in which the facts he relates to the reader cancel out that view. Thus he tells us, straight-faced, that "among the most precious relics" at the cathedral at Milan "were a stone from the Holy Sepulchre, a part of the crown of thorns (they have a whole one at Notre Dame), a fragment of the purple robe worn by the Saviour, a nail from the Cross and a picture of the Virgin and Child painted by the veritable hand of St. Luke" (p. 129). All this is excellent preparation for the writer who will artfully undercut, in 1884, the level of civilization achieved in a household like the Grangerfords', where people are as ready to hang up another sentimental verse about death as they are ready to take another life, or where people pack rifles when they go to church to hear sermons on brotherly love.

It was in the letters he wrote as a traveling correspondent for California and New York newspapers that Twain first strung together within a single narrative a succession of contrasting styles and moods. While a travelogue by definition suggests movement over many terrains, each characterized by its own inhabitants, flora, and fauna, Twain's travelogues covered a wide range of literary and emotional terrains as well, moving from genuine tragedy to mock tragedy, from straight factual description to broad burlesque.

His letter of March 15, 1867, for example,[37] moved from a somber, succinct, factual, and subdued description of the death of a child, and the genuine grief shared by everyone on board, to the amusing tale (told deadpan) of how the ship's resident con-man met his downfall when he tried to swindle the passengers out of their money by affecting very unconvincing false grief for the alleged recent death of his wife. A straightforward description of the landscape comes next, followed by a hilarious tongue-in-cheek rendition of "a legend from the captain" in which an old lady's expectations of a tale ending in death and catastrophe are blasted, much to her irritation, by a surprise happy ending. Nine separate units of narrative (including social diatribes, broad-brushed visual humor, etc.) are strung together in this letter as beads on a necklace, united solely by the thread of the voyage. They relate to each other only by proximity and juxtaposition.

All of this is important preparation for a book that will also include genuine tragedy, grief, and pathos (as in Jim's tale about his family), mock grief (a specialty of the Duke and the Dauphin), straight description (of the river), burlesque (the level to which Tom Sawyer's return sinks the narrative), and numerous other modes as well, each casting its predecessors in new lights. While it is clear that Twain is indebted to his early experiences as a traveling correspondent for having exposed him to the form he would choose for his greatest novel, the contribution was a mixed blessing. One might speculate that without it, perhaps Twain might have put more energy into structuring his novel more conventionally, spending time plotting rather than simply stringing beads. Had the book borrowed less from the "traveling correspondent" tradition, perhaps it might have achieved greater coherence and a less problematical ending. (Of course, however, as long as one is speculating, such differences might have made it less distinctive and unique.)

While Twain's work as a traveling newspaper correspondent allowed him to explore the form he would choose for *Huckleberry Finn*, it was as a freelance journalist for national magazines from 1866 on that he explored the subjects that would be central to the novel and the experiment in style that would lead, eventually, to his decision to let Huck narrate his own adventures. It was in the *Galaxy* magazine in 1870 and 1871 that Twain first explored in depth the dynamics of racial prejudice and persecution and the shameful fact of its persistence in a country founded on principles of equality. He first grappled with the project of casting into print the Mississippi River and life on its shores in a series of pieces he did for the *Atlantic* in 1874 and 1875. And it was in *Harper's New Monthly Magazine* in 1866 and in the *Atlantic* in 1874 that Twain discovered the power and drama of allowing narrators to tell their own stories in their own words.

Twain deplored the fact that the Chinese in San Francisco were systematically stripped of rights promised them by law and treated by the police, courts, tax gatherers, newspapers, and average citizens as some species of less-than-human vermin. His reports of brutality against the Chinese, as we have mentioned, were usually censored by his San Francisco editors, but were occasionally run by newspapers in Nevada and also New York. It was in a series of articles he wrote for the *Galaxy* magazine in 1870 and 1871, however, that Twain was able to explore these issues fully. (He would also explore them in *Roughing It*, the quasi-fictional, quasi-journalistic narrative of the West published in 1872.) In these pieces he profited from a lesson he had first learned as a reporter on the Comstock: the tools of fiction may be fruitfully employed in the service of fact.

In a remarkable satire called "Disgraceful Persecution of a Boy," Twain described a community whose tax gatherers collected unlawful mining taxes from the Chinese not once but twice, whose courts convicted the Chinese not just when guilty but *always*, whose police stood idly by when the Chinese were attacked by dogs, and whose newspapers cheered when the Chinese were mugged or stoned by gangs of youths (all conditions he had personally witnessed in San Francisco).[38] In this piece Twain expresses mock outrage at the nerve of such a community daring to throw "a well-dressed boy, on his way to Sunday-school," into prison for having stoned a Chinese man. The boy, Twain explained, had simply learned from those around him that

> A Chinaman had no rights that any man was bound to respect; that he had no sorrows that any man was bound to pity; that neither his life nor his liberty was worth the purchase of a penny when a white man needed a scape-goat; that nobody loved Chinamen, nobody befriended them, nobody spared them suffering when it was convenient to inflict it; everybody, individuals, communities, the majesty of the State itself, joined in hating, abusing, and persecuting these humble strangers. And therefore what COULD have been more natural than for this sunny-hearted boy, tripping along to Sunday-school, with his mind teeming with freshly-learned incentives to high and virtuous action, to say to himself: "Ah, there goes a Chinaman! God will not love me if I do not stone him." And for this he was arrested and put in the city jail. (p. 717)

"Everything conspired to teach him that it was a high and holy thing to stone a Chinaman," Twain concludes, "and yet he no sooner attempts to do his duty than he is punished FOR it." While the voice that narrates this piece may have more in common with that of Jonathan Swift than of Huckleberry Finn, the moral stance is the same one that will be transformed, with such mastery, in Twain's 1884 novel. The hypothetical young man who is just trying to "do his duty" by stoning a "Chinaman" has much in common with a Huck Finn who wrestles valiantly with his inability to "do his duty" (as he sees it) by returning Jim to slavery. Both boys expect swift punishment if they transgress the values society has drummed into them. The brilliant line in *Huckleberry Finn* "All right, then, I'll *go* to Hell"[39] is a variation on the strategy and theme Twain first explored in the *Galaxy* magazine in 1870.

In another satire published serially in the *Galaxy* in 1870 and 1871, "Goldsmith's Friend Abroad Again," a fictitious Ah Song Hi wrote his fictitious friend Ching-Foo a running description of life in "that noble realm where all are free and equal, and none reviled or abused—America!"[40] While the letters were fictitious, Twain assured his reader that they were based on unadorned reality: "No experience is set down in the following letters which had to be invented," he wrote, "Fancy is not needed to give variety to the history of a Chinaman's sojourn in America. Plain fact is amply sufficient."[41]

Just hours after landing, Ah Song Hi is robbed, beaten, arrested, and thrown into jail (for "disturbing the peace"). When he proposes, at his trial, to call several Chinese witnesses to testify that he did nothing to provoke the attack, the interpreter explains, "That won't work. In this country white men can testify against Chinamen all they want to, but CHINAMEN AIN'T ALLOWED TO TESTIFY AGAINST WHITE MEN."

What a chill went through me! And then I felt the indignant blood rise to my cheek at this libel upon the Home of the Oppressed, where all men are free and equal—perfectly equal—perfectly free and perfectly equal. I despised this Chinese-speaking Spaniard for his mean slander of the land that was sheltering and feeding him. I sorely wanted to sear his eyes with that sentence from the great and good American Declaration of Independence which we have copied in letters of gold in China and keep hung up over our family altars and in our temples—I mean the one about all men being created free and equal.

But woe is me, Ching Foo, the man was right. He was right, after all. There were my witnesses, but I could not use them . . .[42]

(It was not the "Declaration of Independence" itself that Twain was satirizing in this letter, but rather the failure of his country to live up to the ideals it inscribed. Like Dos Passos some fifty years later, Twain would devote an important part of his career as a writer to cleansing, or making new "the clean words our fathers spoke," as Dos Passos put it, which had been allowed to turn "slimy and foul" by intervening generations.)[43]

When Twain returned to the issue of racism and racial persecution in *Adventures of Huckleberry Finn*, the time, the place, and the race would be different. But the central question would be much the same: how can a society which systematically denies the humanity of large numbers of human beings consider itself civilized? How can a society which degrades and debases human lives on a mass scale dare think of itself as refined, genteel, or cultured? As he first did in his *Galaxy* articles of the

1870s, in *Huckleberry Finn* Twain would use the lethal weapon of irony to shame his countrymen into recognizing the gaps between their images of themselves and reality.

It was also as a freelance magazine writer that Twain first explored the issue of slavery directly. "A True Story Repeated Word for Word as I Heard It," which he published in the *Atlantic* in 1874 (his first contribution to that magazine), was his first experiment with sustaining both dialect and an uneducated first-person narrator throughout a fairly lengthy narrative.[44] The piece explored the technique of having a slave tell her own story, in her own words, without the intervention (save at more than one or two minor points) of an educated narrator. Missing from "A True Story" was the condescension normally implicit in the box framework, and missing, too, was the facile humor stemming from the absurd juxtaposition of two levels of language and the views of life embodied by each.[45] "Aunt Rachel" narrates her own story with a moving power and directness:

> Dey put chains on us an' put us on a stan' as high as dis po'ch— twenty foot high—an' all de people stood aroun', crowds an' crowds. An' dey'd come up dah an' look at us all roun', an' squeeze our arm, an' make us git up an' walk, an' den say, "Dis one too ole," or "Dis one lame," or "Dis one don't 'mount to much." An' dey sole my ole man, an' took him away, an' dey begin to sell my chil'en an' take *dem* away, an' I begin to cry, an' de man say, "Shet up yo' damn blubberin'," an' hit me on de mouf wid his han'. An' when de las' one was gone but my little Henry, I grab' *him* clost up to my breas' so, an' I ris up an' says, "You sha'n't take him away," I says; "I'll kill de man dat teches him!" I says. But my little Henry whisper an' say, "I gwyne to run away, an' den I work an' buy yo' freedom." Oh, bless de chile, he always so good! But dey got him—dey got him, de men did; but I took and tear de clo'es mos' off of 'em an' beat 'em over de head wid my chain; an' *dey* give it to *me*, too, but I didn't mine dat.[46]

Twain took great pains to make his reader hear the story as he himself had heard it; he labored long and hard to set down a kind of speech that had not been previously captured in print. "I amend this dialect stuff," he said, "by talking and talking and *talking* it 'til it sounds right."[47] The result was a story of slavery infinitely more powerful than any that had appeared before. As William Dean Howells, then editor of the *Atlantic*, characterized it shortly after it appeared, "The rugged truth of the sketch leaves all other stories of slave life infinitely behind, and reveals a gift in the author for the simple, dramatic report of reality which we have seen equalled in no other American writer."[48] The next time Twain would tell the "simple, dramatic" story of a slave's life, the slave would be Jim, and the place would be Jackson's Island. But for both the experience of translating Missouri Negro dialect into print, and for the chance to see the literary power of having a slave tell his own story, Twain was indebted to his work for the *Atlantic* in 1874.

While Twain had first experimented with a vernacular narrator in his humorous travel-letter satires in the *Keokuk Post*, it was as a magazine writer in the 1860s and 1870s that he was able to explore the serious possibilities of this strategy. Looking back, during his later years, on his first effort in the 1860s to break into the world of national magazines, Twain recalled,

In my view a person who published things in a mere newspaper could not properly claim recognition as a Literary Person: he must rise above that; he must appear in a magazine. He would then be a Literary Person; also, he would be famous—right away. These two ambitions were strong upon me. This was in 1866. I prepared my contributions and then looked around for the best magazine to go up to glory in. I selected the most important one in New York. The contribution was accepted.[49]

The magazine was *Harper's New Monthly Magazine* and the contribution a story about the burning of the clipper-ship *Hornet* on May 3, 1866.[50] Twain had first written up this event as a traveling correspondent for the *Sacramento Daily Union*.[51] Indeed, his story of how fifteen crewmen survived a forty-three-day trip through the tropics in an open boat with ten days' ration of food was Twain's greatest "scoop" as a newspaperman. He had managed to be the first to interview the men when they arrived on shore in Honolulu and was the first as well to tell their story to the world. His newspaper quickly published the account he had thrown on the first boat for the mainland, his distillation of what the men had told him in the initial hours of conversation. It was a significantly different article, however, which would appear in *Harper's New Monthly Magazine*.

Twain booked passage back to San Francisco on the same boat the survivors were to take, and during the voyage he was allowed to peruse and copy the diaries kept by the captain and two members of the crew. While his account for the *Union* had been a competent third-person narrative replete with statements of wonder at the men's remarkable experiences, the article Twain produced several weeks later for *Harper's* was a nearly direct transcription of the diaries. Twain's final "literary" treatment of the event was thus closer to the bare facts of the event than his initial journalistic synthesis. (Hemingway would revise his own journalism along similar lines when he incorporated it into *In Our Time*, as we will see in chapter 5.) Recognizing the incomparable immediacy and power of the unpolished firsthand reports, Twain did not hesitate to substitute them for his own smoother and more structured narrative. Instead of requiring the reader to see the events through Twain's eyes, Twain recognized the benefits of allowing him to encounter the first-person accounts directly. When he returned in *Huckleberry Finn* to material he had first written up in *Life on the Mississippi*, as we will discuss, Twain would follow the same strategy of revision.

In its own distinctive way, Twain's "Old Times on the Mississippi," appearing in the *Atlantic* the same year as "A True Story," was also a "simple, dramatic report of reality." In this work Twain tried to communicate the scrupulous attention to natural fact which was crucial to the work of the pilot and the safety of his passengers. "One cannot easily realize what a tremendous thing it is to know every trivial detail of twelve hundred miles of river and know it with absolute exactness," he wrote.[52]

Twain helps the reader comprehend the mysteries of this attention to concrete detail by allowing him to accompany the "cub pilot" through his river education. As he takes the reader past fog-enveloped plantations and all-important one-limbed cottonwoods, through treacherous snags and reefs, unannounced bluffs, apocryphal sandbars, and constantly changing channels, Twain helps the reader appreciate the supreme respect the river pilot feels for the world of concrete fact. While his purpose in this volume is to introduce the reader to the "wonderful science" of piloting, he would return to the material he documents here in the novel that would appear nearly ten years later. The river is the same river, but the uses to which it is put change deeply.

When Twain expanded "Old Times" into *Life on the Mississippi* his additions fell into two main categories: (1) geographic and political facts about the river, its discovery, its role in history; and (2) social facts about the people along its banks. The first four chapters of the new book, "The Body of the Nation," "The River and Its History," "The

River and Its Explorers," and "Frescoes from the Past," establish a larger context in which the information in "Old Times" might be more meaningfully viewed. Chapters 18 through 60 (also new) deal primarily with the social history of the region Twain knew so well: the way people walked, the way they dressed, their feuds, their architecture, their interior decorations, the books they read, their views of themselves and others' views of them—all these subjects were added to Twain's original chronicle of a boy's piloting experience.[53] Here, even more than in "Old Times," Twain is aware of his role as a chronicler of a fast-fading culture and way of life.

In both "Old Times" and *Life on the Mississippi* Twain establishes the importance of concrete fact and the dangers of failing to attend to fact as closely as one should. But in *Life on the Mississippi* Twain expands his respect for fact to include a hostility toward many of the "fictions" that his compatriots admire and respect. For example, at one point he attacks a southern educator's claim that the "highest type of civilization this continent has seen" may be found in the South;[54] accepting this myth, Twain fears, might blind one to the barbarism and violence underlying that "highest" of cultures. Twain deflates the educator's claims by documenting, without comment, in a two-page footnote, a searing chronicle of mindless, violent crimes committed near that educator's hometown.[55] The fictions which draw Twain's greatest opprobrium in *Life on the Mississippi* are those of Sir Walter Scott, on whom Twain blames much that is false, hypocritical, or worthless in personal values, religion, government, style, and architecture. "The South," Twain wrote, "has not yet recovered from the debilitating influence of his books."

> Admiration of his fantastic heroes and their grotesque "chivalry" doings and romantic juvenilities still survives here . . . traces of its inflated language, and other windy humbuggeries survive along with it. (P. 333)

For early in his life Twain had learned that lies tended to breed lies. Sir Walter's "sham grandeurs, sham gauds and sham chivalries," Twain felt, were likely to breed other shams in a populace that accepted them unquestioningly (pp. 375–76). Twain's heated tirade against Scott-inspired architecture, "with turrets and things—materials all ungenuine within and without, pretending to be what they are not" (p. 333), was less an aesthetic judgment than a moral one. Such an "architectural falsehood" symbolized, for Twain, the presence of a society responsive to things "pretending to be what they are not." He regretted that the restoration funds would not be devoted "to the building of something genuine" instead.

The respect for fact Twain acquired as a journalist led him, throughout his career, to hold other writers to the same standards of accuracy and authenticity to which he held himself. After painstakingly documenting a dozen or so glaring inaccuracies in *The Deerslayer*, for example, Twain concluded, "Cooper's eye was splendidly inaccurate. Cooper seldom saw anything correctly." Evidently his ear was not much better. Twain asserted (in terms much like those that would appear several years later on the *Kansas City Star* style sheet) that it is mandatory that "when the personages of a tale deal in conversation, their talk shall sound like human talk, and be talk such as human beings would be likely to talk in the given circumstances." This requirement "has been ignored from the beginning of *The Deerslayer* to the end of it," Twain wrote, adding that Cooper must have been as verbally "tone-deaf" as he was functionally blind.[56] Twain was wont grandly to assert the accuracy of his own renditions of speech. "As impossible as this conversation may sound to a person who is not an idiot, it is scarcely in any respect an exaggeration of one which one of us actually listened to in an American drawing room."[57] Twain and Charles Dudley Warner put this statement in a footnote in the novel they published in 1873, *The Gilded Age*, a book so densely packed with contemporary realities that it gave the era its name. Twain was good at inventing outrageous scenarios to dramatize the pitfalls of relying on fiction for information about the world of fact. One such scene occurs in "Huck Finn and Tom Sawyer Among the Indians," the sequel to *Huckleberry Finn* that was published posthumously (1968). After a group of Indians have brutally murdered the pioneer family that befriended Huck and Tom, spreading their dismembered limbs across the countryside, Huck asks,

"Tom, where did you learn about the Injuns—how noble they was?"
He gave me a look that showed I had hit him very hard, and so I wished I hadn't said the words. He turned away his head, and after a minute he said "Cooper's novels" . . . and didn't say anything more, and I didn't say anything more, and so that changed the subject.[58]

Later Huck adds, "he had got it through his noodle, by this time, that book Injuns and real Injuns is different" (p. 32).

While Twain's work as a journalist paid his bills, his interest in being known as an imaginative writer seems to date back as far as his earliest years in a newspaper office. His early poetry, like Whitman's, is dismal. His early fiction, while entertaining, is shallow. Only when he returned as an imaginative writer to the subjects, styles, and strategies he had first explored as a journalist would Twain achieve the success for which he is most respected and remembered.

During the same month in which he documented for the *Hannibal Daily Journal* in a competently straightforward, factual manner the grim story of some children with smallpox who were put ashore by a steamboat and "will most probably die,"[59] Twain also published in the *Daily Journal* a piece of sentimental verse called "The Heart's Lament," dedicated "To Bettie W——E, of Tennessee,":

I know thou wilt forget me.
  For that fond soul of thine
Turns boldly from the passionate,
  And ardent love of mine.[60]

Unlike Whitman, young Twain seems to have accepted his submediocrity as a poet and moved on to other genres of literature.

A brief piece of fiction which he published in 1865 against his better judgment but at the insistence of a friend was what earned him his initial nationwide fame as a writer. "The Celebrated Jumping Frog of Calaveras County," Twain's rendition of a Western tall tale related to him by an innkeeper, appeared in the *New York Saturday Press* on November 18, 1865, and was an immediate popular sensation.[61]

Twain was delighted to find himself famous (although since fame brought neither money nor job offers he continued to support himself as a reporter for a number of years). Indeed, his early fame as a humorist was so widespread that it often tended to blind the public, and critics, to the more profound and ambitious role he began to carve out for himself as a writer. Bibliographers even classified the searing satirical record of racial persecution and brutality that he published in the *Galaxy* ("Goldsmith's Friend Abroad Again") under the heading "Whimsical Sketches" despite the total absence of "whimsy" in the pieces.

Twain's earliest efforts as an imaginative writer—bad love poems and fine tall tales—were devoid of moral import. Designed solely to entertain, they succeeded admirably in doing just that. It was only when

Twain welded to his skills as a humorist the depths of profound moral concern he had acquired as a journalist that a masterpiece like *Adventures of Huckleberry Finn* could come into being.

One of Twain's major preoccupations in *Huckleberry Finn*, as we will show, is his familiar concern with documenting facts and deflating fictions; but in this book Twain takes this project a step further than he had in the earlier works. Here Twain succeeds in organizing his respect for fact and suspicion of fiction into a vision broad enough to include the book itself. While poking barbs at the fictions crafted by society, Twain subtly undercuts the fiction he himself has crafted; by highlighting, instead of ignoring, the fictiveness, the made-ness, the concomitant mendaciousness of any text, he succeeds in helping his reader see, as he once put it, "with his own eyes instead of the eyes of those who traveled . . . before him."[62]

Many of the facts in *Adventures of Huckleberry Finn* are familiar ones, encountered previously in Twain's nonfiction. The same stretch of the Mississippi, for example, from St. Louis down past Cairo toward New Orleans, figures centrally in "Old Times" and *Life on the Mississippi* and *Huckleberry Finn*, as do many of the social facts about life on the river's shores. The morals and manners, houses and aesthetics, rites and customs, and varieties of speech which Twain documents in "Old Times" and *Life on the Mississippi* all find their way into *Huckleberry Finn*, as do the facts in Twain's "True Story" of slavery, and the ignorance, brutality, and prejudice which Twain encountered and documented in San Francisco.

As he documents these many real scenes and events in *Huckleberry Finn*, Twain takes pains to avoid the sloppiness and inaccuracy that so irked him in the writings of others; he was determined that his own work never prove deficient in river-craft, that his characters never talk like gilt-edged volumes, that he never use the approximate word when the right one was at hand. Thus Twain shows his firsthand familiarity with procedures such as taking up a "trot line," catching a "wood-flat," and "saddle-bagsing" around a steamboat; he asserts that the seven dialects represented in the book have been done "painstakingly, with the trustworthy guidance and support of personal familiarity with these several forms of speech."[63] Twain welcomes a host of concrete terms rarely if ever included in a work of literature, such as "dog-leg," "bitts," "spondulicks," "galoot," "galluses," and "linsey-woolsey."[64] If the right word is likely to be unfamiliar to his reader, Twain patiently has it explained (a "towhead," Huck tells us at one point, "is a sand-bar that has cottonwoods on it as thick as harrow-teeth").[65]

Precision of observation and expression is as important to the characters in this book as it is to the author. Sensitivity to physical facts—the habits of poisonous snakes, the shape of the river—is necessary for survival; when Huck and Jim manifest insufficient awareness of their physical environment, they are punished for it. When Huck forgets that a rattlesnake tends to seek out its mate, Jim gets bitten; failing to have a river pilot's knowledge of the shape of the river, Huck and Jim miss Cairo in the fog. (The respect for fact Twain acquired as a journalist may be responsible, in part, for his having scuttled the journey to freedom in the novel. As Henry Nash Smith has suggested, Twain may have allowed Huck and Jim to miss Cairo because of his own deficient knowledge of the Ohio Valley. Twain knew the lower Mississippi well, but was almost completely unfamiliar with the area Huck and Jim would have encountered had they boarded a steamer at Cairo and traveled "way up the Ohio amongst the free states" as they had planned.)[66]

Many of the "fictions" deflated in *Huckleberry Finn* are familiar ones for Twain: romantic novels—stories of pirates and robbers, military exploits, and amorous adventure (in particular tales of writers such as Sir Walter Scott, Thomas Moore, Alexandre Dumas, and William Harrison Ainsworth), sentimental verse, political bombast, and Sunday-school primers, to name a few. Throughout the book the dangers (as well as the absurdities) of letting texts serve as guides for action are thoroughly explored.[67]

The literary fabrications of writers such as Alexandre Dumas (as interpreted by Tom Sawyer) defraud Jim of his dignity and transform a genuinely heroic life into a hodgepodge gothic romance. Sunday-school conventions of right and wrong nearly lead Huck to deprive Jim of his hard-earned freedom after their long journey in quest of it. In *Huckleberry Finn* characters continually accept without question the authority of texts which estrange them from the world around them and each other.

The Grangerfords are particularly estranged from themselves and their world, and texts of various sorts contribute a good deal to their self-delusion. The books, the poetry, the verse, and the storybook good manners they have help them feel cultivated and refined; they blind them to the barbarism and brutality underlying their way of life.

Twain had described a household like that of the Grangerfords in *Life on the Mississippi.*[68] There he had deflated the pretensions directly, calling the home "a pathetic sham" (p. 317). In the novel he takes a more circuitous route, and one which forces the reader to see for himself the gaps between the artificial trappings of civilization and civilized behavior.

"Books, piled and disposed, with cast-iron exactness, according to an inherited and unchangeable plan" (p. 317) in the journalism become, in the fiction, simply books "piled up perfectly exact, on each corner of the table."[69] In *Huckleberry Finn* Twain establishes the dangers of acting "according to an inherited and unchangeable plan" not by direct statement, but by subtly reiterating and intertwining, in almost fugal style, the multiple fictions which conspire to kill Buck Grangerford and his family. The "perfectly exact" piles of books introduce the theme of the unexamined rigidity and preordained order which characterize the families' attempts to make the scoreboard of death equally balanced and exact. The sermon on brotherly love in a church lined with guns introduces the theme of hypocrisy, of things masquerading as that which they are not. The charade of chivalry straight out of Walter Scott—seen in the context of the accompanying butchery, cowardice, and general barbarism—echoes this theme. The sentimental verse that so cheapens death in the Grangerford household implicitly reinforces the feud that so cheapens life.

The fictions—the veneer of culture, civilization, refinement, and morality that both families accept as embodiments of their way of life—blind them to the violence at the core of the way they live. The innocent narrator of the novel is much more effective at revealing those contradictions than the wordly narrator of the journalism had been. Twain's editorializing comments on the house in the journalism are deleted in the fiction, replaced by Huck's naïve enthusiasm. The reader is made to see the real nature of the hypocrisy for himself as he takes in both the scene itself and Huck's innocent response to it. Described in *Life on the Mississippi* as "a pathetic sham," the Grangerford home is simply admired by Huck for having "so much style."

If Huck is impressed by "style," the reader is not. Indeed, throughout the book, "style" is associated with artificiality, fabrication, and lies. The absence of "style" is the absence of words. Indeed, when Huck is most in touch with his environment—as he is in the famous daybreak passage on the raft—he is silent. "Not a sound, anywheres," the passage begins, "perfectly still." (pp. 140–41). When confronted by a bloody feud that a romantic novelist might have spun into a lengthy chivalric tome, Huck prefers to use as few words as possible; "style" is incompatible with the fact that people he cares about have just been needlessly killed. "I don't want to talk much about the next day," Huck says, "I reckon I'll cut it pretty short" (p. 135).

While the reader of *Huckleberry Finn* is taught to be suspicious of "style," he is also taught to be suspicious of structures made with "style." Twain throws into question the authority of *any* text by crafting a book composed of multiple fictions, each an ironic commentary on another. *Adventures of Huckleberry Finn* contains scores of tales supposedly invented by the characters—tales which exist as ironic challenges to each other, and as ironic commentaries on Huck's primary text. By making his book a chaotic mélange of fictive forms, Twain prevents any one form from exercising authority or manifesting autonomy and makes his reader conscious of the ultimately fictive and arbitrary nature of all texts, including the one at hand. [70]

Huck invents more than half a dozen fictional life histories for himself, improvised according to expediency. Huck's fictions begin, appropriately, with his staging of his own death. As far as society is concerned, Huck Finn no longer exists after his "murder" in the cabin; any identities Huck now assumes are those he creates for himself. The fictions Huck creates, filled with either sick relations or poor orphans, are themselves artful compressions of the plots and themes of popular sentimental fiction. He becomes, in quick succession, Sarah Williams, whose mother is sick; "runaway 'prentice' " George Peters fleeing a "mean old farmer" in his daughter's clothes; worried kin of "pap, and mam, and sis, and Miss Hooker," who are trapped on the wreck of the "Walter Scott"; frustrated seeker of help for "Pap, Mam and Mary Ann," plagued with smallpox on the raft; Arkansas orphan George Jackson who fell off the steamboat; a Pike County orphan with nothing to his name but his "nigger Jim"; "Adolphus," loyal servant of the brothers Wilks; and "Tom Sawyer."

All of the fictional tales Huck crafts exist as ironic counterparts to the primary text of his allegedly real autobiography, which retains, somehow, a convincing authenticity despite the competing "autobiographies" which exist alongside it. But even the primary text of the book self-consciously acknowledges its own fictive nature. Huck admits in the first paragraph that he owes his existence, as far as the reader is concerned, to a book that was made by Mr. Mark Twain.

Stories invented, repeated, or reported by other characters in the book often serve as ironic commentaries on each other. In two adjacent chapters, for example, Jim relates the story of how he discovered that his daughter was "deef and dumb," and the Duke and King improvise the script for the "deef and dumb" act with which they will try to defraud the daughters of Peter Wilks.[71] Jim's confession of shame and guilt and the two charlatans' shameless plotting thus exist in ironic juxtaposition to one another, highlighting the authentically moving quality of the one, and the outrageously heartless quality of the other.

Another good example of ironic juxtaposition is the relationship between the tale Tom Sawyer tells in chapter 3 and the story Jim relates in chapter 8.

In chapter 3, Tom tells Huck a version of a tale from *Arabian Nights*, explaining where genies come from and what they do. Huck asks, "Who makes them tear around so?" and Tom answers,

"Why, whoever rubs the lamp or ring. They belong to whoever rubs the lamp or ring, and they've got to do whatever he says. If he tells them to build a palace forty miles long, out of di'monds, and fill it full of chewing gum, or whatever you want, and fetch an emperor's daughter from China for you to marry, they've got to do it. And more—they've got to waltz that palace around over the country wherever you want it, you understand."

"Well," say I, "I think they are a pack of flatheads for not keeping the palace themselves 'stead of fooling them away like that. And what's more—if I was one of them I would see a man in Jericho before I would drop my business and come to him for the rubbing of an old tin lamp."

"How you talk, Huck Finn. Why, you'd *have* to come when he rubbed it, whether you wanted to or not."

"What, and I as high as a tree and as big as a church? All right, then: I *would* come; but I lay I'd make that man climb the highest tree there was in the country."

"Shucks, it ain't no use to talk to you, Huck Finn. You don't seem to know anything, somehow—perfect sap-head." (P. 25)

Huck does, in fact, go out in the woods and rub a lamp until he sweats "like an Injun, calculating to build a palace and sell it" before concluding for certain that "all that stuff was only just one of Tom Sawyer's lies."

Not inculcated, as Tom Sawyer is, with genie lore from *Arabian Nights*, Huck takes a fresh view of Tom's tale and finds it patently absurd; he sees no basis for the arbitrary authority the lamp-rubber exercises over a being many times his size and strength.

In chapter 8, Jim tells Huck the story of why he "run off":

> Ole missus—dat's Miss Watson—she pecks on me all de time, en treats
> me pooty rough, but she awluz said she woudn' sell me down to
> Orleans. But I noticed dey wuz a nigger trader roun' de place consid-
> able lately, en I begin to git oneasy. Well, one night I creeps to de
> do' pooty late, en de do' warn't quite shet, en I hear old missus tell
> de widder she gwine to sell me down to Orleans, but she didn' want
> to, but she could git eight hund'd dollars for me, en it 'uz sich a
> big stack o' money she couldn' resis'. De widder she try to git her to
> say she wouldn' do it, but I never waited to hear de res'. I lit out
> mighty quick, I tell you." (P. 58)

While Huck is quick to see the arbitrariness and absurdity inherent in
the lamp-rubber's control over the genie, he fails to see that Miss Watson's control over Jim is equally arbitrary. Jim is as bound (by the legal
documents that let a slaveholder "own" her slaves) to follow Miss Watson's bidding to go to New Orleans as the genie is bound (by the conventions of genie lore) to go wherever the lamp-rubber bids *him* to go.
Huck himself, of course, fails to make this leap of insight. Indeed,
throughout *Huckleberry Finn*, Huck fails to understand that slavery
creates lines of authority and power as arbitrary as any in *Arabian Nights*.

From the first time Huck hears the reason Jim ran off ("people would
call me a low down Ablitionist, and despise me for keeping mum—but
that don't make no difference") (p. 58), to the last time he wrestles with
the problem of giving Jim up ("All right then, I'll *go* to hell") (p. 244),
Huck fails to recognize as arbitrary and illegitimate the system that
keeps Jim in bondage. The brilliantly crafted dramatic irony that results
from the reader's awareness of the limitations of Huck's world view thus
challenges the authority and trustworthiness of the primary text, as the
other ironic juxtapositions in the book challenge the authority of any
given interpolated tale. Instead of presenting a vision of the world, Twain
presents multiple competing visions, many of which cancel each other
out. By crafting a work of art that points up its own limitations, he
thrusts his reader back into the world of fact.

In his travel letters from Europe and the Holy Land, and in the volume in which he collected them, *The Innocents Abroad*, Twain had not
yet figured out how to prevent *his* text from becoming as illegitimate
an authority as all the guidebooks that went before it. His goal was to
help his reader see "with his own eyes,"[72] but Twain's anti-guidebook

guidebook had too many features of the texts it parodied to be wholly successful in this goal. In *Huckleberry Finn*, however, Twain crafted a text that recedes from view just as it seems to be most solidly present. Critics were amply forewarned: "NOTICE," begins the book, the page before chapter 1, "Persons attempting to find a motive in this narrative will be prosecuted; persons attempting to find a moral in it will be banished; persons attempting to find a plot in it will be shot. BY ORDER OF THE AUTHOR."* While no readers seeking these elements have been "prosecuted," "banished," or "shot" as Twain warned, they *have* been sorely tried and coyly evaded. On one level Twain's book seems to be a lesson in the difficulty of reading a book. As he succeeds in crafting an object lesson in how to question the authority of texts, Twain here succeeds, where he earlier failed, in teaching his reader to see "with his own eyes instead of the eyes of those who travelled . . . before him." [73]

---

*Critics disappointed with the ending of *Huckleberry Finn* have focused on Twain's failure to resolve the deep moral and political questions he raised in the first part of the book.

Twain may have been more successful grappling with these problems on a personal level. During the years when he was struggling to complete this troublesome manuscript, he was also attempting to combat the destructive legacy of slavery by supporting the undergraduate and professional education of several promising black students.

In a newly discovered letter that Twain wrote the year *Huckleberry Finn* was published in this country, he explained to the dean of the Yale Law School the reason he wanted to pay the expenses of a black student named Warner T. McGuinn, whom he had met briefly, on one occasion: "I do not believe I would very cheerfully help a white student who would ask a benevolence of a stranger, but I do not feel so about the other color. We have ground the manhood out of them, & the shame is ours, not theirs; & we should pay for it." (SLC to Francis Wayland, December 24, 1885, in the private collection of Nancy and Richard Stiner.) McGuinn went on to become a respected newspaper editor and a renowned Baltimore attorney, community leader, and civil rights activist.

4
THEODORE
DREISER

Theodore Dreiser as a twenty-two-year-old newspaper reporter in St. Louis in 1893, where his assignments included murders, trials, and society balls.

Photo credit: Special Collections, Van Pelt Library, University of Pennsylvania

In timbre, tone, and tempo the world of Chicago journalism that lured young Theodore Dreiser in the 1890s was to the world of journalism Twain had entered in the 1850s what a Sousa march is to a camp hymn. Reporters in the 1890s marched to a beat that was brisk and sassy, flashy and bold. Their ranks had swelled, as had their image of themselves; they made whole cities vibrate with their loud and brassy tunes of sensational murder and sleazy scandal.

During the last third of the nineteenth century, the doubling of America's population combined with increased literacy and education created an unprecedented market for newspapers. By the turn of the century there were six times as many daily papers as there had been in the 1860s, and more than three times as many weeklies. During the century's last two decades, often referred to as "the Age of the Reporter," the increased use of the "by-line," and the signed column, as well as the steady rise in salaries and status, all contributed to reporters' growing sense of their own importance.[1]

Young Theodore Dreiser viewed the world in which they moved as a glamorous and romantic one. As he would later recall in his autobiography, *Newspaper Days,*

> I [thought of] reporters and newspaper men generally as receiving
> fabulous salaries, being sent on the most urgent and interesting
> missions. I think I confused, inextricably, reporters with ambassadors
> and prominent men generally. Their lives were laid among great
> people, the rich and famous, the powerful; and because of their posi-
> tion and facility of expression and mental force they were received
> everywhere as equals. Think of me, new, young, poor, being received
> in that way![2]

The world of journalism attracted Dreiser like a powerful magnet. His highest goal, as a teenager in Chicago, was to somehow become a part of that world: "The newspapers—the newspapers—somehow, by their intimacy with everything that was going on in the world, seemed to be the swiftest approach to all . . . of which I was dreaming. . . . Some paper must give me a place."[3]

When twenty-year-old Dreiser finally did manage to secure a place in one of these august enterprises, he was quickly cured of his illusions. His first newspaper job—obtained in response to a want ad placed by the *Chicago Herald*'s business office—was handing out gimcrack toys to the city's poor during the 1891 Christmas season as part of a "Santa scheme" designed by the paper as a public-relations gambit. When Dreiser was hired as a reporter by the fourth-rate *Chicago Globe* the following summer, the two stories that would garner him great praise both involved the city's poor and powerless—not the rich, famous, and powerful subjects he had imagined to be so central to the reporter's world.

It is one of the charming ironies of American literary history, however, that Dreiser's vague and misinformed notions about the role journalism would play in his life would prove, in time, to be absolutely correct. While "the newspapers" may not have been "the swiftest approach to [all of which he] was dreaming," they *were*, in fact, *the* approach; it was in "the newspapers" (and later, the magazines) that Dreiser would lay the groundwork for a distinguished literary career. His greatest strengths and weaknesses as a writer may be traced to his work in journalism in the 1890s. He would return as a novelist to subjects, styles, and strategies he had first explored as a journalist. His awareness of the limitations of journalism, however, would imbue that return with a special sensitivity to the liberating possibilities of fiction.

In 1892 Dreiser got a part-time job on the *Chicago Daily Globe* gathering political news at the Democratic National Convention being held in Chicago that year; he was soon hired by the *Globe* as a full-time reporter. Five months later he moved to St. Louis to take a higher-paying job as a reporter on the *St. Louis Globe-Democrat*.

One night he was assigned to cover both the opening of several plays in local theaters and a holdup some distance out of town. After giving the typesetter reviews he wrote based on the plays' advance publicity, Dreiser took off to cover the holdup. A flood on the tracks stopped all the actors from reaching the city that night, and none of the shows went on. Dreiser's reviews of the glowing response the audience gave them appeared in the *Globe* the next day nonetheless, much to his own embarrassment and that of his editors. Shamefacedly, he left the *Globe* and took a lower-paying job at its rival, the *Republic*. Brief stints of working as a space-rate reporter for the *Toledo Blade* and the *Cleveland Leader* were followed by six months as a salaried reporter on the *Pittsburgh Dispatch*. In 1894 Dreiser accepted a job as a space-rate reporter for Pulitzer's *New York World*, the largest newspaper in the country at the time, and probably the most competitive. Trivial and depressing assignments, poor health, and general lack of encouragement led Dreiser to leave the *World* for magazine work the following year.

The revolution of the penny press in the 1830s had its counterpart in the periodical revolution of the 1890s. Publishing entrepreneurs in both eras discovered that revenues from high-priced subscription journals could be quickly outpaced by revenues from cheap, mass-circulation publications sold, in large part, by newsboys or at newsstands. In both cases, the appeal of these mass audiences to advertisers was important. While traditional genteel subscription monthlies like *Harper's, Scribner's, Century,* and the *Atlantic* wielded great influence at the beginning of the decade, by 1897 the combined circulation of all four of these journals was exceeded by the circulation of just one of the ten-cent newcomers, *McClure's.*[4] The total number of periodicals in America was rapidly increasing as well. The *Nation* reported in the mid-nineties that magazines were being born "in numbers to make Malthus stare and gasp."[5] In 1897 *National Magazine* exclaimed, "Magazines, magazines, magazines! The news-stands are already groaning under the heavy load, and there are still more coming."[6] The flashy mass-circulation journals that were overshadowing the more traditional monthlies would play a key role in Dreiser's apprenticeship.

In 1895 Dreiser founded a new ten-cent magazine himself, under the auspices of Howley, Haviland & Co., the music-publishing company that issued the songs of his brother, Paul Dresser. Dreiser edited the publication, which he called *Ev'ry Month,* from 1895 to 1897, filling its pages with world and city news, book reviews, fashion and decorating columns, theater notices, and a series of distinctly Dreiserian meditations on city life and other subjects which he signed "The Prophet."[7] Then from 1897 to 1902 Dreiser was a frequent freelance contributor to numerous mass-circulation magazines including *Ainslee's, Munsey's, Metropolitan, Success, Cosmopolitan, Pearson's, Leslie's,* and *Demorest's.* His contributions ranged from profiles of successful businessmen and of contemporary artists, photographers, and musicians, to descriptive pieces about new developments in industry, transportation, education, and science, to discussions of the plight of the city's poor.

After a nervous breakdown that interrupted his writing, Dreiser resumed his editorial career as editor of *Smith's Magazine,* where he told his readers, "*Success* is what counts in the world, and it is little matter how the success is won. . . . No matter how fine our conceptions of art or ethics, we can never see the world as it actually is, until we look this fact in the face . . ." From *Smith's* Dreiser went on to edit *Broadway* magazine, where he attracted subscribers and advertisers with departments such as "Beautiful Women of New York Society."[8] From 1907 to 1910, he occupied the unlikely position of editor-in-chief of Butterick's women magazines, foremost of which was the *Delineator.*[9] Here, sinking perhaps to an all-time low in journalistic integrity (while earning more money than he ever had before), Dreiser allowed himself to be roped into waging an editorial campaign against the teddy bear (in those days, at least, the increasingly popular teddy bears, unlike dolls, had no use for the doll-size dress patterns Butterick's was marketing so successfully through its "Jenny Wren" clubs).

Journalism continued to be Dreiser's primary source of income long after he had begun writing novels. Much of his writing was simply hack work done for the money. Constantly straining to balance his tight monthly budget on what he earned as a freelancer, as Thomas Riggio has noted, Dreiser would feverishly "write in the same week for magazines as diverse as *Masses, Cosmopolitan, The Seven Arts,* and *Saturday Evening Post.*"[10] When he was truly bored he would plagiarize tedious descriptions and statistics from company catalogs or carelessly get his facts twisted; his publishers grew accustomed to receiving letters of complaint. But Dreiser was indebted to the magazines for much more than money. Amid the mindless pieces on carrier pigeons, teddy bears, the apple industry and the homes of famous people were several articles that would later be incorporated, in part or whole, into Dreiser's novels. The seeds of his finest works of fiction were gathered during the twenty years Dreiser spent trafficking in the world of fact.

In the fiercely competitive climate newspaper publishers faced in the 1890s, one did all one could to attract attention. While sensationalism itself was nothing new to the nation's press, the extravagance of its display, the pervasiveness of its presence, and the brassiness of its bravado were unlike anything that had gone before.[11] Every robbery, seduction, adultery, embezzlement, and murder was covered by the press in loving detail; the task of finding appropriate crimes to cover was eased somewhat by the fact that the murder rate in the U.S. would be four times higher by the end of the century than it had been twenty years before.[12] Pulitzer's *New York World* led the pack in featuring sensation and scandal, though the rest of the press quickly followed its example. On January 1, 1894, for example, the year Dreiser took a job on the *World*, two of the most prominent headlines were "Shot His Bride Dead" and "Done by a Fiend." A cartoon published three years later in the comic magazine *Life* titled "In the Old Pit Shaft" satirized the kind of journalism the *World* had come to represent: as two gentlemen descended through an old mine shaft into the snake-infested belly of the earth one excursionist asked the other, "Doesn't it terrify you—the depths to which we are descending?" "Oh, no!" replied his friend, "I'm a reporter for the *New York World.*"[13]

In Chicago, by 1892 the largest city in the country, reporters actively encouraged the public's image of their profession as a romantic one fraught with daring and danger, most at home in the darkest corners of city life. They named their gathering place the "Whitechapel Club" after the London site of some of the crimes of Jack-the-Ripper, and decorated it with a coffin-shaped table, murder weapons, and human skulls—mementos of the world of crime that was their favorite beat. As a young newspaperman in Chicago, he would later recall, Dreiser would often gather with his colleagues in "one of the many small restaurants frequented by newspapermen" and hear "talk of all sorts of scandals: robberies, murders, fornications, incendiarisms, not only in low life but in our so-called high life."[14]

In St. Louis Dreiser learned quickly that writing a good murder story was the swiftest way to win his editor's esteem. Of his editor at the *Republic* he wrote,

> Deaths, murders, great social or political scandals or upheavals, those
> things which presented the rough, raw facts of life, as well as its
> tenderer aspects, seemed to throw him into an ecstasy—not over the
> woes of others but over the fact that he was to have an interesting
> paper tomorrow . . . "Ah, it was a terrible thing, was it? He killed her
> in cold blood you say? There was a great crowd out there, was there?
> Well, well, write it all up. Write it all up. It looks like a pretty good
> story to me—doesn't it to you? Write a good strong introduction for
> it, you know, all the facts in the first paragraph, and then go on
> and tell your story. You can have as much space for it as you want—
> a column, a column and a half, two—just as it runs. Let me look
> at it before you turn it in, though." Then he would begin whistling
> or singing, or would walk up and down in the city-room rubbing
> his hands in obvious satisfaction . . .[15]

"When nothing of immediate importance was to be had," Dreiser recalled in *Newspaper Days*, his editor "proceeded to create news, studying out interesting phases of past romances or crimes which he thought might be worthwhile to work up and publish on Sunday, and handed them to me to do over" (p. 214). One of the earliest crimes Dreiser was sent to cover involved a St. Louis perfume dealer who freed himself of his poor and pregnant sweetheart by murdering her; it was the first of many such crimes Dreiser would encounter. As a reporter in Chicago and St. Louis Dreiser was frequently sent to cover seductions and murders; he was destined to develop, in the process of doing so, a sharp awareness of pattern and problem that his contemporaries largely ignored. It was out of this awareness that *An American Tragedy* would develop.

(Dreiser was not unaware of the cruelty and intrusiveness inherent in the reporter's exploitation of human suffering to get his story. In St. Louis, in 1893, for example, he was sent to cover a lynching in the town of Rich Hill, Missouri. The terse, five-inch story that ran in the *St. Louis Republic* under the headline "A Negro Lynched" began, "Rich Hill's first demonstration of mob violence occurred today although the town is in the fourteenth year of its existence. It resulted in the hanging of a negro rapist."[16] Dreiser later returned to this event in his short story "Nigger Jeff," in which he made a newspaper reporter the central character. The vain, self-centered, ambitious reporter shamelessly exploits the genuine suffering he encounters to get his story on the wire. In the end, however, he recognizes that "before such grief his intrusion seemed cold and unwarranted." He is moved to tears. But the newspaperman within him, as well as "the cruel instinct of the budding artist that he already was," makes him retreat from the prospect of relating to the mother of the dead man as a feeling, grieving, human being and leads him instead to "meditate on the character of the story it would make—the color, the pathos." The story concludes: " 'I'll get it all in!' he exclaimed feelingly, if triumphantly at last. 'I'll get it all in!' "[17])

Scandal and sensation alone did not fill the pages of the nation's dailies. A host of new images, areas, and approaches surfaced in the press in the 1890s and played prominent roles in the papers that would touch Dreiser's life. The physical appearance of the newspapers Dreiser read and wrote for in the 1890s bore little resemblance to that of the papers Twain had known in the 1860s. By the early 1890s technological advances made it relatively fast and simple to produce papers filled with sharp custom-drawn halftones. The massive numbers of new immigrants struggling to master English showed their gratitude to publishers who catered to their needs by buying in record numbers papers with bold headlines and numerous pictures. The voracious appetite for attention-catching graphics helped fuel the impulse to sensationalism and oversimplification that already dominated the way newspapers presented facts of contemporary life.

Artwork gave readers a more dramatic visual awareness of the broad spectrum of fortunes that made up American society, and made more concrete and more vivid what Dreiser would later refer to as the "astounding contrast between wealth and poverty"[18] that pervaded our culture. For example, the face of a slum dweller who tried to murder his family in a feverish frenzy and the look of his dreary home and of his makeshift weapons were vividly sketched in a series of etchings that took up more space than the text of Dreiser's narrative of the event in a St. Louis paper. Again, the artist's sketch, not Dreiser's text, dominated the page when the subject was a local society ball. The artist who rendered the fair features and graceful gowns of the ladies at the ball (Gibson girls all, after the fashion of the time) enabled readers to almost hear the rustle of silk, the hushed tones of refined conversation, the gracious strains of background violins.[19] As a journalist Dreiser constantly moved back and forth between these vastly disparate worlds. The images reflected in such illustrations—emblems of poverty and wealth, misery and contentment—allowed the paper's readers clear glimpses of those worlds as well. Dreiser would later weave such emblematic scenes of slums and society dances into the richly textured fabric of his greatest novel.

By far the largest source of graphics in the papers of the 1890s were the advertisements. In the newspapers for which Twain and Whitman had written, nearly all advertisements had appeared in pages of dense columns filled with small print, close, in appearance, to the "classified" sections familiar to newspaper readers today. By the 1890s, however, papers featured page after page of lavishly illustrated quarter-page, half-page, and full-page ads for the vast range of consumer goods available in specialty shops, and, most important of all, in a young but up-and-coming institution destined to dominate the business end of newspaper publishing in this country to the present day: the department store.

When Wanamaker's in Philadelphia took out the first full-page department-store advertisement in a Philadelphia paper in 1879, other stores were quick to follow suit. Stewart's of New York and Marshall Field's of Chicago were among the many stores bombarding newspaper readers daily with the cornucopia of manufactured goods available within their walls. Newspapers benefited directly from the rising status of consumption in American society; there was four times as much newspaper advertising at the turn of the century as there had been three decades before.[20] As thousands of families used their increased purchasing power to buy goods they had previously made at home, as well as items they never before realized that they needed, newspapers bulged with extra pages, extra sections, and fat and weighty Sunday supplements financed by merchants pushing everything from button hooks to bonbon trays, from fur capes to fine china.

While the papers of the 1890s had more of just about everything than the papers of the 1860s and before the war, the thing they seemed to have the most of was what might be viewed as a running series called the "illustrated 'good life' "—pictures of the many wonderful things one could buy to make life and leisure more gracious, satisfying, and re-fined, things one could buy to show loved ones that they were loved, things one could wear and use proudly as badges of status and esteem. The space the *Chicago Tribune* gave to its lead story on the Homestead strike the day after it began was a fraction of that given to an advertise-ment headlined, "The Important Message." The message detailed the great news that "110,000 Yards of the Best Quality Printed India Silks" were being offered at 68 cents a yard at a local department store.[21] These ubiquitous illustrated advertisements left their impression, even if only a subliminal one, on young Dreiser. They would add, in subtle ways, to his awareness of the role played by "things" in people's images of themselves, of their relationships, and of their society. One item ad-vertised heavily in the Chicago press the year Dreiser began working there as a reporter was a fur coat similar to the one Hortense would covet in *An American Tragedy*.[22] Another item heavily promoted as a Christmas gift by local department stores that year was a toilette set like the one Clyde would present to Roberta in the novel.[23]

The bulky Sunday supplements and fat daily papers that the great spurt of advertising in the last two decades of the century helped make possible were filled with new kinds of stories and styles as well as new kinds of graphics. While European and British journals tended to cater to one or another of the clearly demarcated classes or interest groups of the "old world," a philosophy of "something for everyone" came to dominate America's mass-circulation journals. In addition to lengthy treatments of sensational news, there was new extended theater coverage, detailed interviews, "women's pages," advice columns, and fashion coverage alongside such older newspaper staples as humorous hoaxes, witty and whimsical personal commentaries, and society columns. Dreiser would try his hand at each of these forms, and each played a role in shaping his sensitivity to the ways in which a writer could cast his world into print.

But the two developments that would have the greatest effect on Dreiser's career were (1) the popularity of "color" or "feature" stories, and (2) the new emphasis on "facts." At Pulitzer's *World* posters printed with the words "The Facts—The Color—The Facts" were pasted on the walls to remind reporters of their primary charge. "Facts" had always played a role in newspaper reporting, and "features" were clearly outgrowths of the "human-interest story" Charles Dana had introduced in the *New York Sun* in the late 1860s and early 1870s, but both elements played new and distinctive roles in the world of journalism of the 1890s, and influenced Dreiser's growth as a writer in key ways.

The Sunday supplements financed by department-store advertisements were always hungry for lengthy colorful meandering pieces that vividly evoked the look and sound of a particular chapter of city life or a "human-interest" tale that would capture the reader's imagination. Chicago journalism in the 1890s, as Dreiser would recall in *Newspaper Days*, "was still in that discursive stage which loved long-winded yarns upon almost any topic. Nearly all news stories were padded to make more of them than they deserved, especially as to color and romance. . . . The city editors wanted not so much bare facts as feature stories, color, romance, and although I did not see it clearly at the time I was their man."[24] The "discursive," "long-winded," "padded" leisurely style of 1890s journalism came easily to Dreiser. Indeed, one might argue, this early discouragement of brevity and conciseness might help explain Dreiser's tendency throughout his career (whatever his other faults and virtues may be) to write books which are, indisputably, long.

Dreiser discovered his talent for "feature" stories in the first newspaper special he ever wrote, a piece about Chicago's "vilest slum."

> Saloon lights and smells and lamps gleaming smokily from behind broken lattices and from below wooden sidewalk levels gave it a shameless and dangerous color. Accordions, harmonicas, jew's-harps, clattering tin-pan pianos and stringy violins were forever going; paintless rotting shacks always resounded with a noisy blasphemous life between twelve and four; oaths, foul phrases, a Hogarthian shamelessness and reconciliation to filth everywhere . . .[25]

The piece won high praise from his editor. "You may have your faults,

Theodore," he had told him, "But you do know how to observe. You bring a fresh mind to bear on this stuff."[26]

Dreiser's talent at spinning digressive "color" stories was discovered in Pittsburgh, as well. As he recalls in *Newspaper Days,*

> One day when a spring rain was a magnificent electrical display, I described how the city, dry and smoky and dirty, lay panting in the deadening heat and how out of the west came, like an answer to a prayer, this sudden and seething storm, battalion upon battalion of huge clouds riven with great silvery flashes of light, darkening the sun as they came; and how suddenly, while shutters clapped and papers flew and office windows and doors had to be closed and signs squeaked and swung and people everywhere ran to cover, the thousands who had been enduring the heat heaved a sigh of gratitude. I described how the steel tenements, the homes of the rich, the office buildings, the factories, the hospitals and jails changed under these conditions and then ventured to give specific incidents and pictures of animals and men.
>
> This was received with congratulations, especially from the assistant editor . . . Now, of a sudden, my status was entirely changed. I was a feature man, one who had succeeded where others had apparently failed. . . . (P. 415)

Looking back on his experience as a "feature man" in Pittsburgh, Dreiser recalled that his "mood or word pictures about a summer storm, a spring day, a visit to the hospital, the death of an old switchman's dog, the arrival of the first mosquito . . . gave me my first taste of what it means to be a creative writer . . ." (p. 413).

While accuracy was highly valued in straight news stories, in the feature department, as Dreiser quickly learned, unabashed lying had its own rewards. Like Mark Twain, Dreiser was occasionally prompted to invent stories by the paucity of legitimate news. But unlike Twain, his invention was rarely satirical or directed at a social ill; he was more likely to lie for status and money than for a principle.

Hard-pressed to find any important personage to interview for his "Heard in the Corridors" column in the *St. Louis Globe-Democrat,* Dreiser proceeded to interview imaginary characters who proved infinitely more charming than the real ones who had previously populated his column.[27] The freewheeling journalism of the 1890s easily tolerated the presence of entertaining rambling in its columns, and Dreiser was urged to fill the "Corridors" with imaginary friends as often as he liked. For the *St. Louis Republic* he wrote a lengthy series of burlesques of a baseball game to be played by a fat and thin team.[28] In New York he turned a rather dull tenement fight into a raucous fictional brawl.[29] "I knew now," Dreiser wrote later, "that what my city editors wanted was not merely 'accuracy, accuracy, accuracy,' but a kind of flair for the ridiculous or remarkable even though it had to be invented, so that the pages of the paper and life itself might not seem so dull."[30]

Indeed, the newspaper columnist who had sparked Dreiser's interest in journalism in the first place was a man as famous for the wit of his invention as for the wisdom of his observations, the renowned Eugene Field of the *Chicago Daily News*. "For two years or more" before he got his first job on a newspaper, Dreiser recalled, "I had been reading Eugene Field's 'Sharps and Flats', a column he wrote daily for the *Chicago Daily News*, and through this, the various phases of life which he suggested in a humorous though at times romantic way, I was beginning to suspect, vaguely at first, that I wanted to write, possibly something like that."[31] Field's "Sharps and Flats" included comments in prose and verse on the world he witnessed, literature, drama, politics, and prominent personalities, as well as hoax stories, such as one about a rare imaginary animal recently donated to the local zoo, or "How Milton Dictated to a Typewriter."[32] The varied fare he offered his readers was characterized by a light touch, a distinctively whimsical personal style, and a flair for that which might spark a reader's interest. While he often showed a fine sense of humor and a competent knowledge of history and literature, he was also prone to lapse into cliché and to indulge in sentimentality.

All of Dreiser's pure "inventions" as a journalist—both his extended burlesques and his brief imaginary "interviews" in his "Heard in the Corridors" column—are directly imitative of Field's "Sharps and Flats." But Dreiser borrowed something else from Field, a trait he kept throughout his career as a writer: an inflated, high-sounding diction which Field usually employed for mock-heroic ends, but which Dreiser often seems to have adopted straight, in strictly innocent admiration. When Field referred to a "tangent obliquity of the gifted Texan's ocular organs" his pompous diction was chosen for humorous effect.[33] Or when he let adjectives follow nouns, when he used phrases like "glances arch" and "cunning meek," such artificial "literary" constructions were usually part of a whimsical or incongruous pose on the part of the writer.[34] Dreiser adopted the stilted construction without the humor.

He would see nothing wrong with putting such a ridiculously out-of-place phrase as "a scene more distingué than this" in *An American Tragedy.*[35]

Critics have often berated Dreiser for his tendency to use big words where small ones would do, for his fondness for high-flown, Latinate, inappropriately complicated ways of saying things, and for writing in a manner that must have struck him as pleasingly "literary" or "erudite." Perhaps Dreiser's own lack of formal education prevented him from understanding the nuances of Field's wit. In any event, his uncritical and profuse admiration of Field, combined with his limited understanding of the columnist's games of diction, left indelible marks on his own approach to writing. Field, a journalist who mastered the art of using large words in a small genre, seems to have left one of our greatest novelists the legacy of *mis*using large words in a large genre.

While newspapers in the 1890s gave special prominence to "feature" stories, they also treated facts in a new and significant way. As press historian Michael Schudson has said, "Reporters in the 1890s saw themselves in part, as scientists uncovering the economic and political facts of industrial life more boldly, clearly and realistically than anyone before." Their shift in emphasis, he believes, might be seen as "part of the broader Progressive drive to found political reform on 'facts.'"[36] "Accuracy—Accuracy—Accuracy," read placards on the walls of Pulitzer's *World*. Journalists like Lincoln Steffens, H. L. Mencken, and Jacob Riis all recalled, as Dreiser did, the specific directives of their first editors for factual, impersonal reporting.[37] Dreiser learned the rewards of accuracy early in his newspaper career. The first piece to win him extravagant praise from his editors in Chicago was an exposé he wrote on the fraud practiced by mock auction shops across the city; his carefully accurate, "matter of fact" report closed many of the shops and earned kudos for both Dreiser and the *Globe.*[38]

When critics enumerate Dreiser's greatest virtues as a novelist, the palpable solidity of the world he creates appears near the top of the list; its sheer weight and physical density are not to be denied. Whatever his other faults, Dreiser is renowned for his ability to pile fact upon fact until the reader is dragged almost bodily into the novel's world. Dreiser's appreciation of both the importance and the power of fact is yet another legacy of his background in the journalism of the 1890s.

It was as a reporter in the 1890s that Dreiser first encountered facts that would later prove invaluable to him as a writer of fiction. The year Dreiser became a reporter in Chicago, the local papers were filled with daily investigations into the machinations of a Chicago financier named Charles T. Yerkes. They must have left their impression on young Dreiser, for it was to these same facts that he would return when he wrote his "Trilogy of Desire," *The Financier, The Titan,* and *The Stoic.* In Toledo Dreiser covered a streetcar strike, an event he would incorporate into *Sister Carrie.* It was in St. Louis that Dreiser first wrote about the sumptuous attractions of the grand hotel, and it was here that he first documented the cruel and petty tyrannies that characterized the American court of justice. All of these subjects would find their way into *An American Tragedy.*

Dreiser approached the dense world of fact with an almost pietistic sense of wonder.[39] Indeed, it was his sense of awe before the "roaring, yelling, screaming whirlpool of life" around him that led him to enter journalism in the first place.[40] His deep respect for fact would become a hallmark of his writing when he turned to fiction. Dreiser, known by friend and foe alike as an incorrigible liar, probably spent more time trying to get his facts straight in his novels than any fiction writer of his generation. While his autobiographies are riddled with fictions, his novels are firmly rooted in fact. They are "based upon things actually seen, heard or heard of," as his close friend H. L. Mencken has said. "It was seldom that he departed from what he understood to be the record, and he never did so willingly."[41] Despite his cavalier attitude toward the truth about his personal life, in his novels Dreiser devoted great pains to documenting even the most trivial fact with accuracy and precision. "He would sit down to his desk in the days when I saw him oftenest," Mencken recalled, "and bang away with pen and ink for four or five hours . . . [stopping only] to go to the library to verify a street-name, or to find out when the Pennsylvania Railroad first reached McKeesport, or to establish the precise date of the General Slocum disaster."[42]

While Whitman may have revered the world of fact as emblematic of God and his handiwork, Dreiser stood in awe of the world of fact as emblematic of fate. The parents one had, the seemingly accidental events that crossed one's path, the time in which one lived, determined, in Dreiser's view, the life one lived. Race, moment and milieu (to borrow from Taine) were destiny; any attempt to understand life, Dreiser felt, must document contemporary realities as fully as possible. Thus Dreiser's art came to be so rooted in fact that many had trouble recognizing his novels as products of a creative imagination. His stories were often taken as literal transcripts of their times. Truth was inextricably linked with fact for Theodore Dreiser, and the freedom of the individual to see the world of fact with his own eyes would prove to be as sacred to him as that world itself. The ease with which people allowed attractive illusions to rob them of that freedom would be a major theme of Dreiser's fiction.

The facts that interested Dreiser throughout his career were the facts he had first encountered as a daily-newspaper reporter. His capacity to feel, to sympathize, to understand, was as broad and all-inclusive as the daily newspaper itself—and was molded essentially by exposure, both as reader and reporter, to the facts that medium documented. His sensibility as a novelist was closer than that of any American writer before him to the sensibility of those whose primary reading matter was the newspaper (all the real-life Carries and Hurstwoods and Clyde Griffithses). Largely self-educated, and from "the wrong side of the tracks," Dreiser shared their awe of the Broadway star, of the successful financier, of fashionable clothes and elegant homes. He shared their familiarity with poverty, deprivation, failure, jealousy, and exclusion from the American dream of success; he understood the desperation that often grew out of being poor in a land of plenty. But unlike most newspaper readers and reporters Dreiser constantly searched for meaning in the chaotic jumble of facts that surrounded him, constantly wondered where it all led, and to what end. Pages of Broadway notices; advertisements for luxury goods; sketches of breadlines; stories of strikes; statistics of unemployment, hunger, and death; all contributed to a whole for Theodore Dreiser—a whole which would first come alive in *Sister Carrie*. The triumphs of tycoons, the details of their financial machinations, the activities painted in the society pages—all this bristled with drama for Dreiser, a drama he would evoke in *The Financier*. And he would find, in repeated stories of young men's murder of their girlfriends for social and material advancement, the outlines of a recurring plot all too familiar to an ever-upwardly-mobile America; this story was the blueprint on which *An American Tragedy* was built.

Dreiser's achievement as a novelist was inextricably linked with his ability to assimilate his epoch as recorded in the daily newspaper; no other novelist of his generation was so clearly in touch with its realities and significance. In its jumbled, cacophonous montage, Dreiser found a reality that he endeavored to capture in his art.

Newspaper work forced Dreiser to focus his attention on the contemporary realities that surrounded him. Looking back in later life on his early years in journalism Dreiser readily recognized the important contribution his "newspaper days" had made to his career as a writer. It was the "kaleidoscopic character of newspaper work" which had impressed him most deeply, and "which, in its personal significance to me," he wrote, "cannot be too much emphasized."[43]

In exposing him to a vast "kaleidoscopic" array of facts about American life, journalism also provided Dreiser with an awareness of the extraordinary contrasts that existed in our society. This theme recurs throughout *Newspaper Days*. In Chicago his work took him into the houses of the richest debutantes and those of the poorest slum-dwellers. In St. Louis, the evening he rented his first tuxedo to cover a society ball he was later assigned to cover a grim quadruple murder by a slum-dweller afflicted with brain fever. "My head full of pearls, diamonds, silks, satins, laces, a world of flowers and lights, I was now hustled out along the dark, shabby, lonely streets of South St. Louis to the humblest of cottages in the humblest of streets where, among unpainted shacks with lean-tos at the back for kitchens, was the one which contained this story" (pp. 143–44).

The same contrasts repeated themselves wherever he traveled, working or looking for work. In Buffalo, as in St. Louis, he

> could not help but see that in spite of our boasted democracy and
> equality of opportunity there was as much misery and squalor and as
> little decent balancing of opportunity against energy as anywhere
> else in the world. (P. 380)

In Pittsburgh he witnessed impoverished, struggling miners working and living next door to well-heeled, well-fed, and well-bred robber barons and their flunkies. "It seemed astonishing to me," he wrote,

> that some men could rise and soar about the heavens like eagles,
> while others, drab sparrows all, could only pick among the offal of
> the hot ways below. What were these things called democracy
> and equality about which men prated? Had they any basis in fact?
> (P. 393)

The sharp contrast he saw between rich and poor was paralleled by the sharp contrast he saw between American rhetoric and American realities.

Was God to blame? Dreiser asked. Was government? Dreiser could not answer these questions. His puzzlement runs through his memoirs as a constant refrain. "I had no solution," Dreiser wrote, "and was not willing to accept any, suspecting even then that man is the victim of forces over which he has no control" (pp. 64–65). These contrasts, he wrote, challenged and ultimately destroyed the vestiges of the "dogmatic and religious moral theory [he] had been compelled to listen to [all his] life," and led him to think of American lip service to democracy and equality as simple bandstand patriotism. Clearly, an "omnipotent God" would not tolerate the work of such an "industrious devil" (p. 66). Such contrasts would not exist, Dreiser reasoned, if there were real democracy or equality of opportunity.

Dreiser was supported in his efforts to reexamine these facts for himself by the freethinking atmosphere that pervaded the newsrooms in which he worked. He found newspapermen "nearly all mistrustful of . . . conventional principles in general" (p. 69). Dreiser entered journalism as a romantic dreamer, but reporting taught him to probe under, behind, and through the dream until he reached the solid, brittle fact. The city rooms of the 1890s were filled with cynics—men who admired scientists like Darwin and Spencer, who aspired to a new goal of "objectivity," and who were impatient with conventional codes, accepted systems of belief, socially sanctioned hypocrisy, and mass-produced illusions. Dreiser would emerge from his apprenticeship in journalism as one of them. Science (and pseudoscience) would loom bigger than religion as a force shaping his philosophy of life. The challenge of describing "objective reality," of capturing truth rooted in external verifiable phenomena, would preoccupy and frustrate him throughout his career as a writer. And he would continually pit himself against convention, hypocrisy, and any system of belief that resisted constant testing against experience.

Some of the cynicism that dominated the newsrooms of the 1890s must have been rooted in reporters' awareness of the discrepancies between reality and the representations of it one encountered in the newspapers. As Jacob Riis told young *New York Post* reporter Lincoln Steffens,

> "There's a strike on the East Side, and there are always clubbed strikers here in this [police] office. I'll tell you what to do while you are learning our ways up here; you hang around this office every morning, watch the broken heads brought in, and as the prisoners are discharged, ask them for their stories. No paper will print them, but you yourself might as well see and hear how strikes are broken by the police."[44]

Reporters understood, as Larzer Ziff has noted, that there were many times when "they could not report what they knew."[45] Censorship, particularly self-censorship, was more common than appeared on the surface in a country that paid such prominent lip service to the freedom of its press.[46]

While the papers of the 1890s contained many elements that the papers of the 1860s had not, despite all the added space available to them, their publishers still failed to find room for some of the same subjects that had been missing from the papers of Twain's day. Racial prejudice and pecuniary interest still kept certain kinds of stories from appearing in the papers at all. Twain's publisher in San Francisco, as we have shown, refused to publish a story Twain wrote that struck him as being overly sympathetic to the Chinese. Dreiser encountered a similar climate of racism when he was writing theater reviews in St. Louis in the 1890s. His publisher, less vigilant than Twain's had been, failed to spot a review Dreiser wrote before it appeared in print. It described the talents of a black soprano in terms that clearly captured the wonder and admiration her moving performance had inspired in the reviewer.[47] The publisher was held up to broad public ridicule by the other papers in town the day the review appeared, and passed on to Dreiser his annoyance and disapproval: one simply did not describe achievements by a "Negro" in such glowing terms in St. Louis in 1893.[48] In Pittsburgh, Dreiser would encounter a noteworthy example of self-censorship. "We don't touch on labor conditions except through our labor man," the city editor told him, "and he knows what to say." He went on,

> "There's nothing to be said about the rich or religious in a derogatory sense. They're all right in so far as we know. We don't touch on scandals in high life. The big steel men here just about own the place, so we can't."[49]

Dreiser followed this account in *Newspaper Days* with the comment, "So much for a free press in Pittsburgh, A.D. 1893!"

The host of new periodicals that proliferated in the late 1880s and 1890s brought greater freedom. One of Dreiser's fellow reporters in Pittsburgh introduced him to some labor-oriented magazines in which labor conditions were explored with candor and impressive documentation. Dreiser caught a glimpse of a world where different stories might be told; he would soon seek a way into that world for himself. When the *New York World* could find nothing better for Dreiser to do than track down reports of extraterrestrial manifestations near Elizabeth, New Jersey, Dreiser decided it was time to leave newspaper work.

In 1895, when Dreiser undertook the job of editing *Ev'ry Month*, the "Reflections" column, which he signed "The Prophet," represented the greatest liberation thus far from the limits he had encountered as a newspaperman. Dreiser the reporter had been forced by the conventions of newspaper style to limit his accounts of the tragedies befalling the poor to objective and verifiable facts of an individual's experience. Dreiser "The Prophet," however, could place the stark newspaper account into a larger context, and often he did just that. At a time when the misery of the poor was being eloquently documented by ardent muckraking reformers like Jacob Riis in books like *How the Other Half Lives*, there was still something fresh about Dreiser's perspective on the problem. Time and time again "The Prophet" addressed himself to a dimension of the poor's problems that even someone like Riis touched only obliquely, and others completely ignored. It was a dimension which, though highly familiar to all modern readers, had no name until 1949: the problem of "relative deprivation."[50] "The Prophet" painted, over and over again, scenes of unfortunate individuals not just starving and freezing through no fault of their own, but starving and freezing within sight of a large feast and a warm hearth.

In one piece on this theme Dreiser referred to a story in a New York paper about a woman who was very poor, sick, weak, threatened by hunger, and compelled to sort rags for fourteen hours a day to support herself and her child. One night her strength failed, and "she crept homeward—weak, fevered, blind with pain, and unable to climb the long flight of steps that led to her tenement lodging." Then Dreiser allows the camera to pan back in the closing scene of the article, to expand the context of the woman's misery:

> There she lingered, sick and helpless before her own doorstep, and there they found her, prone and dying, after a time, with a great, wealthy city lying all around her, and the roll of carriages and the laughter of the idle within an arrow's flight away.[51]

In another piece "The Prophet" added to a brief newspaper account of a pauper's suicide in the East River the notion that

> Such a creature may have wandered about all day until that hour. . . . Carriages may have jingled past impressively, and richly garbed

creatures alighted here and there, bent upon expenditures as large and reckless as they are shallow and vain. He may have glanced through gorgeous shop windows, upon wealth of endless value; may have studied the gems in the jeweler's window, the laces in the cloth fancier's, the luxury of books here, the wealth of bric-a-brac there, all barred by polished glass, and at last sadly realized that all was as distant as paradise, as impossible to him as wings. . . . [52]

One can easily view these passages as early literary explorations of what Dreiser would call, in *An American Tragedy*, "that curious stinging sense of what it was to want and not to have."[53]

In other magazine pieces Dreiser would often reiterate this theme. In a piece in *Tom Watson's Magazine* in 1905 on "The Loneliness of the City," he would observe (somewhat clumsily),

So exacting are the conditions under which we are compelled to work, so disturbing the show of pleasures and diversions we cannot obtain, that the normal satisfaction in normal wants is almost entirely destroyed.[54]

And in an editorial in the *Delineator* in 1909 Dreiser would note,

The average person, swept by unknown forces into an unknown, hardly understandable world such as this, finds himself confronted in early youth by a widening field of desire and little or no opportunity to gratify any of its various phases. . . . Only money seems to answer for most of the things which are actually worthwhile. . . . In the face of this, the average individual is born without money and with very little understanding of the subtleties which accompany the acquiring of it.[55]

The contrasts between rich and poor; the agony of being poor not only in a land of plenty, but in a land that held out to everyone the dream of being rich; the staggering array of all that money could buy in our society (status, power, love, sex, freedom, health, and even justice); and the staggering misery that resulted from absence of money—these were some of the themes Dreiser the magazine writer explored frequently. They were themes to which Dreiser the novelist would return on numerous occasions; they were themes that would be central to *An American Tragedy*.

Another theme Dreiser first explored as a magazine journalist which would later feature prominently in his fiction was the deceptive promise of the city and the dreams it both nurtured and destroyed. The evils of the sweatshops and the tenements were already somewhat familiar to the reading public of the 1890s. Journalists had been marshaling grim statistics to support their stances of justified moral outrage for at least six years before Dreiser published a piece called "The City" in *Ev'ry Month* in 1896. But while most of his colleagues focused on the social and moral aspects of the problem, Dreiser alone seems to have been preoccupied by epistemological concerns as well. How do we come to know "the city," "The Prophet" seemed to ask, how might we replace our familiarity with a part of it with an awareness of the whole, what images would help us expand our limited frames of reference?

As in the piece on the suicide of the pauper, Dreiser is more interested here in people's feelings, attitudes, and perceptions about their condition than he is in the objective facts of the condition itself. These distinctive concerns justify a somewhat lengthy excerpt from the piece.[56]

> Usually the thought of miles of streets, lined with glittering shop
> windows; of rumbling vehicles rolling to and fro in noisy counter
> procession, fascinates and hypnotizes the mind, so that reason
> fades to an all-possessing desire to rush forward and join with the
> countless throng . . .

Few men consider, Dreiser notes, that they

> may starve at the base of cold, ornate columns of marble, the cost of
> which would support them and many like them for the remainder
> of their earthly days.

Dreiser reaches for new images for old tales of mystery and magic, of why the city continues to draw ensorcelled seekers and blind them to the shadows beneath the shiny surfaces:

> Perceive first, that what delights you is only the outer semblance,
> the bloom of the plant. These streets and boulevards, these splendid
> mansions and gorgeous hotels, these vast structures about which
> thousands surge and toward which luxurious carriages roll, are the
> fair flowers of a rugged stalk. Not of color and softness and rare
> odor are the masses upon which as a stalk these bloom; not for fresh

air and sunshine are they. Down in the dark earth are the roots,
drawing life and strength and sending them coursing up in the veins;
and down in alleys and byways, in the shop and small dark cham-
bers are the roots of this luxurious high life, starving and toiling the
long year through, that carriages may roll and great palaces stand
brilliant with ornaments. These endless streets which only present
their fascinating surface are the living semblance of the hands and
hearts that lie unseen within them. They are the gay covering which
conceals the sorrow and want and ceaseless toil upon which all
this is built. . . . Like a sinful Magdalen the city decks herself gaily,
fascinating all by her garments of scarlet and silk, awing by her
jewels and perfumes, when in truth there lies hid beneath these a
torn and miserable heart, and a soiled and unhappy conscience
that will not be still but is forever moaning and crying "for shame."

The condition of the city's striking tailors, Dreiser feels, may prove to
"those who are fascinated by dreams of the great metropolis" that the
city's glitter is an illusion for most, and a reality for a very few:

The striking tailors, coat makers, pressers, bushelmen, they are of
this vast substrata on which the city stands; a part of the roots
that are down in the ground, delving, that the vast flowerlike institu-
tions may bloom overhead. They belong to that part of the city
which is never seen and seldom heard. Strange tales could be told of
their miseries, strange pictures drawn of their haunts and habita-
tions, but that is not for here nor now. When they issued their queer
circular it was published as a curiosity because it told a strange
and peculiar story, and to those who are fascinated by the dreams of
the great metropolis it may prove a lesson. All is not gold that
glitters. Neither is the city a place of luxurious abode despite the
brilliancy of its surging streets. Here is the circular:

    Extra.

To the Pressers:
Brethren—the last hour of need, misery and hunger has come. We are
now on the lowest step of the ladder of human life. We can do
nothing more than starve. Take pity on your wives. Are not your
children for whom you have struggled so hard with your sweat

and blood, dear to you? Do you think you have the right to live? Do you think you ought to get pay for your work? We only strive for a miserable piece of bread.

Signed, Coat Pressers Union, No. 17

There is surely no need for comment here, certainly no call for explanation. They are down there in narrow rooms working away again. The great thoroughfares are just as bright as ever. Thousands are lounging idly in cafes, thousands thronging the places of amusements, thousands rolling in gaily caparisoned equipages, and so it will continue. Some imagine this condition can be done away with but it cannot....

Unlike some of his fellow journalists, Dreiser pushes for no reform. The bleak determinism that will play a key role in his novels surfaces here in an early form. But even here, and much more so in a book like *An American Tragedy*, implicit in the writer's project is a sense of how important it is to replace misleading romantic illusions with new metaphors, images, analogies—in short, new visions—rooted not in fantasy, but in fact. Here, as in his finest fiction, Dreiser urges his reader to take a fresh view of familiar surroundings.

As a magazine writer Dreiser had occasion to interview several contemporary artists adept at discriminating the real from the counterfeit in fresh and original ways; his admiration for their freshness of vision was both candid and sincere. Writing for *Ainslee's* on Davenport's caricatures, for example, Dreiser noted that Davenport's version of the politician Hanna

is by no means the person one meeting [Mr. Hanna] casually might imagine, or mayhap that Mr. Hanna would like to be thought; Davenport, . . . looking beyond the glad, joyous, hand-shaking surface, pretends to see the fat, collar-marked, short-term senator with whom everyone is familiar.[57]

And in an interview with Alfred Stieglitz for *Success*, Dreiser admired the photographer's evocation of "the clear crowning reality of the thing" he photographed.[58] Whether capturing clear and solid realities himself, exposing pretense and illusion, or admiring freshness of vision in others, Dreiser cultivated, as a journalist, a distinct taste for what he once referred to as "life as it is."

America, he felt, with its insistence on conformity and conventionality, with its intolerance of unpleasant facts and its determination to see only the good and the beautiful, has encouraged a passive acceptance of "mirage" in place of an active contemplation of actuality—an actuality more complex than his fellow Americans seemed to want to acknowledge. "The actuality of life," Dreiser once wrote in a poem,

> Is like a wraith
> That haunts.
> A shadow that eludes one—
> Escaping by a thousand ways. [59]

Wherever he turned in America, Dreiser found people viewing the world through the blinders of romantic illusions and conventional codes, all passively accepted and rarely questioned or challenged. He felt every individual "should question the things he sees—not some things, but everything."[60] For only then would he be able to think for himself and see the world through his own eyes. The "controlling captains of industry," Dreiser would write in a piece in *The Seven Arts*, did nothing to encourage "the freedom of the individual to think for himself." The dominant religious and commercial organizations similarly did nothing to encourage "a free mental development in individuals." College students, according to one professor Dreiser quoted at length, "do not think; they cannot, because they are bound hard and fast by the iron band of convention."[61] Despite the fact that the platitudes they mouth and the theories they spout bear no relation to American realities, Dreiser felt, Americans accept without question lies about their past and present. "We move," Dreiser wrote, "in a mirage of illusion"; this theme would be central to *An American Tragedy*, a book whose original title, indeed, was to be "Mirage."[62]

Dreiser was appalled by the nation of automatons that he saw, by the lies Americans so willingly lived with, by the facts they so blindly ignored. Americans refused to see facts Dreiser himself had witnessed daily in his years as a journalist:

> the unreliability of human nature; the crass chance which strikes
> down and destroys our finest dreams; the fact that man in all his re-
> lations is neither good nor evil, but both. . . . With the one hand
> the naive American takes and executes with all the brutal insistence
> of Nature itself; with the other he writes glowing platitudes con-
> cerning brotherly love, virtue, purity, truth, etc., etc.[63]

Americans, Dreiser felt, would never allow the fact that they are adept at acting as brutal as Nature itself to tarnish the roseate images of themselves which they so cherished.

In an essay called "Hey, Rub-a-Dub-Dub," published in 1917, Dreiser placed contrasting newspaper clippings side by side in a manner which caused them to clash in harsh cacophony; they could not possibly be reconciled into a meaningful whole. Dreiser's point, in the essay, is that life is simply too complicated to be unraveled. Throughout the essay runs the refrain that it is "all inexplicable," and that "all we know is that we cannot know."[64] In a 1922 essay on "The Scope of Fiction" in the *New Republic* Dreiser voiced his doubts even more directly: "regardless of the realist or romanticist or the most painstaking dispenser of fact in science and history, I know by now that life may not be put down in its entirety even though we had at our command the sum of the arts and the resourcefulness of the master of artifice himself. There are, to begin with, suggestions and intimations just beyond the present scope of the senses that appear forever to elude us. And within the present range of human contact or report there is an immense body of fact that will not be penned. It is of a texture and substance that is beyond the palate and stomach of the race."[65] Even at *Butterick's*, as a colleague recalls, "he was always searching, probing, thinking, delving down for facts, yet acutely conscious that one seldom achieved what one was after."[66] Dreiser was not deterred by this problem, however, and it is responsible for whatever humility shines forth in his art. "He can entertain almost any idea and accept almost any experience," Robert Elias has observed, "so long as the idea or experience does not lay claim to exclusiveness."[67]

Dreiser's suspicions about the limitations inherent in his own fictions led him to form his greatest work, *An American Tragedy*, with peculiar openness and ambiguity (as we will show), as if he were unwilling to assume as narrator a claim to authority over the truth about his characters' lives. For in the end, Dreiser recognized that the role of the artist was not the role of someone who replaces stale and false explanations of life with new explanations soon to become equally stale and false. Rather, it was the role of someone able, in Dreiser's words, to "tear the veil from before [his readers'] eyes"[68] by teaching them how to see on their own, as they had never seen before, the complex life that surrounds them.

This had not been Dreiser's goal as a fiction writer from the start. Indeed, his earliest efforts at fiction were characterized by extravagantly bizarre and outlandish settings that had absolutely nothing to do with the world he was documenting as a journalist. Dreiser's earliest creative effort was a preposterous comic opera in which an Indiana farmer was magically transported back to the Aztec empire where the shocked natives dubbed him their king. He never attempted to get "Jeremiah I" published.[69] In the first story he did submit for publication the main character dreams he is an active participant in a vicious ant war, and is saved from death only by awakening to reality. Dreiser was incensed when *Century Magazine* rejected the story.[70]

When his friend Arthur Henry prevailed upon him to start a novel in 1899, Dreiser made the key decision to place his characters (who were based on members of his family) in scenes he had witnessed and documented as a reporter. The breadlines, the railroad yards, the bustling city streets, the Broadway crowds, the factories, the luxury hotels that would appear in *Sister Carrie* were all familiar to Dreiser from direct observation. Two of his magazine articles, "Curious Shifts of the Poor," which appeared in *Demorest's*, and "Whence the Song," which appeared in *Harper's Weekly*, found their way into *Sister Carrie* with few revisions.[71] Both *Sister Carrie*, and the novel that followed it in 1911, *Jennie Gerhardt* (which was similarly based on people and scenes Dreiser personally knew), forced readers to take a fresh look at some of their society's most accepted assumptions. As Swanberg has noted, the books that were selling when those novels appeared "were the glittering and virtuous costume romances, *When Knighthood Was in Flower, Janis Meredith, Soldier of Fortune*. Lust and vice were allowable only if punished in the end—as they had been in *McTeague*—to furnish the reader a wholesome moral lesson."[72] In Dreiser's novels, however, transgression was presented with tolerance and understanding. Dreiser required his reader to accept, in Jennie Gerhardt's case, the seeming paradox of a virtuous sinner, and in Carrie's, of a successful one. Both images challenged the moral categories implicit in the popular novels of the day.

While Dreiser's profiles of successful businessmen for *Success* and other magazines may have sparked his interest in a businessman as a fruitful subject for a novel, he would incorporate only one of his magazine articles into his next novel, *The Financier* (the piece was "A Lesson from the Aquarium," published in *Tom Watson's Magazine*).[73] Based on the life of financier Charles T. Yerkes, *The Financier* was heavily researched by Dreiser from newspaper files, books, interviews, and public documents. As Robert Penn Warren has observed, the novel's hero, Frank Cowperwood, "is not a fictional creation based on Yerkes;

he is, insofar as Dreiser could make him, the image of Yerkes." [74] In addition to giving his reader an unprecedented inside view of the world of business and finance, Dreiser made Yerkes's life read like the epic poem of the predator-hero by allowing his grandeur and "soul-dignity" to shine through his often sleazy machinations. No conforming Babbitt, Frank Cowperwood came across as both sophisticated and (in his own way) honest. Even in prison he is, fundamentally, free. Yet while Frank Cowperwood may be, in one sense, freer than almost any character that had yet appeared in American literature, in another sense he was a peculiarly modern kind of slave. Dreiser titles the trilogy of Cowperwood books, of which *The Financier* was the first, a "Trilogy of Desire." [75] As the title suggests, Cowperwood was enslaved by a desire which, like Carrie's, would always outstrip its attainments. In his dramatic portrayal of the amoral energy that inhered in the ever-reaching, overreaching desire of a Cowperwood, Dreiser shined a spotlight on an aspect of American life that had been largely absent from both literature and journalism despite the fact that it was the force which animated and dominated the age.

Dreiser would incorporate aspects of several of his magazine articles into *An American Tragedy*. A piece called "Pittsburgh" which he wrote for the *Bohemian* aptly prefigures the walks between the poor and wealthy parts of town that Clyde will take in the novel; a piece Dreiser published in 1910 on "The Factory" is a clear rehearsal for his fictional factory scenes; and the opening of an article called "The Man on the Bench" which Dreiser wrote for the *New York Call* distinctly foreshadows the opening lines of *An American Tragedy*. [76] But Dreiser's initial interest in the subject that would form the core of the novel dates back to his days as a newspaperman in St. Louis.

"In so far as it is possible to explain the genesis of any creative idea, I shall be glad to tell you how *An American Tragedy* came to be," Dreiser wrote two years after the book was published, in response to an inquiry,

I had long brooded upon the story, for it seemed to me not only to include every phase of our national life—politics, society, religion, business, sex—but it was a story so common to every boy reared in the smaller towns of America. It seemed so truly a story of what life does to the individual—and how impotent the individual is against such forces. My purpose was not to moralize—God forbid—but to give, if possible, a background and a psychology of reality which would somehow explain, if not condone, how such murders happen—

and they have happened with surprising frequency in America as long as I can remember. [77]

Dreiser's personal familiarity with a murder like the one Clyde Griffiths would commit dates back to his days as a reporter for the *St. Louis Globe-Democrat.*

In 1892 Dreiser covered the story of a young perfume-dealer who murdered his pregnant sweetheart with poisoned candy. As he would later recall, in a magazine article,

It was in 1892, at which time I began work as a newspaperman, that I first began to observe a certain type of crime in the United States. It seemed to spring from the fact that almost every young person was possessed of an ingrowing ambition to be somebody financially and socially. In short, the general mental mood of America was directed toward escape from any form of poverty. This ambition did not imply merely the attainment of comfort and the wherewithal to make happy one's friends, but rather the accumulation of wealth implying power, social superiority, even social domination. [78]

At this juncture in American history, Dreiser recalls, "Fortune-hunting became a disease," and the frequent result was what Dreiser came to view as a peculiarly American kind of crime.

In the main, as I can show by the records, it was the murder of a young girl by an ambitious young man. But not always. There were many forms of murder for money. . . . [One variation] was that of the young ambitious lover of some poorer girl, who in the earlier state of affairs had been attractive enough to satisfy him both in the matter of love and her social station. But nearly always with the passing of time and the growth of experience on the part of the youth, a more attractive girl with money or position appeared and he quickly discovered that he could no longer care for his first love. What produced this particular type of crime about which I am talking was the fact that it was not always possible to drop the first girl. What usually stood in the way was pregnancy, plus the genuine affection of the girl herself for her love, plus also her determination to hold him. . . .

"These murders," Dreiser wrote, "based upon these facts and conditions, proved very common in my lifetime and my personal experience as a journalist."[79]

From the time he began work as a journalist Dreiser collected clippings about young men who murdered (usually pregnant sweethearts) for social and economic advancement. While there are innumerable inconsistencies among Dreiser scholars regarding the specific cases Dreiser followed, there is evidence that Dreiser was familiar with at least ten murders of this sort, which took place in locales as varied as Missouri, New York, California, West Virginia, South Carolina, Massachusetts, and Illinois. Dreiser continued to collect clippings of this sort even after *An American Tragedy* was published; at one point he claimed that he knew of one crime of this nature that had taken place nearly every year between 1895 and 1935.[80]

One such case interested him particularly when he came to New York to work on Pulitzer's *World* in 1894 and met the criminal's mother. Carlyle Harris, an "intern in one of the leading New York hospitals," seduced

a young girl poorer and less distinguished than he was, or at least hoped to be. No sooner had he done this than the devil, or some anachronistic element in the very essence of life itself presented Carlyle with an attractive girl of a much higher station than his own, one who possessed not only beauty but wealth. The way Carlyle finally sought to rid himself of the other girl was to supply her with a dozen powders, four of which were poisoned, and so intended to bring about her death. One of them did. Result: discovery, trial and execution.[81]

Dreiser became aware of another case while working as a magazine writer in New York in 1911. Clarence Richeson, a young preacher "with a small church in Hyannis,"

had come up from nothing, learned little or nothing, accumulated no money, and was struggling along on a small salary. . . . From all I could gather at the time Avis was a charming and emotionally interesting and attractive girl, but of circumstance and parentage as unnoticed as [Richeson's]. Alas, love, a period of happiness, seduction with a promise of marriage, and then Mephistopheles, with nothing more and nothing less in his hand than a call to one of the richest and most socially distinguished congregations in Boston. There followed

114

his installation as pastor, and soon after that one of the wealthy beauties in his new congregation fixed her eye on him and decided that he was the one for her. Yet in the background was Avis and her approaching motherhood. And his promise of marriage. And so, since his new love moved him to visions of social grandeur far beyond his previous dreams he sought to cast off Avis. Yet she in love and agonized, insisted that he help rid herself of the child or marry her. Once more then, poisoned powders and death. And at last [Richeson] dragged from his grand pulpit to a prison cell. And then trial, and death in an electric chair . . .[82]

Time and time again Dreiser saw history repeat itself.

As early as 1906 Dreiser confided to a friend that he wanted to write a book about a murder.[83] By 1919, he had begun two separate novels dealing, respectively, with a murder in New York City and one in Hyannis, Massachusetts.[84] It was not until 1920, however, that Dreiser decided on the case that deserved his fullest attention: the murder of Grace Brown by Chester Gillette in Herkimer County, New York, in 1906.[85] The first time that he and others heard of the crime, Dreiser recalled,

was when the press in a small dispatch from Old Forge, a small town not far from Big Moose Lake, announced that a boy and girl who had come to Big Moose to spend a holiday had gone out in a boat and both had been drowned. An upturned boat, plus a floating straw hat, was found in a remote part of the lake. The lake was dragged and one body discovered and identified as that of Billy Brown. And then came news of the boy who had been seen with her. He was located as the guest of a smart camping party on one of the adjacent lakes and was none other than Chester Gillette, the nephew of a collar factory owner of Cortland. He was identified as the boy who had been with Billy Brown at the lake. Later still, because of a bundle of letters written by the girl and found in his room at Cortland, their love affair was disclosed, also the fact that she was pregnant, and was begging him to marry her . . .[86]

Inevitably here, as in all the other cases of this sort Dreiser encountered, the newspaper account treated the facts of the case and the trial in the conventional manner. But there was another story which intrigued Dreiser: the story of why this story kept repeating itself, of why this tragic pattern recurred so frequently, and what made it so distinctively American.

Chester Gillette, whose fanatically religious parents had run a slum mission in the West, ran away from home at age fourteen and spent several years working at odd jobs across the country—printer's devil, merchant seaman, and brakeman.[87] He spent two years at Oberlin College before meeting an uncle of his by accident in Illinois who offered him a job in his skirt factory in Cortland, New York. In Cortland Chester seduced Grace Brown, a girl who worked under him at the factory, who was the daughter of a poor South Otselic farmer. Her nickname was "Billy." When their affair began, Billy moved out of the home of the married sister with whom she had been living and rented a room of her own in another part of town.

During this period Chester had begun to advance in Cortland society and had become interested in a wealthy girl named Harriet Benedict, whom he knew only slightly, and who had not returned his love. Yet despite his discouragement, Chester was determined to achieve more status and material well-being than his alliance with Billy Brown could ever offer. When Billy announced her pregnancy, Chester insisted that she return to her parents and ignored her as long as he could. The pathetic letters she sent him from South Otselic moved the jurors to tears.

Unwilling to let Billy Brown hold him back from the prospect of a more comfortable and glamorous life, Chester enticed her into taking a trip with him, presumably to be married. In a rowboat at Big Moose Lake he brutally battered her head with a tennis racket and pushed her overboard. After she drowned, Chester left a straw hat he had bought for the occasion floating on the water to announce his own death. He fled the scene and was apprehended shortly and convicted. He was executed in the electric chair in March 1908, after an unsuccessful appeal.

Dreiser, working as a journalist in New York in 1906, had taken considerable interest in the stories about the Gillette case which he had read in the New York newspapers. The press devoted a great deal of space to every detail of the case, and Dreiser, like other readers, had the chance to learn many specific facts about both Gillette and his victim. The *New York World*'s artists had a heyday with the story as well, often filling a full quarter of the paper's front page (even more on inside pages) with drawings of "Chester Gillette as He Appears on Trial for His Life, and the Girl with Whose Murder He Is Charged," "Chester

Gillette as He Appeared in Court and His Senior Counsel," and "Chester Gillette as He Appeared on the Witness Stand Telling His Version of Grace Brown's Death."[88] In addition, the paper gave prominent play to photos, including a "Group Photograph of Gillette Family Taken When Chester Was Fifteen Years Old," one of the "Jurors Who Will Try Chester Gillette on Charge of Murder," and a picture of the "Prisoner's Handiwork in His Cell at Jail; Corner of Gillette's Parlor-like Cell, Decorated by Himself."[89] It is no wonder that the heavily illustrated, sensational case made an impression on a writer who had been collecting clippings on crimes of this nature for years. Dreiser did not think about basing a novel on the case, however, until four or five years after he had read the newspaper accounts.[90]

Ten years after *An American Tragedy* was published, Dreiser reflected in print on why he had been stirred by the case. "In my examination of such data as I could find in 1924 relating to the Chester Gillette–Billy Brown case," Dreiser wrote, "I had become convinced that there was an entire misunderstanding or perhaps I had better say non-apprehension, of the conditions or circumstances surrounding the victims of that murder *before* the murder was committed."[91]

It was this "misundertanding, or . . . non-apprehension," on the part of Americans, of the context in which the Gillette crime took place that helped prompt Dreiser to write *An American Tragedy*. The context in which the murder must be seen, Dreiser felt, was the fascination, shared by Americans across the nation, with the dream of rising through advantageous marriage from poverty to status and wealth. Versions of this dream had filled the pages of popular magazines Dreiser had encountered in his youth. The dream thrived in the consciousness of average people across America; and it underlay all of those chillingly similar crimes Dreiser had followed since the 1890s. And, almost without exception, it was viewed uncritically by the American public. Gillette, Dreiser wrote in 1935, *"was really doing the kind of thing which Americans should and would have said was the wise and moral thing to do* (attempting to rise socially through the heart) *had he not committed a murder."*[92] Americans were blind, Dreiser felt, to important facts about themselves, their morality, their country, and their dreams. He wrote *An American Tragedy*, in large part, to help them take a fresh look at some of those facts.

While Dreiser departed from Gillette's story in his novel in several significant ways (as we will discuss), he kept extremely close to the record throughout much of the book. Both Chester and Clyde were the children of devout parents who had run a mission, and both came from the West to work for an uncle who had a factory in the East. The initials of the two boys are the same, and both begin affairs with poor farmers' daughters employed under them, who, as it happens, have similar nicknames (Grace Brown was called "Billy"; Roberta Alden was called "Bert"). While Grace's South Otselic becomes Roberta's "Biltz," the backgrounds of the two girls are nearly identical. In the novel Big Moose Lake, complete with its strange wier-wier birds, is changed, only in name, to "Big Bittern." Chester Gillette's tennis racket is changed to Clyde Griffiths's camera, but the trips planned by the two boys (save for the nature of the girls' deaths) are the same; both Chester Gillette and Clyde Griffiths use the pseudonym of "Carl Graham" during their travels.[93]

The letters from Grace Brown which made jurors weep at the Gillette trial are extremely close to those which evoke the same pathos at the Griffiths trial:

(last letter from Grace Brown)	(last letter from Roberta Alden)
If you fail to keep your promise, Chester, to come to me Saturday, I will surely come to Cortland and you will have to see me there.	This is to tell you that unless I hear from you either by telephone or letter before noon, Friday, I shall be in Lycurgus that same night, and the world will know how you have treated me.

In the Gillette trial, the prosecutor states in his opening statement to the jury, ". . . there was another person on the lake as they struggled, and when Grace Brown's death cry sounded over the water of Big Moose Lake this witness heard it. And she will be here." In the Griffiths trial in the novel, the prosecutor states in his opening statement to the jury, ". . . as her last death cry rang out over the waters of Big Bittern, there was a witness, and before the prosecution has closed its case that witness will be here to tell you the story."[94]

Newspaper reports of the Gillette trial say that "this announcement astounded the crowded, breathless courtroom as if the roof had fallen. Gillette, who had been watching the prosecutor speak without the slightest expression on his face, suddenly quailed, then straightened up in his chair and threw his head back." After the prosecutor's announcement in the novel, Dreiser writes, "the result was all that could be expected and more. For Clyde, who up to this time . . . had been seeking to face it all with an imperturbable look of patient innocence, now stiffened and then wilted. . . . His hands now gripped the sides of his chair and his head went back with a jerk as if from a powerful blow." At both the Gillette trial and the Griffiths trial, the round-bottomed rowboat and strands of the dead girl's hair are produced as evidence. Chester and Clyde each went through a forest after fleeing the lake, and each had the misfortune to meet three men who later testified against him.[95]

Judge Devendorf's charge to the jury at the Gillette trial and Judge Oberwaltzer's charge at the Griffiths trial are nearly identical:

(Gillette trial)

"If any of the material facts of a case were at variance with the probability of guilt, it would be the duty of the jury to give the defendant the benefit of the doubt raised.

Gentlemen, evidence is not to be discredited or descried because it is circumstantial. It may often be more reliable evidence than direct evidence . . .

While I do not say that you must agree upon your verdict, I would suggest that you ought not, any of you, place your minds in a position which will not yield if, after careful deliberation, you find you are wrong."

(Griffiths trial)

"If any of the material facts of the case are at variance with the probability of guilt, it would be the duty of you gentlemen to give the defendant the benefit of the doubt raised.

And it must be remembered that evidence is not to be discredited or descried because it is circumstantial. It may often be more reliable evidence than direct evidence.

While I do not say that you must agree upon your verdict, I would suggest that you ought not, any of you, place your minds in a position which will not yield if after careful deliberation you find you are wrong."

A New York newspaper had reported Chester Gillette's reaction to the verdict as follows: "He leaned over a nearby table, he drew toward him a bit of white paper and, taking a pencil from his pocket, wrote deliberately this message: 'Father, I am convicted. Chester.' It went to his father in Denver." Clyde Griffiths in *An American Tragedy*, similarly, asking his lawyer "for a piece of paper and pencil . . . wrote: 'Mrs. Asa

Griffiths, care of Star of Hope Mission, Denver, Col. Dear Mother—I am convicted. Clyde.' "[96]

While no one knows the precise material relating to the Gillette trial to which Dreiser had access, it is clear from the above citations that Dreiser was familiar with at least the trial proceedings reported in the New York newspapers.[97] He also had available a small pamphlet called "Grace Brown's Love Letters," which reprinted the letters Grace Brown sent to Chester Gillette in the early summer of 1906, shortly before her death.[98]

In addition to doing extensive research in newspaper files, Dreiser personally visited the region of upstate New York where the Gillette crime had taken place. He collected vivid personal impressions of the drab and isolated farmhouses of South Otselic, of the sounds the birds made at Big Moose Lake, of the shape of the upstate woods to which Chester had fled. He visited a factory in Troy, New York.[99] And he even took his cousin-consort Helen Richardson out in a rowboat on Big Moose Lake presumably to help him capture more authentically the crime that took place there.[100] Dreiser also finagled his way into the death block at Sing Sing to get "the physical lay" of the place. (On this occasion—as, on others—Dreiser was less than overwhelmed by what he saw. He commented, about his visit there, "My imagination was better— (more true to the fact)—than what I saw.")[101]

Before examining the ways in which Dreiser departed from the facts of the Gillette case in *An American Tragedy*, I would like to suggest some hypotheses as to why he stayed as close to them as he did.

One important reason was his conviction, reiterated throughout the book, that fact is fate. In all of the clippings Dreiser collected, the young murderer sought to eradicate the fact of his initial sexual transgression and the need for any responsibility for its consequences.[102] But, repeatedly, fact would prove to be destiny; the young man's deeds and words would follow him regardless of the cleverness of his attempts to evade them.

In keeping with the pattern he observed in these crimes, Dreiser insists in *An American Tragedy*, that fact cannot be avoided; there is no turning away from the concrete events which shackle one's past to one's future. Clyde never really succeeds in running away from the automobile accident he had in Kansas City (it comes back to haunt him at his trial). He finds that ignoring Roberta does not make her (or the fact of her pregnancy) go away; neither does murdering her. The travel folders he bought, the photographs he took, the questions he asked, the letter Roberta wrote to her mother but had not had time to mail—all conspire to convict Clyde at his trial.

A second reason for staying close to the facts of the Gillette case in his novel was Dreiser's desire to make his story not merely an absorbing imaginative creation, but the story of America as well, at a particular juncture in its history. Dreiser wanted to document the time in which he lived; he wanted to synthesize what he saw as key aspects of the culture he had come to know since his childhood. He wanted to encompass in his novel "every phase of our national life—politics, society, religion, business, sex."[103]

By rooting his book as firmly in actuality as he did, he could be more confident of achieving the referential power he wanted to achieve. He wanted the lakes and poor farmhouses to be the lakes and farmhouses of upstate New York. He wanted Roberta to *be* all of those poor country girls who came to work in factories in the nearest city. He wanted Clyde Griffiths to be all of those ill-fated young American boys who had committed similar crimes—and all those who might never commit crimes, but who shared his ambition, his insatiable cravings, his youth, optimism, and illusion.

Dreiser succeeded in giving his novel the referential power to which he aspired, both on the social and the individual level. As Robert Penn Warren has observed, one feels, in the novel,

> a historical moment, the moment of the Great Boom which climaxed the period from Grant to Coolidge, the half century in which the new America of industry and finance-capitalism was hardening into shape and its secret forces were emerging to dominate all life.[104]

Dreiser himself proudly boasted of the letters he received from young men all over the country who saw portraits of themselves in Clyde Griffiths.

Dreiser's many minor changes in the Gillette story—such as his switching a skirt factory to a collar factory, changing a tennis racket to a camera, adding a local political battle to the trial—are useful and interesting,[105] but the most important changes in *An American Tragedy* are: (1) the description of Clyde's character and background; (2) the description of American culture that emerges from the shared values of other invented characters in the novel; and (3) the description of the drowning. For it is through the first two of these elements that Dreiser succeeds in exposing as illusions some of the conventional assumptions and explanations which dominate American society. And it is through the last that he challenges the possibility of *any* completely adequate explanation of reality. By pointing up the inadequacies of this and any one version of reality, Dreiser forces the reader to "go back, in so far as we may, to the primary sources of thought, i.e. the visible scene, the actions and thoughts of people, the movements of Nature and its chemical and physical subtleties, in order to draw original and radical conclusions for ourselves."[106]

Clyde Griffiths's background and character are very different from the background and character of Chester Gillette. Clyde's parents were poorer, and his childhood more circumscribed and deprived. Clyde was less scheming than Chester was. His formal education was inferior to that of his real-life model; he was less well-traveled and sophisticated. In many ways, as some critics have observed, he was more like Theodore Dreiser than he was like Chester Gillette.

He was also more like another American figure as well: the hero in a Horatio Alger novel. Dreiser knew the Alger novels well, having started reading them avidly at age ten.[107] The plot of *An American Tragedy* up to the point when Clyde goes to Lycurgus—in other words, the portion of the book that relied most heavily on Dreiser's powers of invention—bears a striking resemblance to the standard Alger plot, as the chart below indicates. In many ways, of course, the young man Samuel Griffiths meets at the Union League Club is not at all like an Alger hero: he is selfish and weak and has not done anything specifically heroic. But even Alger heroes are known to have their faults;[108] what counts is that Clyde's uncle *perceives* him as a youth characterized by those qualities typical of Alger heroes. Indeed, while not sparing the reader a view of Clyde's flaws, Dreiser emphasizes his virtues throughout the first part of the novel, making the resemblance between his own plot and the Alger plot even stronger. The plot summary of the typical Alger novel (in the column on the left) was constructed by Alger's most recent biographer; the plot summary on the right (my own) is that of *An American Tragedy*:

Alger's plot:	Dreiser's plot:
A teen-aged boy whose experience of the sinister adult world is slight, yet whose virtue entitles him to the reader's respect . . . enters the City, both a fabled	Clyde Griffiths, a teen-aged boy who knows little of the adult world but who is sensitive and thoughtful (if confused), and loyal to and respectful of his

land of opportunity and a potentially corrupting environment.

mother, gets a job at Kansas City's Green-Davidson Hotel, a place of great opportunity, and of potential corruption.

His exemplary struggle to maintain his social respectability, . . . to gain a measure of economic independence, . . . this is the substance of the standard Alger plot.

While Clyde's struggle is not "exemplary" (he leaves town when he is a passenger in a car that is involved in a hit-and-run accident), even Alger's heroes sometimes commit crimes in their youth for which they repent. Clyde is "terribly sorry" about the accident, and especially regrets the pain it caused his mother. He gets a series of solid, honest jobs, and sends money home whenever he can; he's determined to "make his own way as best he might" and rise above the oppressive poverty of his parents. He avoids the hotel business ("too high-flying, I guess"), and by chance (a contrivance common to Alger plots) he meets an old chum who helps him get a job at Chicago's Union League Club.

At length the hero earns the admiration of an adult patron who rewards him with elevated social station, usually a job or reunion with his patrician family, and the trappings of respectability . . .

As luck would have it (again an Algerism), Clyde's rich uncle turns up there. He is "obviously impressed" by Clyde's association with such a distinguished club, and also admires Clyde's neat appearance and "efficient and unobtrusive manners." Finding him bright and ambitious he offers him a job at his collar factory. The offer brings Clyde the standard Alger rewards

> listed at left: "elevated social
> station . . . reunion with his
> patrician family, and the trap-
> pings of respectability.[109]

Clyde's fantasies, incidentally, when he gets a job at the Union League Club, resemble the fantasies of the millions of young people who, thinking to themselves, "this might happen to me," pushed Alger's novels into best-sellerdom:

> And who knows? What if he worked very steadily and made only
> the right sort of contacts and conducted himself with the greatest
> care here, one of those remarkable men whom he saw entering
> or departing from here might take a fancy to him and offer him a
> connection with something important somewhere, such as he had
> never had before, and that might lift him into a world such as he had
> never known.[110]

(In addition, Clyde's fantasies of marrying Sondra are rooted in the "reality" of the world of Alger's heroes. The character of Sondra is nearly totally invented by Dreiser; there was no one like her in the Gillette case.[111] However, in Alger's books there were many girls like her. As one of Alger's biographers described a familiar variety of female in an Alger novel, these wealthy young ladies "invited the hero to their homes for tea, and he took dancing lessons to acquit himself satisfactorily at their parties. But when they spoke to him, he fumbled for words; when they complimented him, he blushed."[112] The hero usually ended up marrying such a girl—but implicitly, beyond the close of the book.)

While Alger always "abandoned his hero on the threshold of his good fortune, at the cultural boundary delimiting his place, rather than following him into that strange new world of opulence,"[113] Dreiser follows his hero into that "strange new world." He takes the remainder of his plot (from the point at which the Alger plot ends) from the story of the Gillette murder that appeared in the newspapers.

By merging the world of the Alger romance with the world reported in the daily newspaper, Dreiser forces his reader to see *both* texts in a new way. His strategy highlights the *incompleteness* of both the Alger plot *and* the newspaper story. The former ignores what happens to the young man after his fortunes are elevated; the latter ignores, for the most part, the early experiences that helped make him the way he is.

The reader of the Alger story is not required to consider the repercussions of the hero's rapid rise; the formulaic structure of Alger plots encourages passive acceptance, on the part of the reader, of the author's "happily-ever-after" intimations. The reader of the newspaper story is similarly not required to become engaged with the material reported in more than a passive way; the young man described has already committed a crime, and, as a criminal, may be dismissed as a very different sort of person from the reader.[114] Dreiser's strategy, however, produces very different results.

Dreiser lets the reader see Clyde's life through Clyde's own eyes in a way which evokes both sympathy and compassion. He lets the reader witness the parched and thirsting feelings Clyde has in the poor and musty rooms of his parents' mission, stifling in their bareness. And he lets the reader share Clyde's amazement at the luxury and comfort that surround him at the Green-Davidson Hotel. The reader has trouble condemning Clyde too harshly for allowing himself to be seduced by glitter and glamor.

Clyde is not perverse. He is not driven by any desires that are considered abnormal in society. He is not given to irrational outbursts; he is not even particularly passionate. He is a typical adolescent with typical adolescent "yearnings" and fantasies. He simply puts one foot in front of the other and suddenly finds himself tumbling down a mountainside from which there is no escape.

Telling Clyde's story the way he did, Dreiser challenged his readers' most unquestioned assumptions. The crimes Americans read about in the newspapers, in the 1890s, were "supposed to represent the false state of things, merely passing indecencies, accidental errors that did not count," Dreiser wrote.[115] In short, crimes were considered curious aberrations from an otherwise good, honest, virtuous norm; and criminals were aberrant monsters whose exploits resembled those of beasts that had escaped from the zoo. In *An American Tragedy* Dreiser explores the *normality* underlying the criminal. And his notion forced his readers to take a fresh look at aspects of American life which they had grown accustomed to distorting or ignoring. While the reader of a Horatio Alger novel is soothed by the dream that anyone (including himself) can become a millionaire, the reader of *An American Tragedy* is disturbed by the nightmare that anyone (including himself) can become a murderer.

In exploring the normality underlying the criminal, Dreiser also dared to explore the criminality underlying the normal. The thirsting after wealth and respectability that motivated Clyde is identical to that which motivates other characters in the book, from all strata of American society. What separates them from Clyde is simply a matter of degree, not kind.

Hortense Briggs lies and schemes to get Clyde to buy her a new and expensive coat that is guaranteed to raise her social standing and hence her self-worth. (Meanwhile the coat-store proprietor lies and schemes to extract from her the maximum price.) Bella Griffiths tries to manipulate her father into building a bungalow at Twelfth Lake because she craves the status that summering there involves; she longs to be part of that set of families in Lycurgus that advertises its wealth and status with flashy cars, homes, and summer cottages. When simple shopgirls and the daughters of sophisticated factory owners are seen doggedly pursuing the same ends, the universality of these goals and of the often unsavory means these characters use to pursue their ends—lying, cheating, manipulating—is clearly established. There is a distinct aspect of criminality that underlies the normal throughout the book, and Dreiser constantly emphasizes it through such parallels.

The America portrayed in this novel is a grasping, greedy, and ever-thirsting culture that rarely, if ever, questions where it is going, or why. It is a society that accepts without question the validity of the American dream—the quest for success as defined by wealth and status. If his better-educated, higher-born compatriots have little reason to doubt the validity of striving for these goals, how can we expect Clyde to do so? For Clyde, as for most of the characters in the novel, "material success" was "a type of success that was almost without flaw, as he saw it."[116]

While the reader is made aware of the multiple blemishes inherent in lives ruled solely by the dream of material success, Dreiser points out, evenhandedly, that such quests had valid aspects as well. For money solves many if not all problems in American society. Indeed, in American society as it is portrayed in the novel, money and status, in addition to providing comforts and glittering delights, can, in fact, get one out of almost any conceivable scrape.

Thus Belknap, one of the defense attorneys at Clyde's trial, had extricated himself as a young man from a problem similar to Clyde's with little difficulty. A college graduate who derived high social status from his father's position—"his father had been a judge as well as a national senator" (p. 592)—Belknap had run away from his problem as Clyde had, but without adverse consequences.

In his twentieth year, [Belknap] had been trapped between two girls, with one of whom he was merely playing while being seriously in love with the other. And having seduced the first and being confronted with an engagement or flight, he had chosen flight. But not before laying the matter before his father, by whom he was advised to take a vacation, during which time the services of the family doctor were engaged with the result that for a thousand dollars and expenses necessary to house the pregnant girl in Utica, the father had finally extricated his son and made possible his return, and eventual marriage to the other girl. (Pp. 592–93)

In contrast to Belknap's easy solution, Clyde and Roberta are left to grapple with "the enormous handicaps imposed by ignorance, youth, poverty and fear" (p. 384). A doctor who was known to have performed an abortion for a girl "of a pretty good family" (p. 393) summarily refuses to have anything to do with a poverty-stricken girl like Roberta (p. 408). Both of these episodes were invented by Dreiser to highlight a fact he did not want his reader to ignore. As he would later observe, looking back on Chester Gillette's plight, "you may depend upon it that if he had had money and more experience in the ways of immorality, he would have known ways and means of indulging himself in the relationship with Billy Brown without bringing upon himself the morally compulsive relation of prospective fatherhood."[117]

In the society Dreiser documents in the novel, the pain and complexity of life's problems are constantly denied in favor of the "easy solution." Dreiser knew, however, that the easy solutions available to the rich were usually denied the poor. Despite the lip service America paid to the notion of equality, the poor were, for all practical purposes, treated as less equal than the rich. This reality (first encountered by Dreiser as a newspaper reporter) was denied by the roseate hues that permeated the pictures of American life that appeared in literature and by the rhetoric of politicians who trumpeted that all Americans were free and equal. But Dreiser was determined to prevent his reader from ignoring realities which popular fictions and rhetoric conspired to repress. It was vital to understand what money and status bought in America if one was to understand the manic acquisitiveness that ruled the day.

When Clyde first arrives in Lycurgus he walks down streets lined with elegant mansions and then reports for work at his uncle's factory. After work he strolls down River Street past more factories, and then he came finally upon a miserable slum, the like of which, small as it was, he had not seen outside of Chicago or Kansas City. He was so irritated and depressed by the poverty and social angularity and crudeness of it—all spelling but one thing, social misery, to him— that he at once retraced his steps and recrossing the Mohawk by a bridge farther west soon found himself in an area which was very different indeed—a region once more of just such homes as he had been admiring before he left for the factory. . . . (Pp. 187–88)

Clyde continues to believe, throughout his life, that he can turn his back on poverty and deprivation as easily as he can retrace his steps out of this slum. The rich do it, after all. Why shouldn't he?

Embodying the "youth, optimism and illusion" that Dreiser felt characterized America as a whole, Clyde constantly assumes that there will be an easy way out of potential misery.[118] His tragedy, in part, is the tragedy that stems from denying life its untidy complexity.

Clyde's catalog of problems and solutions reads almost like a parody of the advertisements that fill the magazines to which Dreiser contributed. Have you a pain? the ad would ask. Take our pill. Are you going bald? Use our cream. For Clyde, and for most of those around him, life itself seems filled with equally simple solutions. Poor? Get a job. In trouble with the law? Get a pseudonym in a new city for a fresh start. Caught in a rut? Find a rich uncle. Got a poor girl pregnant? Throw her overboard. Convicted for murder? Appeal. Appeal denied? Take Jesus.[119] (This final "solution" brings one full circle to the hymn Clyde's family sings in chapter 1: "The love of Jesus save me whole, / The love of God my steps control") (p. 9). Each of these "solutions," however, is obviously inadequate and unsatisfactory, though Clyde has neither the mental nor the moral resources to understand why. Like millions of other Americans whose follies Dreiser often criticized, Clyde had never learned to think for himself.

Clyde comes by his inadequate mental equipment naturally, through no fault of his own. His father, we learn, "poorly knit mentally as well as physically," was the "product of an environment and a religious theory, but with no guiding or mental insight of his own" (pp. 172, 13). His mother accepts without question the religious maxims that hang on her mission walls despite daily challenges to their wisdom. It is not surprising that Clyde lacks the mental and moral faculties to view his surroundings critically. He has been told all his life that he is free to choose the road to heaven or hell, and he assumes he is as free to choose

success or failure, wealth or poverty, happiness or misery. He is unaware of the extent to which he is not free. Like so many other characters in the book, Clyde is bound up in a morass of illusions that impede
his ability to deal effectively with the realities he encounters.

Dreiser is well aware of the inadequacy of Clyde's perspective on himself and his actions; for Dreiser knows that simplistic solutions, framed
mottoes, and dreams of status and wealth fail to contain the complexities of life in the modern world. It is with stunning humility that Dreiser
suggests that perhaps even a novel as long and dense and intricate as his
may prove, in the end, to be equally incapable of containing those
complexities.

Dreiser, willing to admit the possibility that some of the complexities
which elude Clyde may elude him as well, makes the drowning of
Roberta indeterminate and ambiguous, as if he were unwilling to
assume authority as narrator over the truth about his characters'
actions.

In the Gillette case, the murder was a rather straightforward one.
There was clear evidence of heavy blows, obviously deliberate, upon the
victim's face: "one whole side of her face had been bashed in, there
had been brain damage from a three inch gash behind her ear."[120] Chester
Gillette insisted throughout the trial that Grace Brown had committed
suicide by jumping into the lake after he told her he would not marry
her, but a physician who testified at the trial ruled out that possibility:
"Dr. Edward Douglass testified that she was beaten over the head with
a blunt instrument (such as a tennis racket) and that she was dead when
she entered the water."[121] There was clear evidence that Chester Gillette
had murdered Grace Brown.

The evidence presented to the court in *An American Tragedy* is much
more ambiguous. No "three-inch gash" announced that a brutal crime
had been committed.

> While the joint report of the five doctors showed: "An injury to the
> mouth and nose; the top of the nose appears to have been slightly
> flattened, the lips swollen, one front tooth slightly loosened, and an
> abrasion of the mucous membrane with the lips"—all agreed that
> these injuries were by no means fatal. (P. 573)

Grace Brown's skull appeared to have been severely damaged by the
heavy blows she received from the tennis racket; Roberta's head injuries,
as well as the grasping position of her hands, however, indicated to the

lawyers that Clyde's story about her having been hit in the head by the boat may have been true (p. 573).

Strands of Grace Brown's hair which had stuck in the rowboat had been produced at the Gillette trial; one of the most incriminating pieces of evidence presented at Clyde Griffiths's trial is the bit of Roberta's hair supposedly found attached to Clyde's camera. But while there is no reason to doubt the authenticity of the hair exhibited at the Gillette trial, it is clear that the hair exhibited at the Griffiths trial was placed in the camera (some time after Roberta's death) by a morally overzealous backwoodsman named Burton Burleigh who desired to speed Clyde's conviction (pp. 575–76). The evidence that convicts Clyde Griffiths is thus, in part, more shadowy than that which convicted Chester Gillette.

The ambiguity of the evidence presented at Clyde's trial echoes the ambiguity of the events that took place in the rowboat. By a series of subtle maneuvers of syntax and diction, Dreiser manages to leave these events remarkably indeterminate, as we will show. The key sequence of events centering around Roberta's death occurs in the final five pages of book 2. These pages warrant a close examination. For here Dreiser shows himself to be more of a conscious stylist than he is credited with being. While Dreiser's literary career is spotted with innumerable instances of his insensitivity to the finer points of syntax and diction, in these pages he proves himself to be a master craftsman.

After an hour of rowing on Big Bittern, Clyde begins to experience the strange sensation that he, as well as the boat, is "drifting, drifting" (p. 489). Clyde is, indeed, drifting, emotionally as well as physically at this time, caught up in the flow of currents he does not fully understand. Dreiser evokes Clyde's passivity and lack of decision by narrating events through a shadowy fog of participial sentence fragments, passive constructions, static noun clusters, and other carefully chosen grammatical structures. In subtle ways, he inhibits the establishment of Clyde as an acting subject.

Shortly after Clyde feels this "drifting" sensation, he begins to drift grammatically through the narrative: "And suddenly becoming conscious that his courage, on which he had counted so much this long while to sustain him here, was leaving him, and he instantly and consciously plumbing the depths of his being in a vain search to recapture it" (p. 490). There is neither an active nor a passive verb in this "sentence" (which, from a syntactic standpoint, is not a sentence at all). One finds rather two drifting participial phrases connected by "and":

(1) " . . . becoming conscious that his courage . . . was leaving him, and he (2) . . . consciously plumbing the depths of his being . . ."

One of several more standard constructions might have eliminated the "and" and changed "plumbing" to "plumbed," thus connecting these two phrases into a sentence. But Dreiser fractures his grammar consciously and not accidentally. For while a normal sentence structure might make Clyde the subject of an active verb (he . . . plumbed), Dreiser's floating participles allow Clyde simply to find himself in a state of doing something, set adrift in that state by forces beyond his awareness and control.[122]

The pages following this passage are filled with many analogous examples of such "floating participles."[123] By this term we mean participial phrases cut off from the larger sentences of which they would normally be a part and set adrift on their own. (They are not "dangling participles" since they correctly modify the nouns to which they implicitly or explicitly refer.) In the following passage, the participles italicized for easy identification are those which have Clyde alone as their subject:

And Clyde, instantly *sensing* the profoundness of his own failure, his own cowardice or inadequateness for such an occasion, as instantly *yielding* to a tide of submerged hate, not only for himself, but Roberta—her power—or that of life to restrain him in this way. And yet *fearing* to act in any way—*being unwilling* to—*being willing* only to say that never, never would he marry her—that never, even should she expose him, would he leave here with her to marry her— that he was in love with Sondra and would cling only to her—and yet not *being able* to say that even. But angry and confused and *glowering*. And then, as she drew near him, seeking to take his hand in hers and the camera from him in order to put it in the boat, he *flinging* out at her, but not even then with any intention to do other than free himself of her—her touch—her pleading—consoling sympathy—her presence forever—God!

Yet (the camera still unconsciously held tight) *pushing* at her with so much vehemence as not only to strike her lips and nose and chin with it, but to throw her back sidewise toward the left wale which caused the boat to career to the very water's edge. And then he, stirred by her sharp scream, (as much due to the lurch of the boat, as the cut on her nose and lip), *rising* and *reaching* half to assist

131

or recapture her and half to apologize for the unintended blow—yet
in doing so completely *capsizing* the boat—himself and Roberta
being as instantly thrown into the water. . . . (Pp. 492-93)

Thus Clyde does not fling, push, reach, or capsize; rather, he somehow
finds himself flinging, pushing, reaching, capsizing. The difference is
vital.

Dreiser further intensifies Clyde's passivity by moving, in the final
phrases of this passage, from active present participle ("rising" and
"reaching") to passive present participle ("being thrown"). There are a
number of other passive constructions in these pages, as well, many of
which contribute directly to the ambiguity of Clyde's responsibility.
Thus Dreiser refers to the moment of contemplated murder as "the
moment [Clyde] or something had planned for him" (p. 491), rather
than referring to the moment Clyde had planned; Clyde is the passive
recipient here, of his own former plans, or of the plans of some force
outside himself. After Roberta falls into the water, a voice at Clyde's
ear tells him, "this—has been done for you"; again, it does not say,
"this you have done" (p. 493).

The static nature of this important scene is established, in part, by
Dreiser's direct references to "a static between a powerful compulsion to
do and yet not to do" (p. 492), and to "the stillness of his position, the
balanced immobility of the mood" (p. 492). But Dreiser also evokes
stasis by frequently pasting noun clusters on the page, cut off from any
verbs, active or passive: "the weird, haunting cry of that unearthly bird
again," "His wet, damp, nervous hands!," "A sudden palsy of the will"
(p. 491) are all treated as if they were sentences. These and the many
disconnected images that appear in these pages help evoke a "weird"
tableau of "balanced immobility."

On those few occasions in these pages when Dreiser does employ
complete sentences and not sentence fragments, he almost always
makes statements indicating necessity, possibility, or a future state—
and not actions actually taken. These statements involve the words
"would," "could," "might," "must," "needed to." For example, Dreiser
writes, "All that [Clyde] needed to do now was to turn swiftly and
savagely to one side or the other . . . It could be done—it could be
done . . ." (p. 491). But indicating the possibility of completing an
action is very different from saying that that action has been completed.
Again, Clyde has "done" nothing.

Clyde himself is unsure of the role he has played in Roberta's death.

She sinks for the final time not after he has decided not to save her, but as he floats in his interminable indecision. "Had he [killed her]? Or, had he not?" Clyde ponders (p. 494). From the moment Clyde is seen "becoming conscious that his courage . . . was leaving him," to the end of book 2, he ceases to be the subject of any active verb. Clyde's thoughts flow in sentence fragments and images. The reader sees him *in the process* of doing things (consciously or unconsciously), yet unaware of how he came to be doing them.

In a final effort to evoke the murkiness of the scene he relates, Dreiser constructs several masterfully ambiguous phrases. Dreiser shows Clyde "rising and reaching half to assist or recapture" Roberta when she falls into the water (p. 492). The word "recapture" suggests that she is his captive; "assisting" (implicitly to save) and "recapturing" (implictly to be able to destroy her himself) are thus polarly charged words, and the meaning of the sentence is ambiguous. Dreiser also refers to the blow Clyde "had so accidentally and all but unconsciously administered" (p. 493). Clyde's action was not completely unconscious; does this mean that it was somewhat conscious? Can something be *somewhat* conscious? If an action is somewhat conscious, can it also be accidental? The answers to these questions remain as clear as the silt on the bottom of Big Bittern.[124]

Throughout *An American Tragedy*, as we have indicated earlier, Dreiser suggests the limitations of Clyde's outlook on life. But when it comes to the death of Roberta, the reader has no reason to believe that Dreiser knows more than Clyde does. Dreiser, supremely humble as an author despite his often pompous pride as a man, prefers to remain at Clyde's side, in the dark waters of his confusion, leaving the reader to postulate an explanation of the events on his own from the ambiguous cues offered.

Few writers of fiction have elicited the amount of literal reader participation that Dreiser elicited in this volume. The opinions of readers as to what "really happened" in the rowboat were so strong and diverse that Boni and Liveright decided to capitalize on them by running a contest. The essay contest they ran, on the topic, "Was Clyde Griffiths Guilty of Murder in the First Degree?," drew hundreds of entries from readers across the country and was eventually won by a law professor in Virginia.[125] Because of the special openness and ambiguity with which Dreiser narrated the death of Roberta, readers were attracted to the idea of constructing interpretations of the event on their own.

Dreiser himself, in *An American Tragedy*, seemed to be unwilling to assume authority as narrator over what really happened to Clyde because he knew the complex facts of the event were unlikely to yield to any simple explanation. He preferred to admit that even he, as narrator, could not capture the "truth" about his characters, that they, like "the actuality of life," were

A shadow
That eludes one—
Escaping by a thousand ways.[126]

And rather than end his novel with the kind of resonant finality that is the novelist's prerogative, Dreiser chose to leave *An American Tragedy* peculiarly open-ended. In his final chapter Dreiser circles back to the words with which the novel began: "Dusk, of a summer night";[127] he then proceeds to begin the story of Russell (the child of Clyde's sister), who is being raised by Clyde's parents, and who is likely to relive, in his own way, Clyde's story. Implicit in this strategy is Dreiser's admission of the limitations of his novel: it contains the story of Clyde—but also of Russell? His final chapter reflects his belief that even a text as panoramic and dense as this one is destined to be incomplete, that life (and the experiences, tragedies, dreams, and mysteries it entails) resists containment in the writer's forms.

5

ERNEST HEMINGWAY

Ernest Hemingway as foreign correspondent for the *Toronto Star* in Paris in 1923. Photo credit: Helen Breaker, Paris; The Kennedy Library

Hemingway, covering the Spanish civil war for the North American Newspaper Alliance, looking out over a battlefield in Spain in 1938.
Photo credit: The Kennedy Library

Nobel Prize winner Ernest Hemingway is on record as having told the *Paris Review* that "the most essential gift for a good writer is a built-in shockproof, shit detector."[1] It was not the first time he had been this blunt. Indeed, in *Death in the Afternoon*, Hemingway defined "any overmetaphysical tendency in speech" as "horseshit."[2] For Hemingway, it is important to stick to the facts, even if you are Robert Jordan and you are dying,[3] to fix your attention on "the real thing" and not on some secondhand characterization of it.[4]

The scatological expletives Hemingway often uses to label what he views as false, overblown, illusory, or artificial would seem, at first glance, to set him in a world far removed from that inhabited by the church-going, civic-spirited, turn-of-the-century editor and publisher of the "first class . . . family journal"[5] that gave him his first job as a reporter. The legendary founder of the *Kansas City Star*, William Rockhill Nelson, had died more than two years before Hemingway joined the paper. However, his standards and his attitudes permeated every aspect of the *Star* long after his death.[6] What had been important to him was passed on to new recruits through the style sheet, the nature of assignments, and the directives of editors. Hemingway probably never knew precisely where these notions came from; they were simply prescriptions for success at the *Star*. He might have been surprised to learn that one of Nelson's famous favorite expressions had been "the real thing."[7] Hemingway similarly might not have known that "freshness of vision" was another theme on which Nelson had been known to harp frequently.[8] Or that Nelson had often claimed that the central figure in the entire newspaper operation was "the reporter who can get facts straight and put them into plain, concise language."[9] During his brief apprenticeship at the *Star*, Hemingway would learn to be that kind of reporter. The style with which Hemingway would transform American fiction reflected in diction, syntax, and subject the lessons that he first learned in Kansas City.

Throughout his career as a writer, as he constantly moved back and forth between journalism and fiction, Hemingway would adhere firmly to the rules of diction and grammar that he was taught at the *Kansas City Star*.

The first rule on the *Star*'s style sheet stressed brevity and compression, two qualities for which Hemingway's prose would become famous: "Use short first paragraphs. Use vigorous English. Be positive, not negative," it urged.[10] Whatever tendencies toward verbosity and expansiveness

Hemingway may have brought with him from high school were quickly checked by rules such as this one.

Other rules prescribed high standards of lean, simple, condensed writing:

> The style of the *Star* is . . . he walked "twelve miles," not "a distance of twelve miles"; "he earned $10" not he earned "the amount" or "sum of $10"; he went there "to see his wife," not "for the purpose of seeing his wife." He was absent "during June," not "during the month of June.". . .

> Eliminate every superfluous word as "Funeral services will be held at 2 o'clock Tuesday," not "*The* Funeral services will be held at *the hour of* 2 o'clock *on* Tuesday." He "said" is better than he "said in the course of the conversation."[11]

Adjectives in general were classed with other nonessential words as "superfluous." "Avoid the use of adjectives," the style sheet admonished, "especially such extravagant ones as splendid, gorgeous, grand, magnificent, etc."

Accuracy in grammar and diction was another key feature of the *Star*'s style sheet. In addition to urging writers to watch their tenses and connectors, the sheet stressed the importance of keeping the tone of a quotation consistent with speaker and subject: "Try to preserve the atmosphere of the speech in your quotation, for instance, in quoting a child, do not let him say, 'Inadvertently, I picked up the stone and threw it.' "

The sheet stressed the importance of freshness of expression by warning writers to "watch out for trite phrases" and to avoid "old slang." "Slang to be enjoyable," it concluded, "must be fresh."

As a young writer of fiction in 1926, Hemingway echoed those rules when he defined his aims for his editors. To Samuel Putnam he stated his commitment to an ethos of simplicity; he wanted to "put down what I see and what I feel in the best and simplest way I can tell it."[12] And to Maxwell Perkins he wrote that one of his great aims was "trying to write books without any extra words in them."[13]

Hemingway's later comments on writing often reflect the style sheet's concern with consistency of tone. "If the people a writer is making talk of old masters; of music; of modern painting; of letters; or of science then they should talk of those subjects in the novel," Hemingway wrote,

"If they do not talk of those subjects and the writer makes them talk of them he is a faker, and if he talks about them himself to show how much he knows, then he is showing off."[14]

The high value Hemingway placed on freshness throughout his career may be seen clearly in works such as *Death in the Afternoon*, where he laments the fact that "all our words from loose using [*sic*] have lost their edge,"[15] and tries to extricate words from the stale, conventional patterns of usage into which they have fallen.

Hemingway's early work on the *Star* conformed to the high standards of the style sheet. His articles were concise and clear, his grammar and diction were accurate, and his images were often fresh and vivid. His editor, Pete Wellington, recalls that he took "great pains" with his work and labored carefully in fashioning "even the one-paragraph news story."[16] During his seven months on the *Star*, Hemingway told an interviewer in 1940, his goal had been "to tell simple things simply."[17] He recalled that he had been "enormously excited under Pete Wellington's guidance to learn that the English language yields to simplicity through brevity."[18]

In an era when, in the name of attracting the goodwill of subscribers, the *Chicago News* handed out toys and the *New York World* gave away coal, the *Kansas City Star* gave subscribers an unprecedented thirteen papers a week for ten cents. William Rockhill Nelson had a no-nonsense approach to circulation that was unique at the turn of the century: "If we have to give away alarm clocks to get people to take the *Star*, we'll go out of business."[19] Horrified by the trend toward sensational exaggeration, large headlines, profuse illustration, comic supplements, and gaudy promotional schemes, he believed the business of a newspaper should simply be news.

Nelson's gamble paid off. Despite its conservative layout and typography, its restrained tone and its no-frills approach to wooing subscribers, the *Star* was a huge success. The dogged way in which it emphasized local news, the incorruptible energy with which it attacked any case of fraud or deceit it found (regardless of whose ox was gored in the process), and the seriousness with which it took its mission of informing the public earned the *Star* widespread loyalty and respect. By the time Ernest Hemingway got his job on the *Star* after graduating from high school in 1918, it had become one of the most admired and influential newspapers in the country.

Hemingway describes his early activities:

I covered the short-stop run, which included the 15th Street Police Station, Union Station, and the General Hospital. At the 15th Street Station you covered crime, usually small, but you never knew when you might hit on something larger. Union Station was everybody going in and out of town . . . some shady characters I got to know, and interviews with celebrities going through. The General Hospital was a long hill from Union Station and there you got accidents and a double check on crimes of violence.[20]

His editor recalled that Hemingway "liked action. . . . He always wanted to be on the scene himself."[21]

By being "on the scene himself," Hemingway found he was able to capture the vivid nuances of speech and behavior that added color and substance to his narratives. Thus, at the hospital he carefully documented the ironic image of the failed bank robber, defeated, dejected, but concerned not with his failure or his fate, but with how to stop his clean clothes from being stained by his dripping blood. And here, too, he records the $10 receipt in the pocket of "George," the unfortunate casualty, for payment on the Nebraska home he'll not live to finish paying for. The myriad details of half a dozen precisely observed, carefully etched vignettes are meshed as Hemingway shapes them into the ongoing human tragedy that takes place nightly at the General Hospital.[22]

At the army recruiting office, Hemingway listens (as Whitman might have listened) to the comments of the men waiting on line; he captures the rhythms and tones of their speech with accuracy and immediacy.[23] He brings the same sensitivity and perception to the scene when he records the way the warm bustle at a local dance hall must have looked to a lonely prostitute walking the street outside.[24]

Hemingway returned to his Kansas City experiences on several occasions. Two of the interchapters in *In Our Time*—one dealing with the cigar-store robbery, and the other with the local jail—have their roots in Hemingway's life in Kansas City. The first of these incidents was covered by Hemingway as a reporter; the second, though largely invented, was firmly set in a scene Hemingway had often covered.

Ernest Hemingway worked on the *Star* for less than a year before taking off to drive ambulances in Europe. But the brevity of his stay at the *Star* should not belittle its significance. It was at the *Star* that Hemingway learned lessons of style and habits of thought that he would retain and profit from throughout his career as a writer. Indeed, the hallmarks of the style which made him famous were precisely those qualities of accuracy, conciseness, and concreteness which were nurtured during this apprenticeship in journalism. The attitudes that the *Star* instilled in its reporters—a respect for fact and its documentation, and a suspicion of liars, phonies, frauds, and the words behind which they so often hid— would become vital to the worlds of fiction Hemingway would create.

In addition to his work on the *Kansas City Star*, two other chapters of Hemingway's journalism deserve attention: his stint as a correspondent for the *Toronto Star* after World War I, and his coverage of the Spanish civil war, both as a correspondent for the North American Newspaper Alliance, and as scriptwriter for a documentary film. These experiences exposed Hemingway to themes and subjects to which he would return as a writer of fiction. They offer instructive examples of the problems Hemingway encountered as a journalist, and help highlight the roots of many special strengths of his fiction.

When Hemingway returned to the United States in 1919 after having enlisted as an ambulance driver he was a hero: the first American wounded on the Italian front. Hemingway's homecoming was a celebrated event. The young hero thought of himself as a writer and considered himself "qualified to take a job on any New York newspaper that wants a man that is not afraid of work and wounds."[25] No New York newspaper, however, had a place for him. He returned home instead, and spent several frustrating months in Chicago and Petoskey, Michigan, trying to write as best he could. He took a job as a reporter for the *Toronto Daily Star* in 1920.

Though the standards of brevity, accuracy, and freshness demanded by the *Kansas City Star* were largely absent from the Toronto papers for which Hemingway went to work,[26] they were maintained, for the most part, by Hemingway himself. He explored satire and humor with greater freedom than he had in Kansas City, and wrote five lengthy pieces on fishing and camping. Throughout all of his work a concern for accurately observed and precisely recorded fact is evident, as is a commitment to discriminate (and to help his reader learn to discriminate) between the facts and counterfeit representations of them.

He enjoyed exposing myth, fraud, or misrepresentation wherever he found them. In Toronto he condemned Canadian outdoor magazines for passing on to their readers deceptive and intentionally misleading information that served their advertisers;[27] he deflated the pretensions of a former hired gunman who posed as a fine, upstanding citizen.[28] As a foreign correspondent for the *Toronto Star* in Europe, Hemingway continued to spot the chinks in the armor of the "great" and showed that they were, after all, like everyone else. The renowned Turkish leader Ismet Pasha, Hemingway noted, concealed his poor French by pretending to be deaf.[29] He concluded a sketch of the Greek king with the words, "Like all Greeks he wanted to get over to the States."[30] And it was the same resolute objectivity that unmasked the pretensions of the Russian diplomat George Tchitcherin, militarist defender of the Russian empire, who, despite the fact that he was always photographed in uniform, had never been a soldier.[31]

The concern with accuracy that would pervade all of Hemingway's fiction dominated his early journalism as well. In an article for the *Toronto Star* on "The Best Rainbow Trout Fishing,"[32] for example, he placed a strong emphasis on getting the facts right and knowing the right way of doing something. Correct knowledge and accurate technique, Hemingway implied, determine more than whether or not one snares a fish: they determine whether one survives the project. In a place where "a mis-step will take the angler over his head in the rapids" (p. 9), it is important to know one's terrain. (Hemingway further refined his images of the relationship between risk and skill in his articles several years later on bullfighting, in which he observed that with its stupendous stakes, it was a bit like the Grand Opera; if one misses the equivalent of high C, however, he is likely to pay for it with his life!)

In this article Hemingway explores the literary use he can make of a technique borrowed from film in an effort to describe with documentary precision a great river for trout fishing near the Sault Sainte Marie canals:

> . . . to get the proper picture you want to image in rapid succession the following fade-ins:
> A high pine covered bluff that rises up out of the shadows. A short sand slope down to the river and a quick elbow turn with a little floor wood jammed in the bend and then a pool.
> A pool where the moselle colored water sweeps into a dark swirl and expanse that is blue-brown with depth and fifty feet across.
> There is the setting. (P. 10)

Hemingway continues to narrate his story as he would a screenplay, and he corrects his own inaccuracies as he goes along:

> The action is supplied by two figures that slog into the picture up the trail along the river bank with loads on their backs that would tire

a pack horse. These loads are pitched over the heads onto the patch
of ferns by the edge of the deep pool. That is incorrect. Really
the figures lurch a little forward and the tump line looses and the
pack slumps onto the ground. Men don't pitch loads at the end
of an eight mile hike.

Hemingway's interest in narrowing the gap between reality and his description of it would become a hallmark of his craft.

When he was assigned to cover the Greco-Turkish conflict in 1922,
Hemingway was pleased to have the chance to be at the scene of so much
action.[33] In fact, as Jeffrey Meyers has noted, the war ended before
Hemingway arrived, and it was the aftermath of the conflict—especially
the flight of refugees after the Greek defeat—that Hemingway witnessed
and described for the *Star.*[34] Far from being an experienced war reporter,
as Charles Fenton has observed, Hemingway was prone to take short-
cuts, detouring or condensing the "various journalistic drudgeries" that
would normally preface his assignments.[35] He specialized in etching vivid
scenes, in painting carefully observed vignettes of the aftermath of the
war.

Hemingway breathed life into the terms "refugees" and "evacuation,"
as few of his fellow reporters had been able to do. His Asia Minor assign-
ment prompted some of his most forceful prose, and articles such as
this one (which would play a key role in one of his first works of fiction
and in later works as well) won him praise from such veteran journalists
as Lincoln Steffens:

ADRIANOPLE.—In a never-ending, staggering march the Christian
population of Eastern Thrace is jamming the roads to Macedonia.
The main column across the Maritza River at Adrianople is twenty
miles long. Twenty miles of carts drawn by cows, bullocks and
muddy-flanked water buffalo, with exhausted, staggering men, wom-
en and children, blankets over their heads, walking blindly along
with the rain beside their worldly goods.

This main stream is being swelled from all the back country. They
don't know where they are going. They left their farms, villages
and ripe, brown fields and joined the main stream of refugees when
they heard the Turk was coming. Now they can only keep their
places in the ghastly procession while mud-splashed Greek cavalry
herd them along like cow-punchers driving steers.

It is a silent procession. Nobody even grunts. It is all they can do to keep moving. Their brilliant peasant costumes are soaked and draggled. Chickens dangle by their feet from carts. Calves nuzzle at the drought cattle wherever a dam halts the stream. An old man marches bent under a pig, a scythe and a gun, with a chicken tied to his scythe. A husband spreads a blanket over a woman in labor in one of the carts to keep off the driving rain. She is the only person making a sound. Her little daughter looks at her in horror and begins to cry. And the procession keeps moving . . . [36]

While his counterpart at the *London Times* had described carts "piled high with all the portable goods of the owners—tables, chairs, blankets, chickens, children, carpets, agricultural implements, cooking utensils, all heaped together in reckless confusion and bearing down heavily upon the rickety patched-up wheels" (October 25, 1922), Hemingway simply noted "women and kids were in the carts crouched with mattresses, mirrors, sewing machines, bundles." It was an early instance of Hemingway's aesthetic theory of omission. As he would put it in *Death in the Afternoon*, "If a writer of prose knows enough about what he is writing about he may omit things that he knows and the reader, if the writer is writing truly enough, will have a feeling of those things as strongly as though the writer had stated them. The dignity of movement of an iceberg is due to only one-eighth of it being above water" (p. 192). Lincoln Steffens recounts in his autobiography that as a correspondent during the Greco-Turkish conflict Hemingway took greatest pride not in the substance of his observations but in their compression; look at "the cablese," he had exclaimed to Steffens, "Isn't it a great language?"[37] He later confessed to Steffens his fear that his fascination with the lingo of the transatlantic cable might prove too seductive. He was becoming too adept, he feared, at "compressing his observations into such economical form."

It was precisely the vivid, economical compression of the transatlantic cable that captured Hemingway's imagination most fully during his early years in Paris. Indeed, it was on telegraph blanks that Hemingway recorded carefully etched cameos of scenes he had witnessed in the Latin Quarter. (Despite their resemblances to his dispatches to the *Star*, these longhand, image-strewn cables were never meant to be sent. They represented, instead, some of the reporter's earliest efforts to record that which interested *him*, and not necessarily his editors, or his readers in Toronto.)

What continued to interest Hemingway throughout his writing career, in fiction as well as journalism, was the search for the precisely correct concrete image that would evoke a specific scene vividly and economically. His reports on the Spanish civil war as a correspondent for the North American Newspaper Alliance, for example, were filled with highly evocative images that helped the reader sense the experience of a city under siege, of a people plunged into battle. In a piece on "The Shelling of Madrid," for example, Hemingway writes,

MADRID.—At the front, a mile and a quarter away, the noise came as a heavy coughing grunt from the green pine-studded hillside opposite. There was only a gray wisp of smoke to mark the Insurgent battery position. Then came the high inrushing sound, like the ripping of a bale of silk. It was all going well over into the town, so, out there, nobody cared.

But in the town, where all the streets were full of Sunday crowds, the shells came with the sudden flash that a short circuit makes and then the roaring crash of granite-dust. During the morning, twenty-two shells came into Madrid.

They killed an old woman returning home from the market, dropping her in a huddled black heap of clothing, with one leg, suddenly detached, whirling against the wall of an adjoining house.

They killed three people in another square, who lay like so many torn bundles of old clothing in the dust and rubble when the fragments of the "155" had burst against the curbing . . . [38]

While Hemingway was not the only foreign correspondent to cover the shelling of Madrid, he was the only one to write about it in this way. Hemingway, too, made passing references to military strength and the strategic implications of the battle; but he was alone in giving the reader a sense of actually being on the scene.

Like Whitman covering the fire at Broome and Christie streets, Hemingway seems more concerned with evoking what it *felt* like to *be* on the streets of Madrid than with reporting the dry facts and figures of casualties and damage. Images of "the ripping of a bale of silk" stunning the calm "Sunday crowds" and turning live human beings into "so many torn bundles of old clothing" do more to communicate the impact of war than do any of the accounts of Hemingway's colleagues. It is interesting to note, however, that just as Whitman's account of the Broome and Christie streets fire seemed to be as much an account of the nature of all fires as of a specific fire, Hemingway's account of the assault on Madrid seems to be as much an account of the nature of war's impact on civilians as it is of the particular war at hand. The universal qualities inherent in each writer's record of the particular event hint at the kind of special talent he was destined to realize most fully as an imaginative writer.

Hemingway had begun to become more and more disillusioned with journalism as early as 1923, his second year in Paris. "I am going to chuck journalism, I think," he wrote to Gertrude Stein in November of that year, "You ruined me as a journalist last winter. Have been no good since."[39] Stein had encouraged Hemingway to move on to more creative endeavors, and he longed to follow her advice single-mindedly. Despite the fact that he began spending more and more time working on fiction after 1923, he never "chucked" journalism completely. Indeed, Hemingway would continue writing for newspapers and magazines for more than thirty years, often relying upon his journalistic talents to put food on his table and pay his rent.

In later years, Hemingway looked back on his career as a journalist and tried to understand what had left him dissatisfied. "On a newspaper ... you have to sponge your memory clean like a slate every day," he observed, "In newspaper work you have to learn to forget every day what happened the day before. . . . Newspaper work is valuable up until the point that it forcibly begins to destroy your memory. A writer must leave it before that point."[40]

By 1924, Hemingway was convinced it was time to devote more energy to the stories he "made up" than to those he reported. The time he spent wandering through the Musée du Luxembourg fueled those energies: "I was learning something from the painting of Cezanne that made writing simple true sentences far from enough to make the stories have the dimensions that I was trying to put in them."[41] But the strict attention he had learned to pay to the task of recording the accurately observed fact in "simple true sentences" would stand him in good stead in his fiction; it would, indeed, become the cornerstone of his greatest achievements as an artist.

When Hemingway arrived in Paris in 1921 determined to "write the truest sentence that you know,"[42] his own interest in fact found support in the views of many of his contemporaries in the arts. At the end of 1921 and in early 1922 Hemingway gave Ezra Pound boxing lessons in exchange for writing lessons.[43] Nearly ten years before, in an essay called "The Serious Artist," Pound had asserted the importance of accuracy, truthfulness, and authenticity in writing; elsewhere he had declared his opposition to all "rhetorical din and luxurious [verbal] riot," and called for a kind of writing characterized by directness, simplicity, and freedom from "emotional slither." "Bad art is inaccurate art," Pound had written, "it is art that makes false reports."[44] Hemingway has acknowledged his debt to Pound, "the man who believed in the 'mot juste'—the one and only correct word to use, the man who taught me to distrust adjectives as I would later learn to distrust certain people in certain situations."[45] Pound's emphasis on accuracy and simplicity impressed Hemingway, who had been taught to value those qualities as a journalist. While Pete Wellington taught him that they were at the core of good reporting, Pound asserted they were central to the production of good art.

From his earliest "Nick Adams" stories to his last novels, Hemingway would pay careful attention to concrete sensation, accurate technique, and precisely observed fact. "Facts march through all his pages in a stream as continuous as the refugee wagons in Thrace or the military camions on the road from the Isonzo," Baker writes, "Speculation, whether by the author or by the characters, is ordinarily kept to a minimum. But facts, visible or audible or tangible facts, facts baldly stated, facts without verbal paraphernalia to inhibit their striking power, are the stuff of Hemingway's prose."[46]

Many of the facts upon which he bases his stories are familiar to his readers; some of his books have been read as romans à clef. But more important than the correspondences between real people and scenes and those in his books is the very solid and tangible nature of all he evokes, his insistence on focusing his reader's attention upon the concrete fact.

And, from the start of his career to its end, Hemingway would show concern about the potential of verbal structures and of words themselves to "lie," to move one away from the realities he thought it so crucial to confront. Like Krebs in Hemingway's story, "Soldier's Home," many of Hemingway's characters would find that talking about an experience somehow robbed it of its essence. Time and time again, whether in Africa or Switzerland or Pamplona, they warn each other against words with variations of Jake's comment to Brett in *The Sun Also Rises*: "You'll lose it if you talk about it."[47] Like his character Frederic Henry in *A Farewell to Arms*, "embarrassed by the words sacred, glorious, and sacrifice and the expression in vain," Hemingway felt "there were many words that you could not stand to hear. . . . Abstract words such as glory, honor, courage, or hallow were obscene beside the concrete names of villages, the numbers of roads, the names of rivers, the number of regiments and the dates."[48]

His belief that "words are at least potentially lies" leads him to strive for the starkest understatement, to eschew the slightest expansiveness and elaboration.[49] Hemingway would have his characters, and his reader, learn to confront the world of fact directly, immediately—for only then, in Hemingway's view, can that world be fully known and explored. Thus, like Whitman, Twain, and Dreiser before him, he crafts an art devoted to helping the reader turn away from art, toward life. And, like Whitman, Twain, and Dreiser he recognized that the power of his inventions helps his readers to achieve fresh views of the distinctly "noninvented" world around them; he recognized the power of fiction to focus the reader's attention upon the world of fact.

It is fitting, perhaps, that Hemingway's debut as a literary figure took the form of a book pervaded by images of, allusions to, and insights gleaned from journalism. While one previous book had been published by his friends Bird and McAlmon in 1923 (*Three Stories and Ten Poems*) it had received little attention and can hardly be considered the volume that launched him as an author. *In Our Time*, on the other hand, was reviewed by Edmund Wilson and others; its publication in 1925 put Hemingway on the map of American literati.

As it was originally conceived by its publishers (with Hemingway's blessings), the first version of the book, *in our time* (for the first edition, published in 1924, was thus printed) would have smacked of journalism on every page. Bill Bird had considered the idea of framing every page of the book with a border of newsprint, emphasizing the book's intimate connection with the contemporary realities its author had become so adept at recording. He settled, in the end, for a cover design consisting of a montage of scrambled newspaper clippings.[50] The cover montage and the title both boasted that the book would be documentary in significant ways; and the reader, upon opening the cover, was not disappointed.

The 1925 volume which brought Hemingway international attention was a montage of two modes: short story and apparently documentary vignette. Hemingway's fascination with the possibilities for mixing fact with fiction blossomed for the first time in this volume. For the short stories, while primarily "invented," were closely rooted in experiences Hemingway had actually had, and the brief documentary narratives, while largely based on facts Hemingway had observed and recorded previously in his journalism, were artfully molded by their author's imagination. Tightly harnessed to the world of fact on every page, *In Our Time* simultaneously includes significant departures from that world. It succeeds, as we will show, in its primary mission of thrusting the reader into the world of fact on his own.

Much of the material in the 1925 *In Our Time* had been published earlier. Two of the interchapter vignettes were taken from Hemingway's experiences on the *Kansas City Star*.[51] Six of the remaining vignettes deal with Hemingway's recent observations on bullfighting, and particularly on the careers of stars Maera and Villalta. Seven may be thought to deal primarily with experiences he encountered fighting in World War I. And two (including the "Quays at Smyrna" piece he inserted at the beginning of the 1930 volume) deal with subjects he had recorded as a journalist in Asia Minor.

Of the short stories, eight deal with the main character Nick Adams (whose resemblance to Hemingway has been duly noted by critics) and are set primarily in the northern Michigan familiar to Hemingway from his youth. One story takes place mainly in Padua ("A Very Short Story") and is rather frankly autobiographical, as is "Soldier's Home," ostensibly set in a hometown in Oklahoma, which could easily be Hemingway's hometown in Illinois. Five stories deal with Americans in Europe (often friends and acquaintances of Hemingway's, thinly disguised), and one with a Hungarian revolutionist.

While only a small portion of the journalism Hemingway absorbed into his book remains intact as journalism, enough exists to enable one to draw some conclusions about the nature of Hemingway's efforts in *In Our Time*. I would suggest that the transformations from journalism into fiction involve, primarily, two parallel processes: sharpening, and expansion of context.

Here, and throughout his career, when Hemingway approached as an artist facts he had documented as a journalist, he did two things: on the one hand, he made his narrative more concise and more precise and strung his images together more freshly; and on the other, he cast his observations, by artfully juxtaposing them in ways which reflected and refracted them in new lights, into a context much larger than the one in which they had originated.

These processes are in keeping with Hemingway's own description of his goals in a letter he wrote to Edmund Wilson in 1924. He wrote that he had finished the book of 14 stories with a chapter of *in our time* between each story—that is the way they were meant to go—to give the picture of the whole between examining it in detail. Like looking with

your eyes at something, say, a passing coastline, and then looking at it
with 15X binoculars. Or rather, maybe, looking at it and then going in
and living in it—and then coming out and looking at it again."[52] Perhaps
the least cumbersome way of envisioning the process Hemingway describes is looking through his 15X binoculars both ways, through the
magnifying and reducing sides, the former heightening one's awareness
of the concrete detail (sharpening), the latter broadening the context
in which an object or event is seen (expansion of context). A comparison
of Hemingway's 1922 dispatch from Adrianople[53] and chapter 2 of *In
Our Time* shows both of these processes at work.

The sharpening process, as Fenton has noted, is apparent from Hemingway's condensation of a 343-word dispatch into a 131-word paragraph. But even more significant than the change in the number of
words is the change in the kind of words. The cabled first draft of
Hemingway's article, clear and crisp as it was, had contained nearly
thirty adjectives as well as an abundance of compound modifiers
which functioned as adjectives. The effect of such charged modifiers
as "staggering," "never-ending," and "ghastly" was to relieve the reader
of the task of coming up with his own responses to the scene the writer
painted. The adjectives summed up the emotional impact of the scene
on a firsthand observer. The reader was able to take it in at a distance,
accepting the writer's subjective reactions as appropriate rather than
responding with his own subjectivity to the panorama itself.

In *In Our Time*,[54] on the other hand, the description of the same
scene—the procession of refugees along the Karakatch road—contained
only ten adjectives, and no compound adjectival phrases. Rather than
supplying the reader with reactions to the scene, Hemingway here
simply etches the scene itself. The vague and general descriptive phrases
with which the newspaper dispatch had ended—"never-ending, staggering march"—are eliminated; instead the "never-ending" and "staggering"
qualities of the scene are allowed to emerge from the piling up of
specific details.

Chapter II

Minarets stuck up in the rain out of Adrianople across the mud flats.
The carts were jammed for thirty miles along the Karakatch road.
Water buffalo and cattle were hauling carts loaded with everything
they owned. The old men and women, soaked through, walked
along keeping the cattle moving. The Maritza was running yellow
almost up to the bridge. Carts were jammed solid on the bridge

with camels bobbing along through them. Greek cavalry herded along the procession. Women and kids were in the carts crouched with mattresses, mirrors, sewing machines, bundles. There was a woman having a kid with a young girl holding a blanket over her and crying. Scared sick looking at it. It rained all through the evacuation. (P. 21)

Rather than manipulate the reader's sentiments with adjectives as he had done in the journalism, Hemingway here allows him to respond on his own to a sequence of vividly etched images.

While the article titled "A Silent, Ghastly Procession Wends Way from Thrace" existed in the context of the other world events covered by the *Toronto Star* in October of 1922, chapter 2 of *In Our Time* exists in the context of the other factual vignettes and fictional narratives that comprise the book. Both the minute particulars of the piece and their large-scale implications take on new and special significance when informed by the context of the whole. The experience of the refugees radiates out toward the experiences of many others in the book, both taking on and casting forth, in the process, new shadows and new lights.

The world that is pictured in the Adrianople sketch finds its echoes in other sketches throughout the book: in the casualties of other wars, in the defeat of a failed bullfighter and of an ex-prizefighter; in the powerlessness of all victims of war, of crime, of overzealous law enforcers; in the messiness of plans going constantly awry, of dreams being constantly thwarted, of life being ever "out of season"; and in the fears of soldiers and of children. Yet in the context of the book as a whole, certain aspects of this scene stand out in a new light. While others in the book are dead, the refugees are alive. They are taking control over what is left of their lives; others in the book are not able to do so. They are giving birth to new life; others in the book want to do just that, but can't. They are plagued by rain and mud but not defeated by it; others are submerged in total defeat.

The scene of the refugees' procession along the Karakatch road is no less "ghastly" than it was when Hemingway wrote about it for the first time. But the world it inhabits is more complicated, and more whole. The world of the dispatch was a world of war, defeat, powerlessness, messiness, and fear. The world of *In Our Time* is all of that and more, but it is also a world that contains interludes of peace, victory, order, and trust—qualities which can only really be known, Hemingway implies, after one has acknowledged the existence of their opposites.

In Our Time culminates in a paean to the project of paying careful attention to concrete sensation, to accurate technique, to precisely observed fact. But rather than being a simple story of a fishing trip, as so many of Hemingway's newspaper articles had been, the "Big Two-Hearted River" sequence with which the book concludes takes its meaning from all that has gone before.

It is only *after* Nick has confronted death and pain firsthand in the war that he can truly appreciate the miracle of that which is peaceful and beautiful and good in life. It is significant that "Cross Country Snow," an idyll permeated by friendship, trust, and exhilaration with living, is placed *after* the chapters dealing with the war. It is not an innocent's idyll. It is a reverie of two men fully aware of the impermanence of life, and thus the value of the present; of two men familiar with the world's imperfections savoring the perfect moment. It is almost a Blakean "higher innocence" that seems to be the goal of Hemingway's heroes—a commitment to the miraculous that is possible only after one has denied the existence of miracles. One must confront a world of chaos and war to understand the value of order and peace. All that is positive and meaningful in *In Our Time* takes its meaning, in part, from the near-by presence of its opposite.

Thus the revolutionist who suffered greatly for his dream and who, "in spite of Hungary . . . believed altogether in the world revolution" knows enough about life to settle for whatever small joys it offers him (p. 81). Denied the world revolution in which he fervently believes, he nevertheless "was very eager to walk over the pass while the weather held good. He loved the mountains in the autumn" (p. 82). Knowing pain, he can appreciate pleasure. Knowing the likelihood of ultimate defeat, he enjoys the successes of the moment. While his dream may be doomed to destruction, he is determined to deny that fact all along the way, relishing both the dream and its foe, reality.

His choices are further validated by Hemingway's description of two people who take an opposite course. The Eliots, in the section following the one dealing with the revolutionist, find themselves devotees of an equally ill-fated dream. But while the revolutionist's life is saturated with a knowledge of reality, the Eliots' lives are enmeshed in a vague romanticism. Unprepared for life, they disintegrate totally as reality mars their dreams. Denied fertility, they create a sterile world around them. Denied their dream, they block out reality as well.

Much as the revolutionist's approach to life is seen as more adequate than that of the Eliots, Villalta's approach to bullfighting is seen as more adequate than that of his Mexican colleague. Unlike the scared Mexican bullfighter who evades the challenge of the ring by getting drunk the day of a fight, Villalta faces his bull with a direct, sober intensity: "the bull charged and Villalta charged and just for a moment they become one. Villalta became one with the bull and then it was over" (p. 105). It is by tempting death, by accepting its possibility, and by challenging it fairly, that Villalta succeeds, for a moment at least, in transcending it. It is by concentrating on the fact of death that he becomes preternaturally alive.

While death is never mentioned in the "Big Two-Hearted River" sequence, it is very much in the background of the stories. Nick's camping trip takes place after he has returned from the war, after he has experienced its desolation and destruction. Fittingly, almost as a reminder of the experiences he has survived, Nick's trip begins in a charred and empty ghost town where even the grasshoppers have turned black:

> There was no town, nothing but the rails and the burned-over
> country. The thirteen saloons that had lined the one street of Seney
> had not left a trace. The foundations of the Mansion House hotel
> stuck up above the ground. The stone was chipped and split by
> the fire. (P. 133)

"Two hundred yards down the hillside the fire line stopped," Nick continued, "Then it was sweet fern, growing ankle high, to walk through, and clumps of jack pines; a long undulating country with frequent rises and descents, sandy underfoot and the country alive again" (p. 136). Like his physical progression from a terrain that was sterile and dead to one burgeoning with life, Nick's psychological and spiritual progression during this trip leads him away from the pains of war, into the regeneration of peace. Against a background of war, death, duplicity, defeat, powerlessness, messiness, lies, violence, fear, shame, and finality, the miracle of this idyll of peaceful solitary living, where no lies must be told, where one is in complete control of one's fate, where order, calm, dignity, and hope pervade the scene, stands out in sharp relief.

The reader knows by the mention of "St. Ignace" that the scene of the story is not far from that of the first story of the book, "Indian Camp," which concluded with Nick's feeling "quite sure that he would never die" (p. 19). At the end of the "Big Two-Hearted River," Nick takes solace in the thought that "There were plenty of days coming when he could fish in the swamp" (p. 156). There is an important difference between these two observations, one the scared denial of death by a young boy, the other a secure acceptance of life by a young man. The stakes are scaled down; but the first dream, built on air, will be exploded, while the second, firmly grounded in the world of fact, will be realized in the here and now. It is an appreciation of the world of fact in its actuality that has, indeed, been the primary focus of the book. In "Big Two-Hearted River" Hemingway shows the benefits to be had by concentrating deeply on the world as it is.

While at the start of the story Nick sees "back of him" a charred and burned world in which there is "the need for thinking, the need to write, other needs," as the story progresses that world recedes further and further both physically and psychologically as Nick finds himself in a world which demands neither thought nor words, but simply intense concentration on the present. By the end of the story he looks "back to see only his camp, and the river showing through the trees" (p. 156).

The world of "Big Two-Hearted River" is a world where one is required to tell no lies, where one is not even required to speak to compare the present with the past, to abstract from what one is experiencing. There is no disjunction here between words and things; words themselves are simply superfluous.

> He took the ax out of the pack and chopped out two projecting roots. That leveled a piece of ground large enough to sleep on. He smoothed out the sandy soil with his hand and pulled all the sweet fern bushes by their roots. His hands smelled good from the sweet fern. He smoothed the uprooted earth . . .
>
> Across the open mouth of the tent Nick fixed cheesecloth to keep out mosquitoes. He crawled inside under the mosquito bar with various things from the pack to put at the head of the bed under the slant of the canvas. Inside the tent the light came through the brown canvas. It smelled mysterious and homelike. Nick was happy as he crawled inside the tent. He had not been unhappy all day. This was different though. Now things were done. There had been this to do. Now it was done. It had been a hard trip. He was very tired. That was done. He had made his camp. He was settled. Nothing could touch him. It was a good place to camp. (Pp. 138–39)

In the larger context of violence and trauma, of duplicity and brutality, of war and death and powerlessness and pain, that exists in *In Our Time*, Nick's peaceful "good place" takes on new and special significance. It is a place where problems have solutions, where obstacles yield to competent levelers of them. While many of the scenes in this story have their roots in Hemingway's earlier articles on trout fishing, nowhere in the earlier journalism are they etched with the sharpness and clarity they manifest here, and nowhere do they achieve the significance they have here. Having experienced pain, Nick can appreciate the lack of pain. Having known what it is to be powerless, he can appreciate the control he exercises here over his fate. Having witnessed the lies words can tell, he can relish direct experience unmediated by words. Having been brushed by death, he can appreciate the sensations of being "alive again."

Edmund Wilson has remarked that "with the descriptions in *In Our Time* of American wood and water, Hemingway has brought into literature a new pair of eyes for landscape, as in his sketches of the War where . . . he catches as they have never yet been caught the blind excited emotions of the Americans of 1917 and thereafter."[55] Hemingway's goal in *In Our Time*, I would suggest, is precisely that which earned him Wilson's praise. In his effort to help his reader confront the world around him freshly and directly, Hemingway found it necessary to utilize nothing less than "a new pair of eyes," eyes able, like 15X binoculars, both to focus on the minute concrete details, and to scan those details in the largest possible context. While as a journalist he was content with vividly evoking a scene, as an artist he would settle for nothing less than communicating a new way of seeing.

By 1937, Hemingway was an accomplished writer of fiction, having four novels and two collections of short stories behind him (in addition to two extended nonfiction works). But it was as a newspaper reporter that he returned to Spain, under contract to write for the North American Newspaper Alliance. And it was as a reporter that he first wrote about the way the Spanish civil war was being fought in the mountains in which he would later set his novel, *For Whom the Bell Tolls.*[56] Hemingway, like his character Robert Jordan, saw the Loyalists' cause as a fight "for all the poor in the world, against all the tyranny."[57] In the States he helped the Loyalists by raising substantial funds for ambulances and medical supplies; in Spain he tried to help them by reporting their struggle accurately in the American press.

As a number of journalists and historians have observed, Franco's rebels had widespread support in the American press throughout the Spanish war. "The Loyalist side got the worst of it in the battle of propaganda," noted *New York Times* reporter Herbert Matthews, who covered the front alongside Hemingway.[58] Matthews attributes this to the fact that "in the first wild, mad popular reaction, the flaming pressures of anti-clericalism were uncontrollable." Others take a more conspiratorial view of why the American press tended to print as true a multitude of lies that the rebels circulated as fact.[59]

In a piece titled "Who Lied About Spain?" in the *New Republic* which appeared in 1939, specific untruths and distortions—all in Franco's favor—were pinned on Matthews's fellow *Times*man William Carney, on a prominent Catholic weekly, and on others.[60] "The few men who told the truth about Spain (and got it printed)," the article went on, "were denounced and libeled by Franco partisans" (p. 212). Press historian George Seldes also documents numerous occasions on which the American press printed without question untruths, half-truths, and distortions put forth by the rebels during the war.[61] "The complete list of individuals or spokesmen for organizations who lied about the facts of the Spanish Civil War," the *New Republic* piece concluded, "would fill a small volume."[62]

In his entire career as a reporter, Hemingway had never before encountered the kind of press distortion he encountered in Spain. It was with incredulity that he wrote to his ex-wife Hadley after covering a major Loyalist victory, "the *Times* re-took the town for Franco on the strength of [what I know to be a phony] Salamanca communique."[63]

In February of 1939, he wrote in another letter,

> I read in the Sunday *Visitor* about the atrocities of the Reds, the wickedness of the Spanish "Communist" government, and the humaneness of General Franco who could have ended the war months ago if he had not been afraid of harming the civilian population after having seen town after town bombed to the ground, the inhabitants killed, the columns of refugees on the roads bombed and machine gunned again and again. . . . But that sort of lying kills things inside of you.[64]

It was in response, in part, to "that sort of lying," that a group of American intellectuals conceived of the notion of making their own documentary film about Spain and getting it to the American people directly, through local movie houses. Hemingway would play a key role in that project. Indeed, all of his writings on the Spanish civil war—some twenty-eight newspaper articles, a film script, four short stories, a play, and a novel—may be seen, in part, as his effort, in the context of widespread lies, to set the record straight by telling the truth.

The Spanish Earth, produced in 1937, resulted from the efforts of a group that called itself the "Contemporary Historians," and which included John Dos Passos, Archibald MacLeish and Lillian Hellman.[65] Dutch director Joris Ivens and his photographer John Ferno were charged by the group with producing "a picture of the true state of affairs in Spain along a general theme provided by Hemingway." Hemingway wrote the script.

According to Ivens, Hemingway "showed a quick comprehension and understanding of the documentary film and a very helpful humility towards this new profession."[66] He insisted on accompanying Ivens and the film crew wherever they went and was fascinated by the ways in which they were required "to become so involved in actual life." While Ivens had arrived in Spain with elaborate visions of reenactments and story line, he quickly realized the folly of asking a people fighting a war for their lives to become actors for a film; *The Spanish Earth* quickly became a record of "actual life" in an embattled land.

The Spanish Earth attempted to communicate to the viewer the facts about the current war in Spain. The camera panned freshly irrigated fields, outposts of the rebels in the distance, breadlines, civilians walking the streets, rebel attempts to capture a bridge, Loyalist efforts to defeat fascist forces lodged in University City, villagers returning to their bombed homes, various battles. Close-up shots focused on the faces of men before the battle, the faces of orators who inspired the populace, and the face of a young man who was to be the central dramatic focus of the film.

But the film was beset by problems from the start. The thin line of continuity on which the film makers finally agreed centered on a young soldier named Julian from Fuentedueña. Julian was filmed in a trench in front of the university in Madrid, and his homecoming during a furlough was reenacted in Fuentedueña. But when Ivens and Hemingway and company tried to find him at the front, he seemed to have disappeared. For all their efforts to trace Julian's regiment and division, the film's hero simply vanished into the chaos that was the civil war. So much for continuity. Before the filming of the battle around University City in Madrid, Hemingway took pains to scout out the perfect observation post for Ivens and the crew. When the group arrived they were harassed by what they first thought were stray bullets; the bullets were not stray at all, and the film shooting had to be abandoned. The film makers resigned themselves to using a big telephoto lens at a place where both the view and the enemy fire were considerably less dramatic. (Compromises became necessary in the editing room as well when, in the absence of tapes of the actual battle of Madrid, the sound of the battle was approximated quite ingeniously in the final versions of the film by running the sound track of a film about the San Francisco earthquake backward.)[67]

The film was less successful than its producers had hoped it would be. The *Daily News* found it "without beginning or end, without continuity or order." The *New York Sun* charged that "the producers have erred gravely in believing that pictures of soil, Spanish or any other kind, make very exciting screen fare." And the *Motion Picture Herald* called it ineffective: "Its partisanship and propagandistic non-objectivity tend to vitiate whatever message it may carry."[68]

Hemingway had his own doubts about the film's ability to communicate the truth. As he watched a battle from the side of a cameraman, he observed how little the black specks in the distance resembled men and tanks. At a thousand yards, Hemingway observed, "the tanks looked like small, mud-colored beetles bustling in the trees and spitting tiny flashes, and the men behind them were toy men who lay flat, then crouched and ran . . . spotting the hillside as the tanks moved on."[69] The cameraman had no choice: film tanks from sufficient distance, or run the risk of being killed by one.

While the footage that emerged was actual footage of the battle, it must have seemed more like a B-rated film than the story of the dusty, dangerous, and bloody encounter that really took place. As scriptwriter, Hemingway made the best he could of the inadequate footage. But the experience confirmed his suspicions of the potential limitations of the purely documentary record of an event. Even though the film was visually exact, Hemingway told its viewers at the Writers' Congress, he thought the "limitations of the medium made it impossible to re-create the total experience of living in wartime Spain."[70] Hemingway's narrative for the film reflects his suspicions about these limitations.

Aware of the fact that the image of "toy men" dodging "tiny flashes" emitted from "small, mud-colored beetles" failed to communicate the terror and the danger the men faced (and the bravery with which they faced it), Hemingway was forced to emphasize the seriousness of their situation in other ways. He tried to make up for the fact that he couldn't get close enough to the battle to show men actually facing death by noting in his commentary that this danger lurked in the future. Thus he accompanied close-up shots of faces with a rather heavy-handed narration that underlined the danger the men faced: "This is the true face of men going into action. It is a little different from any other face you will ever see. Men cannot act before the camera in the presence of death."[71] And he would add a grim epilogue to the images that passed on the screen at a later point in the film, also to emphasize the reality of the threat of death: "The bearded man is Commander Martinez de Aragon. Before the war he was a lawyer. He was a brave and skillful commander and he died in the attack on the Casa del Campo on the day we filmed the battle there."[72]

In both of these instances, Hemingway is aware of his handicap in not being able to follow an individual into battle, to stay with him until he meets his end. Thus, despite the fact that the film is documenting actual men about to face their destinies, the film's treatment of that fateful confrontation itself is of necessity much less immediate than a novel's treatment might be. In his rather self-conscious references to the camera and to the act of filming, Hemingway reveals his need to stress in words the *realness* of that which is represented on the screen; he shows he is uneasy about potential gaps between reality and his representations of it on film, much as he was uneasy at an earlier time about gaps between reality and his representations of it in words.

Here, too, words posed a problem. For the heroes and heroines of the Loyalist cause were fond of some of the very abstractions Hemingway found it most difficult to stomach, such as "sacrifice" and "valor"— words which Frederic Henry in *A Farewell to Arms* called obscene. In *The Spanish Earth* Hemingway allows the popular leaders to speak for themselves on the film's sound track. The words are then translated for the viewers by the narrator—who, in this case, was Hemingway himself. (Orson Welles originally read Hemingway's commentary on the sound track, but the results disappointed the Contemporary Historians, who asked Hemingway to read his own script instead.) Thus Hemingway found himself in the position of having to repeat, himself, the flowery patriotic rhetoric of "La Pasionaria" and others, a role which must have made him uncomfortable given his distaste for such language.[73]

Fascism, as Hemingway defined it in his 1937 speech to the Writers' Congress, was "a lie told by bullies,"[74] and *The Spanish Earth* was a film made to help the world learn to reject that lie. The novel Hemingway published in 1939 would try to do even more. Rather than simply replacing fascist rhetoric and propaganda with Loyalist rhetoric and propaganda as *The Spanish Earth* did, it would try to teach its reader how to be suspicious of all rhetoric and propaganda. It would teach its reader not only how to reject the lie that was fascism, but how to reject all lies. It was a book which strived to reaffirm the significance of the world of fact, and the importance of confronting that world in its actuality. It was a book which preached suspicion toward all books, including itself.

Concrete facts of all sorts are supremely important to the characters in *For Whom the Bell Tolls*. It is as important that Robert Jordan be able to judge from the split in a horse's hoof that "the sorrel is lame in the off foot," as it is crucial for him to remember to check "that the grenades, lashed on their sides, had room for the levers to spring when the pins were pulled." [75] The first fact enables him to withstand the test of having "his papers . . . examined by the man who could not read," [76] the second insures that the bridge will be destroyed. Both are necessary for survival.

But facts matter ultimately in *For Whom the Bell Tolls* because they are seen to be the basic morphemes of existence. The proximity of death evokes paeans to the earthen jars, the pastries and prawns, the timber-covered slopes that make up life. Against the empty background of death, the sharp outlines of the concrete minutiae of life glow with a luminous intensity.

El Sordo, dying, muses on his hilltop,

> Dying was nothing and he had no picture of it nor fear of it in his mind. But living was a field of grain blowing in the wind on the side of a hill. Living was a hawk in the sky. Living was an earthen jar of water in the dust of the threshing with the grain flailed out and the chaff blowing. Living was a horse between your legs and a carbine under one leg and a hill and a valley and a stream with trees along it and the far side of the valley and the hills beyond. (Pp. 212–13)

Pilar, after Finito has brought news from La Granja that spells doom for them all, pays tribute to the succulent delights of Valencia:

> We ate in pavilions on the sand. Pastries made of cooked and shredded fish and red and green peppers and small nuts like grains of rice. Pastries delicate and flaky and the fish of a richness that was incredible. Prawns fresh from the sea sprinkled with lime juice. They

were pink and sweet and there were four bites to a prawn. Of those
we ate many. Then we ate "paella" with fresh sea food, clams
in their shells, mussels, crayfish, and small eels. Then we ate even
smaller eels alone cooked in oil and as tiny as bean sprouts and
curled in all directions and so tender they disappeared in the mouth
without chewing. All the time drinking a white wine, cold, light
and good at thirty centimos the bottle. And for an end melon. That
is the home of the melon . . . When I think of those melons as
long as one's arm, green like the sea and crisp and juicy to cut and
sweeter than the early morning in summer. Aye, when I think of
those smallest eels, tiny, delicate and in mounds on the plate. Also
the beer in pitchers all through the afternoon, the beer sweating
in its coldness in pitchers the size of water jugs. (P. 85)

And Robert Jordan, dying,

looked across the green slope, seeing the gray horse where Agustin
had shot him, and on down the slope to the road with the timber-
covered country behind it . . . He touched the lower part of his
leg and it was as though it were not a part of his body. He looked
down the hill slope again and he thought, I hate to leave it, is
all. (Pp. 466–67)

For El Sordo's band, Pilar, and Robert Jordan, life itself is seen as
those things one can see and touch and taste in their concreteness; death
is simply their absence: nothing. And for El Sordo, Pilar, and Robert
Jordan it is important to pay proper respect to the world of fact. It is
important to see it for what it is and not for what it is not, for it is all
one has got.

Thus when Joaquin, a member of El Sordo's band, quotes slogans of
the Communist party and of La Pasionaria, the rhetoric is ignored or
deflated by his comrades in battle:

"'Resistir y fortificar es vencer,'" Joaquin said, his mouth stiff
with the dryness of fear which surpassed the normal thirst of battle.
It was one of the slogans of the Communist party and it meant,
"Hold out and fortify, and you will win."
Sordo looked away and down the slope at where a cavalryman
was sniping from behind a boulder. He was very fond of this boy and
he was in no mood for slogans.

"What did you say?"

One of the men turned from the building that he was doing. This man was lying flat on his face, reaching carefully up with his hands to put a rock in place while keeping his chin flat against the ground.

Joaquin repeated the slogan in his dried-up boy's voice without checking his digging for a moment.

"What was the last word?" the man with his chin on the ground asked.

"Vencer," the boy said. "Win."

"Mierda," the man with his chin on the ground said.

"There is another that applies to here," Joaquin said, bringing them out as though they were talismans, "Pasionaria says it is better to die on your feet than to live on your knees."

"'Mierda' again," the man said and another man said, over his shoulders, "We're on our bellies, not our knees." (Pp. 308–9)

The man with his chin on the ground is determined to see his situation for what it is—a desperate and exceedingly uncomfortable one that cannot be dismissed or glorified by a slogan.

And when Primitivo remembers that "with the blowing of the trains the lamp of the engine blew over my head and pieces of steel flew by like swallows," Pilar corrects him: "'Thou hast poetic memories,' Pilar said, 'Like swallows. Joder! They were like wash boilers'" (p. 444). Pilar has little use for poetry. She shoots balloons of figurative language to earth in a second:

They stood in the high mouth of the cave and watched them. The bombers were high now in fast, ugly arrowheads beating the sky apart with the noise of their motors. They *are* shaped like sharks, Robert Jordan thought, the wide-finned, sharp-nosed sharks of the Gulf Stream. But these, wide-finned, in silver, roaring, the light mist of their propellers in the sun, these do not move like sharks. They move like no thing there has ever been. They move like mechanized doom.

You ought to write, he told himself. Maybe you will again some time. He felt Maria holding to his arm. She was looking up and he said to her, "What do they look like to you, 'guapa'?"

"I don't know," she said. "Death, I think."

"They look like planes to me," the woman of Pablo said. (P. 87)

Robert Jordan, too, for all his visions of "mechanized doom," is committed to seeing the world around him clearly, for what it is. Dying, he thinks to himself,

> Well, we had all our luck in four days. Not four days. It was afternoon when I first got there and it will not be noon today. That makes not quite three days and three nights. Keep it accurate, he said. Quite accurate . . .
> He looked down the hill slope again and he thought, I hate to leave it, is all. I hate to leave it very much and I hope I have done some good in it. I have tried to with what talent I had. *Have, you mean. All right, have.* (Pp. 466–67)

As he feels himself losing his hold on life, the value Robert Jordan refuses to relinquish to the end is accuracy.

Throughout his life Robert Jordan has been troubled by the difficulty of putting his experience into words. He is troubled by his own tendency to think in a "catch phrase," instead of thinking for himself (p. 163). He wants to learn to reject "any sort of *clichés* both revolutionary and patriotic" (p. 164). He was uncomfortable with dialectics, and with slogans (p. 305), and was puzzled by the fact that something might be "true no matter how trite it sounded" (p. 162). He wanted to write a "true book" when he got through with the war, but doubted that he was a good-enough writer to handle even those things which "he knew, truly" (pp. 163, 248). He knew he had a tendency to rationalize or idealize or romanticize when he tried to explain the war to himself: "Don't lie to yourself, he thought. Nor make up literature about it" (p. 287).

"There's no *one* thing that is true," Jordan tells himself as he is dying, "It's all true" (p. 467). And since no work of "literature" can get it "all" in, any work of "literature" that fails to acknowledge its own limitations is a "lie." There is always more than can be encompassed in any volume; there is always another story to tell; there is always more experience left out than put in. The reader knows the story of Pilar, but of the fascist Lieutenant Berrendo? The reader knows that Spain looks different in Spanish than it does in English (Jordan constantly muses on the way language determines what one thinks and what one sees). What did this world look like in Russian, to Karkov? Or in Italian, to a bomber flying overhead? By providing a small sampling of the infinite stories-within-a-story that any story inevitably holds, *For Whom the Bell Tolls* challenges the ultimate authority of any fiction, including itself.

Throughout the book Robert Jordan often muses on the problems of knowing enough about the varied dimensions of the war to write "truly" about it. "I wish I could write well enough to write [Pilar's] story," he thinks at one point,

> What we did. Not what the others did to us. He knew enough about that. He knew plenty about that behind the lines. But you had to have known the people before. You had to know what they had been in the villages. (Pp. 134-35)

By discussing Robert Jordan's sense of the limitations likely to mar any text he might write, Hemingway suggests, indirectly, that his own text as well may have analogous limitations.

There was, in fact, much that Hemingway did not know about what his characters "had been in the villages," before the war, that mars his treatment of them in the novel. Arturo Barea, former minister of information for the Loyalists, has observed that Hemingway is guilty of some major misunderstandings of Spanish culture.[77] Given his preoccupation with accuracy throughout his career, Hemingway would undoubtedly be disturbed by the specific litany of "grave mistakes" that Barea enumerates. He would also be disturbed by additional inaccuracies noted by scholars more recently.[78] But his errors simply confirm the doubts Robert Jordan continually expresses about the possibility of writing a "true book." Despite Karkov's claim that Jordan writes "absolutely truly," Jordan knows, by his death, that there is no such thing as an absolutely true book. Any book, the novel implies, is only provisionally true; and it is true, at that, only to the extent that it acknowledges its own potential limitations.

6

JOHN
D O S
PASSOS

John Dos Passos being arrested in front of the
Massachusetts State House during a protest against
the Sacco-Vanzetti death sentence in 1927. Bailed
out by a friend, he later appealed his $10 fine in
court on the grounds that he had been covering
the demonstration as a reporter for the *Daily
Worker*.

Photo credit: UPI/Bettman Archives

Herman Melville once remarked that a whaling ship was his Harvard College. As we have seen, the newspaper city room was Harvard for Walt Whitman, Mark Twain, Theodore Dreiser, and Ernest Hemingway. For John Dos Passos, however, Harvard University was his Harvard. His career encompassed other striking departures, as well, from the now familiar pattern.

The other writers supported themselves as journalists for significant periods during which they tailored their writing to the preferences of their editors and publishers. John Dos Passos, on the other hand, was insulated by family wealth from the need to assume a full-time apprenticeship in journalism. As a freelance writer (nearly always for magazines and not newspapers), Dos Passos wrote what he wished, as he wished; if his editors turned down his work and no checks came in the mail, there was always a wealthy aunt to wire him funds.

At the age when Whitman, Twain, Dreiser, and Hemingway were carefully documenting the raw and complex city life that swirled around them, Dos Passos was sipping tea in an incense-filled room in Cambridge, Massachusetts, debating the merits of "rimeless sonnets" and of Oscar Wilde, who expressed the fear, in his much-admired book *The Decay of Lying*, that art stood in danger of being reduced by some current practitioners to "a mess of facts."[1] Facts were as far from Dos Passos's thoughts in 1916 as "the massacres round Verdun" were from Cambridge.[2] He recalled, years later in his memoirs, that he and his friends "chose to live in the 1890's."[3] "Poetry," he recalled, "was more important than submarines or war guilt or brave little Belgium or the big Board on the New York Stock Exchange."[4]

John Dos Passos, the Harvard "aesthete" whose first project out of college was arranging the publication (with substantial financial help from his father) of a rather effete collection of poems by himself and his friends, might seem, at first glance, to be an unlikely subject in a discussion of journalists turned novelists. But between his graduation from college in 1916 and his publication in 1930 of the first volume of the trilogy that would ensure his place in American literary history, John Dos Passos published some sixty pieces of nonfiction in publications including the *Dial*, the *Liberator*, the *Freeman*, the *Seven Arts*, the *Nation*, *Bookman*, the *New York Tribune*, *Asia*, *Broom*, *Mentor*, the *Arts*, *Vanity Fair*, the *New Masses*, the *Daily Worker*, the *Saturday Review of Literature*, and the *New Republic*. While Dos Passos managed to publish four novels, three plays, and a book of poems during this period, some of which are still read and still worth reading, these early imaginative works would probably be largely forgotten now were it not for the stunning trilogy which followed them. Dos Passos's greatest success as an imaginative writer came when he returned in fiction to subjects, themes, and strategies he had first explored as a journalist. Rooted, as none of the earlier books had been, in material the author had first documented in nonfiction, *U.S.A.* is a book whose unique strength stems from its firm footing in the world of fact and its brilliant restructuring of that world to extricate the reader from preconditioned patterns of perception.

Dos Passos's experiences as a journalist played a vital role in exposing him to the vast range of human activity that would become part of *U.S.A.* He seemed to enjoy the role of observer with notebook in hand. Even when he was personally attracted to the idea of involvement in a cause or event, he often chose "covering" it for some magazine as the most appealing mode of involvement. Two aspects of his experiences as a journalist will receive special attention in this chapter—his reports on Spain from 1917 to 1922 for such magazines as the *Seven Arts*, the *Dial*, the *Freeman*, the *Liberator*, and *Bookman*, and his reports on the Sacco-Vanzetti case in 1926 and 1927 for the *New Masses*, the *Daily Worker*, and the Sacco-Vanzetti Defense Committee. But other chapters contributed to his education as well.

It was as a journalist that Dos Passos first explored certain subjects which would later play a key role in *U.S.A.* A convention of the unemployed that he covered for the *New Masses* in 1934 in an article called "The Unemployment Report,"[5] for example, would find its way two years later into *The Big Money* in several sections, including Newsreel XLVII ("boy seeking future offered opportunity . . .") and the concluding section, "Vag."[6] A 1931 piece Dos Passos wrote for the *New Republic* called "Back to Red Hysteria"[7] explored a theme that would later figure prominently in *The Big Money*, particularly in the last third of the novel.[8]

It was as a journalist, too, that Dos Passos first became familiar with places and events which would later play key roles in his trilogy. For example, Dos Passos would return, in the story of Mary French in *The Big Money*, to a textile-workers' strike in Passaic, New Jersey, that he had covered for the *New Masses* in a 1926 piece, "300 N.Y. Agitators Reach Passaic."[9] Some of the scenes of Mexico Dos Passos had reported in articles like "Paint the Revolution," "Relief Map of Mexico," and "Zapata's Ghost Walks" in the *New Masses* in 1927[10] would be transmuted into the fictional experiences of Mac, a major character in *The*

Forty-Second Parallel. Dos Passos first visited Detroit in the course of writing an article about that city for the *New Republic* in 1932;[11] in *The Big Money* the Detroit that Dos Passos had first documented as a journalist—the nature of the city, and its image of itself—would become the subject of a newsreel,[12] and would figure prominently in the story of Charley Anderson, a major character in the book. Three pieces Dos Passos wrote in the *New Republic* in 1931 on the coal strike in Harlan County, Kentucky,[13] would contribute to the final newsreel in *The Big Money*,[14] in which the verses of blues Dos Passos quotes echo distinctly those he quoted in the *New Republic* piece in which celebrated blues-singer Aunt Molly Jackson movingly articulated the miners' plight; Dos Passos's reporting on the Harlan strike also contributed effectively to the final "Camera Eye" section of *The Big Money* set in the valley of "dark strikesilent hills," in which the powerless miners "have only words against POWER SUPERPOWER."[15]

It was in the *New Masses* that Dos Passos first explored the project of writing tightly knit, vivid, and succinct biographies of famous people of his day. Pieces of this nature appeared so frequently in the *New Masses* that one might almost consider them a small genre to which that publication gave special encouragement. Biographies of such contemporary figures as Joe Hill, Paxton Hibben, and Isadora Duncan—none of which were written by Dos Passos—appeared in the *New Masses* between 1926 and 1928, years when Dos Passos was a frequent contributor. Dos Passos himself first published in the *New Masses* many of the biographies that would later appear in *U.S.A.*[16]

In addition to his many pieces of reportage, Dos Passos contributed book reviews and essays in the 1920s and the early 1930s to such publications as *Vanity Fair*, the *New Masses*, the *Daily Worker*, *Bookman*, and the *New Republic*. In these pieces he had the opportunity to explore in nonfiction personalities destined to play important roles in *U.S.A.* For example, Dos Passos first wrote on the lives of Edison and Steinmetz, whose biographies would appear in *The Forty-Second Parallel* and *The Big Money*, respectively, when he reviewed three books about them in the *New Republic* in 1929.[17]

It was also in the *New Republic* that Dos Passos first wrote about Ivy Lee, the father of modern public relations on whom he based the only fictional character to span all three volumes of his trilogy, J. Ward Moorehouse.[18] In this 1930 article (titled "Wanted: An Ivy Lee for Liberals") Dos Passos expressed a somewhat ambivalent attitude toward the industry that had come to dominate American life to such a great extent during the first three decades of the twentieth century that John Dewey was moved to assert, in 1929, that the publicity agent "is perhaps the most significant symbol of our present social life."[19] During this period advertising had grown into a \$3.5 billion industry.[20] President Coolidge had called it "the most potent influence in adopting and changing what we eat, what we wear, and the work and play of the whole nation," and embraced it as "part of the greater work of the regeneration and redemption of mankind."[21] Press agents for corporations, banks, railroads, and politicians had come to outnumber journalists in New York City by 1930, and, as Michael Schudson has noted, were probably responsible for at least half of all news items in the papers.[22] Dos Passos appreciated the power of advertising and public relations. "After all, if by propaganda you can make women wear corsets and everybody believe cigarettes are good for the voice," he wrote, "it's conceivable that by propaganda you can make them hate cruelty or tolerate the idea of change."[23] But Dos Passos understood that the talents of the new "super-public-relations counsels" were for sale, and were thus most likely to end up serving the highest bidder, the big corporations who could afford them, who had little economic stake in making people "hate cruelty or tolerate the idea of" the kind of "change" Dos Passos had in mind. Advertising and public relations would play a key role in *U.S.A.* not only through the characters of J. Ward Moorehouse and Richard Savage, but also through the ubiquitous bits of ads and public-relations rhetoric that appear in the newsreels and biographies. In the newsreels in the final volume of the trilogy alone, for example, one finds headlines about Coolidge's praise for advertising, ads for Chesterfield cigarettes, Ford motorcars, Frank E. Campbell funeral parlors, and a variety of other products, and public-relations blurbs about the steel industry, railroads, the city of Detroit, Florida real estate, investment-counseling services, and installment buying.[24]

It was in the *New Republic*, the *New Masses*, and the *Daily Worker* that Dos Passos first explored literary aesthetics which he would continue to grapple with in *U.S.A.* In an essay called "Against American Literature"[25] which he wrote in 1916 for the *New Republic*, Dos Passos came out strongly in favor of a literature which was concrete, tangible, solid, and rooted in American "soil." He also implied that America stood in need of the artist to help her understand herself. American literature, he wrote, was "a strangely unstimulating diet" characterized by thinness, vague gentility, and lack of depth, texture, and substantiality, "a rootless product" which had succumbed to a "cult of the abstract" in a land where everything *but* literature was dominated by an "inane matter-of-factness" (pp. 269–71). America needed its artist, he wrote, to help it transcend its "inane matter-of-factness." While the artist must accept the challenge of dealing directly and concretely with the world of fact, his art must transcend that world and help its inhabitants to see themselves. The resistance likely to greet him in this endeavor is alluded to humorously in the closing words of the essay:

> Shall we pick up the glove Walt Whitman threw at the feet of posterity? Or shall we stagnate forever, the Sicily of the modern world, rich in this world's goods, absorbing the thought, patronizing the art of other peoples, but producing nothing from amid our jumble of races but steel and oil and grain?
> "Well, isn't that enough?" I hear someone say.

For Dos Passos, clearly, it is not.

In an essay he wrote in 1922 Dos Passos reflected further on the kind of writing America required. "We need writing that shall be acid, with sharp edges on it," he wrote, "yeasty to leaven the lump of glucose that the combination of the ideals of the man in the swivel chair with decayed puritanism has made of our national consciousness."[26] Dos Passos saw American newspapers, in the twenties and the decades before, as dominated by two kinds of misguided "hype": the sales pitches of "the man in the swivel chair," or the "public relations counsel" as he preferred to be called, and the misplaced moral outrage of a "decayed puritanism" that produced headlines about colleges banning chewing gum and society matrons being shocked by the latest Paris fashions while ignoring (or burying in the back pages) subjects that warranted genuine moral outrage. As a novelist, Dos Passos would be more attentive than any of his colleagues to the way in which newspaper headlines, advertising, and public relations in general were shaping Americans' consciousness of themselves and their world during the first third of the twentieth century. In *U.S.A.* he would shoulder the challenge of liberating his reader's consciousness from the stultifying clichés of newspaper headlines, government and industry propaganda, public relations, and popular songs that had turned our national consciousness into a "lump of glucose." He would indeed, pick up Whitman's gauntlet.

Dos Passos frequently wrote book reviews in the twenties and thirties in which he discussed the various modes of literary expression available to the writer. In a review of Robert Cantwell's *The Land of Plenty* he explored the difference between nonfiction and fiction.

> To get the difference between imaginative creation and successful journalism, all you have to do is compare ["The Land of Plenty"] with a work of clever reporting like "I Went to Pit College." "The Land of Plenty" really molds your perceptions and leaves them different from what they were when you began it; when you have read it you have undergone the town and the forest fires, the noise and sweat and grease of the big plant, of the mud flats, the feel of the dirty overalls and the tremor of the panels going under the saw . . . Reading "I Went to Pit College" leaves you as far away from the miners it describes as you are from a bum you've felt sorry for and slipped a nickel to; "The Land of Plenty" puts you right in the shoes of the men and women who work in and exploit the lumber business . . . [27]

Dos Passos was groping toward the task of fiction. "The writer has to be continually transforming his tools while he's using them," he wrote. The central task of the writer, he stated in this review, was "the invention of a new way of looking at the world about us, a new and unique imaginative classification of the hodge-podge of consciousness" (p. 25). "The invention of a new way of looking at the world about us" would become Dos Passos's central project in *U.S.A.*

Between 1917 and 1922, Dos Passos contributed some sixteen articles about Spain to magazines including the *Seven Arts*, the *Liberator*, the *Freeman*, *Bookman*, the *Nation*, the *Dial*, *Mentor*, and *Broom*. (Most of these articles were reprinted in the volume published in 1922, *Rosinante to the Road Again*.) In these pieces Dos Passos set out to document the culture of Spain and the processes by which one may come to know and express that culture. The explorations of Spain's past and present, of its artists and its anarchists, of its dreams, its illusions, and its realities, would prove to be (although he hardly knew it at the time) an important rehearsal for his study of American culture in *U.S.A.*

Dos Passos's first article, published in *Seven Arts* in August of 1917, was a piece called "Young Spain."[28] (Most, but not all of this article, appears in *Rosinante to the Road Again* as "The Baker of Almorox.") "Young Spain" is a clearly written, well-conceived article about one individual Dos Passos met in Spain, and about the difficulties of trying to write about the culture as a whole.

The article begins with a finely etched profile of the village baker of Almorox (a town Dos Passos had visited on a Sunday excursion from Madrid). In its careful description of the baker's appearance, of that of his wife and of their home, in its sensitive portrayal of the values which animated their lives, of that which made them proud, of that which puzzled them, and of their relation to their fellow villagers and to the past, the profile takes on the characteristics of the best of the genre the *New Yorker* would later make famous.

Dos Passos entered into the life of this man in all its concrete detail in an effort to understand the culture of which he was a part. The technique was valid not only because of his own view that a culture might best be understood by a close look at the individuals that comprised it, but also because "predominant in the Iberian mind," as he saw it, was the thought that "only the individual, or that part of life which is in the firm grasp of the individual, is real" (p. 476).

Dos Passos realized that the "love for the place, the strong anarchistic reliance on the individual man" that he found in the baker of Almorox could be found in all regions of Spain, that all Spaniards placed similar emphasis upon the importance of the concrete and the local.

> In trying to hammer some sort of unified impression out of the scattered pictures of Spain in my mind, one of the first things I realize is that there are many Spains. Indeed every village hidden in the golds of the great barren hills, or shadowed by its massive church in the middle of one of the great upland plains, every fertile "huerta" of the seacoast is a Spain. (P. 477)

It was precisely the fierce regionalism of Spain, the unwillingness of any part of the land to acquiesce culturally or politically to Madrid, that attracted Dos Passos; but it is also this emphasis on the particular and individual that made the task of writing about Spain an extraordinarily complex one.

The problem, for Dos Passos, was that this tendency to emphasize the diverse specifics of topography, culture, language, and traditions was about the only generalization one could make about Spain with any confidence. The land "is essentially centrifugal" (p. 480), he observed, seeking to describe in abstract generalities Spain's relentless insistence upon the concrete and the local. Dos Passos was aware that any effort to impose unity upon Spain—whether by the government or by a writer—is bound to be fraught with difficulties. Despite the ambitious whirlwind tour of Spain's political history which follows his profile of the baker of Almorox, and despite his broad overview of all the Spanish arts, the results were, in the end, unsatisfactory, as Dos Passos himself must have realized. "Young Spain" had not stood still for him. It had eluded him as it had eluded its rulers and artists throughout the ages.

In the course of writing the fifteen other pieces on Spain that he produced during the next few years, Dos Passos puzzled over the complicated challenge of documenting the spirit and culture of a country.[29] Some of the people and events that he covered in the process later had direct bearing on subjects featured in his trilogy; it was here, for example, that Dos Passos covered his first strike, and here that he first explored the nature of Mediterranean anarchists, two subjects central to *U.S.A.* But more important than these specific subjects were the questions Dos Passos had to ask himself as he set about trying to capture Spain on paper. Who are the culture's heroes? Why are they admired? How do they embody qualities that are special to that culture? What literary approaches are best suited to capturing what is most Spanish about Spain?

Dos Passos probed popular songs, and common speech, politics and literature, art and commerce, and the topography of greatly different geographic regions in an attempt to get Spain to stand still for him. Aware of the way Spanish culture (and perhaps all cultures) resists abstractions, he grew adept at stringing together vast numbers of concrete images to capture the look and taste and feel of the culture in his prose. Dos Passos wrote straightforward factual reportage, autobiographical reminiscences, cultural history, literary criticism, and allegorical fictional narratives. Each of these modes highlighted and illuminated unique aspects of Spanish culture; some were more effective than others. When the George H. Doran Company published a number of his pieces on Spain in a single volume, these diverse modes came to serve as interesting commentaries on each other. The notion that sections of autobiography, current events and popular songs, cultural history, and fiction might be interwoven to document the culture of a nation was one which would prove more useful to Dos Passos than he had any reason to suspect when he published *Rosinante to the Road Again* in 1922. He would publish a volume of poetry, three novels, two books of nonfiction, two plays, and countless articles before returning to this idea again. But when he did, eight years later, he met with spectacular results.

In 1926 Dos Passos went to Boston to look into the facts of the Sacco and Vanzetti case for a piece in the *New Masses*. It is unlikely that he suspected, at the time, that this case, and its implications for American society, would preoccupy him as a writer for the next ten years and would inspire the climax of the trilogy that would earn him his greatest literary acclaim.

The straightforward, factual article that appeared in the *New Masses* in August of 1926 told succinctly and clearly the story of two Italian immigrants, a fish peddler and a shoemaker, who had been convicted, on the basis of circumstantial and contradictory evidence, of a crime Dos Passos was sure they had not committed.[30] The guilty verdict handed down in 1923 still stood in 1926, despite repeated motions for a new trial. Dos Passos believed that Nicola Sacco and Bartolomeo Vanzetti were being sentenced to death not for their actions, but for their political views. Vanzetti had tried to organize a strike once. Both men, morally opposed to World War I, had failed to register for military service. But most important of all, Dos Passos felt, they were anarchists.

Dos Passos described Vanzetti in the *New Masses* as follows:

> He was an anarchist, after the school of Galeani. Between the houses he could see the gleaming stretch of Plymouth bay, the sandy islands beyond, the white dories at anchor. About three hundred years before, men from the west of England had first sailed into the grey shimmering bay that smelt of woods and wild grape, looking for something; liberty . . . freedom to worship God in their own manner . . . space to breathe. Thinking of these things, worrying as he pushed the little cart loaded with eels, haddock, cod, halibut, swordfish, Vanzetti spent his mornings making change, weighing out fish, joking with the housewives. It was better than working at the great cordage works that own North Plymouth. Some years before he had tried to organize a strike there and had been blacklisted. The officials and detectives at the Plymouth Cordage Works, the largest cordage works in the world, thought of him as a Red, a slacker and a troublemaker. (P. 10)

And of Sacco, Dos Passos wrote,

> He was an anarchist. He loved the earth and people, he wanted them to walk straight over the free hills, not to stagger bowed under the

ordained machinery of industry; he worried mornings working in his garden at the lethargy of the working people. It was not enough that he was happy and had fifteen hundred or more dollars in the bank for a trip home to Italy. (P. 10)

Dos Passos tried to outline for his reader the social factors which would make such views so threatening that two men who held them would have to be sentenced to death. At the time of their arrests in 1920, Dos Passos wrote in his 1926 *New Masses* piece, "any foreigner seemed a potential Bolshevik, a menace to the security of Old Glory and liberty bonds and the bonus" (p. 10). He then proceeded to document the process by which two men he considered innocent were being "inexorably pushed towards the Chair by the blind hatred of thousands of well-meaning citizens, by the superhuman involved stealthy soulless mechanism of the law."[31]

Despite the worldwide attention focused on the case, the verdict continued to stand throughout the following year. After months of painstaking research, including interviews with both Sacco and Vanzetti in jail, and with a number of witnesses for the defense, Dos Passos expanded his *New Masses* article into a 127-page pamphlet for the Sacco-Vanzetti Defense Committee. "Facing the Chair: Story of the Americanization of Two Foreignborn Workmen" was published in Boston in 1927 as part of the final effort to win a stay of execution.[32]

Dos Passos's book, while meticulously accurate, is much more readable than the other accounts of the trial that were published around the same time. It is the product of Dos Passos's careful attention to detail, the fruits of his patient sifting through voluminous court records of testimony.

While in "The Pit and the Pendulum," Dos Passos tells his story in a single narrative voice, many voices narrate the facts in "Facing the Chair." They include: Defense Attorney Thompson, Anatole France, Eugene V. Debs, FBI agent Felix Feri Weiss, the American Federation of Labor, Justice Department employees Lawrence Letherman and Fred J. Weyand, journalist John Dos Passos, Judge Webster Thayer, convict Celestino Madeiros, FBI informer John Ruzzamenti, Assistant Secretary of Labor Louis Post, lawyers of the National Popular Government League, scores of court witnesses, and state-police head-captain William Proctor. Some of these people believed the defendants to be innocent; others felt they were guilty. Still others knew them to be innocent of this particular crime, yet seemed to want them to die.[33]

By presenting a montage of documents including court testimony and trial and hearing transcripts, public statements by famous people and by organizations, factual narratives assembled by Dos Passos, excerpts from Vanzetti's "Story of a Proletarian Life," and essays in which Dos Passos dissects the social forces involved in the case, Dos Passos allows the same raw facts to be seen from dozens of perspectives. Dos Passos came to understand that the ways in which one understood the facts were determined, for the most part, by one's vision of America. Thus "Facing the Chair" became, in addition to a documentation of facts, an anatomy of visions. There are many visions of America that emerge from "Facing the Chair," but those that claim our special attention here are those of the accused and of their accusers.

Sacco and Vanzetti, like the ancestors of the Dedham jurors who wanted them to die, viewed America as a land of freedom and opportunity, a land where new peaceful and equitable relations might exist between neighbors, a land free from the oppressions and deprivations of the Old World, where men might develop their potential in liberty and peace. "What is this criminal garlic-smelling creed that the people of Massachusetts will not face openly?" Dos Passos asks. "This outlaw creed . . . anarchy," he says, is the same dream of implanting the "City of God" on earth that was sustained in the hearts of America's first settlers.[34]

"In the tough memories of peasants and fishermen," in the twentieth century, Dos Passos wrote,

> there remained a faint trace of the vanished brightness of the City of God. All our citydwelling instinct and culture has been handed down to us from these countless urban generations, Cretans, Greeks, Phoenicians, Latins of the Mediterranean basin, Italians of the hill-towns. It is natural that the dwellers on those scraggy hills in sight of that always blue sea should have kept alive in their hearts the perfect city, where the strong did not oppress the weak, where every man lived by his own work at peace with his neighbors, the white Commune where man could reach his full height free from the old snarling obsessions of god and master.
>
> It is this inner picture that is the core of feeling behind all anarchist theory and doctrine. Many Italians planted the perfect city of their imagination in America. When they came to this country they either killed the perfect city in their hearts and submitted to the system of dawg eat dawg or else they found themselves anarchists. There have been terrorists among them, as in every other oppressed

and despised sect since the world began. Good people generally have contended that anarchism and terrorism were the same thing, a silly and usually malicious error much fostered by private detectives and the police bomb squads.

An anarchist workman who works for the organization of his fellow workmen is a man who costs the factory owners money; thereby he is a bomb-thrower and possible murderer in the minds of American employers . . .

Yet under the conflict between employer and workman, and the racial misunderstanding, . . . might there not be a deeper bitterness?

The people of Massachusetts centuries ago suffered and hoped terribly for the City of God. This little white courthouse town of Dedham, neat and exquisite under its elms, is the symbol of a withered hope, mortgaged at six per cent to the kingdoms of this world. It is natural that New Englanders, who feel in themselves a lingering of the passionate barbed desire of perfection of their ancestors, should hate with particular bitterness, anarchists, votaries of the Perfect Commune on earth. The irrational features of this case of attempted communal murder can only be explained by a bitterness so deep that it has been forgotten by the very people it moves most fervidly. . . . (Pp. 57–58)

Dos Passos finds the ironies of their fate chilling. Who might have believed that men filled with hopes of freedom in the land of engines and opportunity would find their lives ground into nothingness by the frighteningly efficient, opportunistic engines of the law? Who might have dreamed, when young Sacco set out for the land of machines and dollars, that the men who owned the machines and controlled the dollars would find his dreams so threatening they would want him dead? Who would have suspected that the descendants of the men who settled a new land in search of liberty and freedom would feel so threatened by others who did the same that they would want to deprive them of their lives? These ironies strike Dos Passos as being at the core of the gigantic misunderstanding involved in the Sacco-Vanzetti case, a misunderstanding which, in his view, extends far beyond it, which pervades all parts of American society.

While Americans may envision their land as a land committed to freedom and opportunity, to equality and justice, an event like the Sacco-Vanzetti trial throws facts which undercut this vision into sharp relief. Somehow, somewhere in the course of American history, Dos Passos feels, those who came here fleeing oppression became themselves the oppressors. The Sacco-Vanzetti case became, for people all over the world, "a focus in the unending fight for human rights of oppressed individuals and masses against oppressing individuals and masses" (p. 20). But the "oppressing individuals and masses" in America are different from their counterparts elsewhere in a significant respect: they *believe in* the dreams they daily violate. "There is a smouldering tradition of freedom," Dos Passos writes, that makes those who abridge it "feel guilty. After all everyone learnt the Declaration of Independence and 'Give me Liberty or Give me Death'" (p. 20).

Throughout "Facing the Chair" there is a starkly evident and often reiterated gap between rhetoric and reality, between image and act, between dreams of what might be and facts of what is. Authorities who avow, in patriotic rhetoric, their loyalty to the principles on which America is founded fail to see the ways in which their actions go counter to those very principles. The "neatly-swept courtroom in Dedham with everything so varnished and genteel," surrounded by "white old-time houses . . . pious Georgian doorways" (p. 20), is the good and pure and genteel and religious façade behind which senseless murder will be committed. The dream of freedom and of a "saner social order" (p. 45) that prompted the settlement of Massachusetts by its first citizens has been transformed, by their descendants, into a license to quash those dreams when more recent immigrants dare to dream them.

"Circumstances sometimes force men into situations so dramatic, thrust their puny frames so far into the burning bright searchlights of history that they or their shadows on men's minds become enormous symbols," Dos Passos writes,

> Sacco and Vanzetti are all the immigrants who have built this nation's industries with their sweat and their blood and have gotten for it nothing but the smallest wage it was possible to give them and a helot's position under the bootheels of the arrow collar social order. They are all the wops, hunkies, bohunks, factory fodder that hunger drives into the American mills through the painful sieve of Ellis Island. They are the dreams of a saner social order of those who can't stand the law of dawg eat dawg. . . . (P. 45)

In "Facing the Chair" Dos Passos tried to fathom these mysteries in nonfiction narrative. He tried to give some insight into the ways in which the minds of the prosecutors and the FBI agents worked; he established the context of the "red hysteria" and fear of anarchist bombings that dominated the headlines of the day. He inserted grim reminders of the history of repression in America: "Don't forget that people had been arrested and beaten up for distributing the Declaration of Independence" (p. 54). And he offered a concise sociology of Eastern Massachusetts as an explanation for the "atmosphere of rancor and suspicion, fear of holdups and social overturn" that pervaded that part of the country when the South Braintree murders (for which Sacco and Vanzetti were charged) were committed. "Pent-up hatred found an outlet when the police in Brockton arrested Sacco and Vanzetti, wops who spoke broken English, anarchists who believed neither in the Pope nor in the Puritan God, slackers and agitators, charged with a peculiarly brutal and impudent crime. . . . The people of Norfolk county and of all Massachusetts decided they wanted these men to die" (p. 53).

In "Facing the Chair" Dos Passos dissected and reassembled the facts of the Sacco-Vanzetti trial and the facts of the lives of the two men involved into a compellingly moving narrative lucid in its clear and finely etched evocation of the concrete. In 1927 he still shared the faith in the propensity of his fellow Americans to respond to fact that Whitman had expressed in the *Brooklyn Eagle* some eighty years earlier. "Once open the eyes of men to the *fact* of the intimate connection between *poor pay* for women, and *crime among women*," Whitman had written, "and the greatest difficulty is overcome. The remedy will somehow or other follow."[35] Dos Passos concludes "Facing the Chair" with the assertion, "All that is needed is that the facts of the case be generally known."[36]

Dos Passos began to doubt the truth of this assertion by the middle of the summer of 1927. He had been sending daily reports on the Boston demonstrations in support of Sacco and Vanzetti to the *Daily Worker*.[37] Next to his reports the paper printed details of mass demonstrations in New York, Chicago, Seattle, Mexico, Belgium, Uruguay, Germany, and Czechoslovakia. Yet no stay of execution was in sight. Clearly, the facts alone were *not* enough.

On August 9, Dos Passos sent the *Nation* a piece called "An Open Letter to President Lowell" which "no publication in Boston," he wrote, "seems willing to publish."[38] In place of factual narrative or montage of documents, his "Letter" was a direct, impassioned plea directed to Lowell, the president of Harvard and a member of the advisory committee appointed by the governor of Massachusetts to review the case. He accused Lowell of being an accomplice to a massive "whitewash." Despite the fact that serious irregularities in the trial warranted thorough investigation, he accused Lowell of having produced "an apology for the conduct of the trial rather than an impartial investigation." He referred to the case, in now familiar terms, as an important part of "the world struggle between . . . those who have power and those who are struggling to get it." He concluded the piece by accusing Lowell of having made himself an accessory to a "foul crime against humanity and civilization." The letter was printed in the August 24 issue of the *Nation*, two days after Nicola Sacco and Bartolomeo Vanzetti were executed in the electric chair.

In November 1927 Dos Passos returned to the Sacco and Vanzetti case in a review he published in the *New Masses* of a new book about the case by Eugene Lyons. "In this excellent pamphlet," Dos Passos wrote, "Lyons has done exactly what he set out to do, which was to write an account of these seven years of agony of the working class that would be immediately available to men of all languages and conditions. I can't imagine how his particular job could have been done better."[39] But less than one-third of the review dealt with the book which was its ostensible subject. The piece focused much more on Dos Passos's plea that writers not let the case fade into memory, that they formulate new ways of helping the country understand, remember, and transcend the dark chapter of American history that the Sacco and Vanzetti trial represented.

> The names of Sacco and Vanzetti are fading fast into the cloudland of myth where they are in danger of becoming vague symbols like God, country and Americanism. One of the most extraordinary things about industrial society of the present day is its idiot lack of memory. Tabloids and movies take the place of mental processes, and revolts, crimes, despairs pass off in a dribble of vague words and rubber stamp phrases without leaving a scratch on the mind of the driven, installment-paying, subway-packing mass. It is up to the writers now to see to it that America does not forget Sacco and Vanzetti so soon as it would like to . . .
>
> Every detail must be told and retold. Sacco and Vanzetti must not have died in vain. We must have writing so fiery and accurate that it will sear through the pall of numb imbecility that we are again swaddled in after the few moments of sane awakening that followed the shock of the executions. . . . (P. 25)

He ended the review with a challenge—to his readers, and also to himself: "Well, it has come to pass. Well, we have protested. Our blood has curdled. What are we going to do now?"

Dos Passos's own answer to this question did not spring into his consciousness full-blown in 1927. He was thinking, at the time, of writing a book which was "sort of on the edge between [fiction and nonfiction], moving from one field to the other very rapidly."[40] The book, which he also thought of as a "series of reportages of the time," was to be "a contemporary commentary on history's changes, always as seen by some individual's ears, felt through some individual's nerves and tissues."[41] While he may not have envisioned at the time the massive trilogy that this effort would produce, the work he was planning was *U.S.A.*

As so many American writers had realized before him, Dos Passos came to realize that if his reader was to develop the ability to see the facts of his world freshly, the artist must first help him extricate himself from the "vague words and rubber stamp phrases" which pervaded his culture; he must write a book which "made new" the words that generations of misuse and malice had turned "slimy and foul."[42] It was a problem Dos Passos had addressed before, and it was one he would continue to address throughout his career.

During his senior year at Harvard, he condemned a friend's use of "vague worn-out terms."[43] A few years later, he would watch a jumble of worn-out "phrases" turn a group of humane people into murdering automatons,[44] and would witness "the physical power of lies to kill and destroy."[45] World War I was called "the first press agents' war" by the *New York Times;* to one historian it represented "the first modern effort at systematic nationwide manipulation of collective passions."[46] "It was the astounding success of propaganda during the war," wrote public relations magnate Edward Bernays, "which opened the eyes of the intelligent few in all departments of life to the possibilities for regimenting the public mind."[47] Dos Passos was one of "the intelligent few" who found his eyes opened to "the possibilities for regimenting the public mind" during the war—but he was horrified by the prospect that cheered Bernays. As Martin Howe, the main character in his first novel complained, "What terrifies me . . . is their power to enslave our minds . . ."

> "I shall never forget the . . . gradual lulling to sleep of people's humanity and sense by the phrases, the phrases . . . People seem to love to be fooled . . . We are slaves of bought intellect, willing slaves."

"But Howe, the minute you see that and laugh at it, you're not a slave."[48]

In *U.S.A.* Dos Passos would give his reader the tools to understand directly the nature of "the phrases, the phrases," that enslaved him. Suspicious of all members of the "word-slinging" classes,[49] he wanted his reader to learn to step back from the "cloudy masses of unattached verbiage"[50] that surrounded him and see his world not as some "word-slinging" intermediary may have seen it, but with his own eyes.

When he returned in *U.S.A.* to the facts he had first documented in the *New Masses*, the *Daily Worker*, "Facing the Chair," and the *Nation*, Dos Passos shouldered directly the challenge of liberating his reader's consciousness from the various texts that shackled his thought—from the clichés of newspaper headlines, government and industry propaganda, advertising, public-relations puffs, and the lyrics of popular song. His goal was to create readers who would no longer passively accept without question the stale and worn-out texts that blazoned their own authority all around him. In place of the straightforward authorial essay that characterized much of Dos Passos's journalism, the reader of *U.S.A.* confronts conflicting signals, competing messages, contradictory opinions, each limited in its own way. He must wade through facts and visions constantly at war, ideals as promptly deflated as they are proudly proclaimed, dreams that recur with the regularity of a phoenix, and real-life nightmares as punctual as a factory time clock. The reader is required, by Dos Passos's artful juxtapositions, to construct a pattern of meaning on his own. He is forced to forge, out of the facts and visions that he confronts, his own vision of what is, and of what might be.

Like a Greek chorus commenting upon the events which touch every character's life, the Newsreels of *U.S.A.* rivet every moment to its specific place in history. They lay out the "phrases" which channel people's thoughts; they paint their visions of themselves and their world and the facts which undercut those visions. Assembled through many hours of research in the Chicago Public Library,[51] each Newsreel documents with painstaking exactness the concrete facts that made headlines during a given year. Each Newsreel covers approximately one year, although events are often mentioned when they begin to impinge on the American public's awareness rather than when they were actually in the news. The news stories are often familiar ones.[52] The item in Newsreel XII, for example, about the murder of nineteen-year-old Avis Linnell by a minister named Richeson in Boston, had been collected by

Theodore Dreiser as a possible source for his novel about a murderer.[53] The popular songs quoted in the Newsreels are usually appropriate to the time frame with which they are associated.

Facts stated in the biographies of well-known people are carefully researched as well, and are corroborated by other accounts of their lives. Several of the biographies appeared originally as journalism in the *New Masses* and other publications. (Some of them, indeed, bear striking resemblances to biographies written by other writers in the *New Masses*, with which Dos Passos was undoubtedly familiar. Dos Passos's biography of Isadora Duncan, for example, has much in common with a brief biography of Duncan that Michael Gold wrote in the *New Masses* in 1929.)[54]

The autobiographical material in each Camera Eye section documents specific facts of Dos Passos's life in chronological order; it is consistent with facts known about Dos Passos's life, and with his own accounts elsewhere, in letters and memoirs. In the Camera Eye sections of *U.S.A.* the reader is exposed to the processes by which Dos Passos's own consciousness was molded. The reader shares the ways in which Dos Passos became aware of the dominant patterns underlying American culture and also the ways in which he weaves these themes together into the volume at hand; for *U.S.A.*, like *Leaves of Grass* and *Adventures of Huckleberry Finn*, is very much a book about writing a book, a book about itself. By sharing his insights into the processes of consciousness and creativity with his reader, Dos Passos further stimulates his reader to observe and structure reality for himself.

While several of the fictional characters in *U.S.A.* are based on historical figures, for the most part the characters are products of the writer's imagination. Yet even when totally "made-up" characters participate in events which existed outside the novel, Dos Passos shows a familiar concern for accuracy. Accounts of such events as the Passaic textile strike and the Sacco and Vanzetti demonstrations in Boston bear out his sense of responsibility to what Hemingway would have called "the way it was." It is through his fictional characters that Dos Passos allows his reader to see contemporary history as heard "by some individual's ears, felt through some individual's nerves and tissues."[55] By helping his reader see the ways in which one's intellect is shaped by one's environment, Dos Passos helps him acquire the tools he needs to step beyond those powerful shaping mechanisms himself.

The concept of "montage" was being developed by the Russian film director Sergei Eisenstein while Dos Passos was at work on *U.S.A.* Dos

Passos had met Eisenstein during a trip to Russia and was impressed by his films (particularly by the *Cruiser Potemkin* of 1925).[56] Dos Passos had already experimented with the literary potential of montage on his own to a limited extent in *Rosinante to the Road Again* and "Facing the Chair," as we have shown (and also in an early novel, *Manhattan Transfer*);[57] but in *U.S.A.* the concept of montage was to be instrumental in the masterful and complex structure Dos Passos evolved. In Eisenstein's description of "the principles of conflict" which create montage, the word "counterpoint" constantly recurs. The structure of *U.S.A.* may be seen, from one perspective, as analogous to that of a fugue: "a polyphonic composition based upon one, two or more themes, which are enunciated by several voices or parts in turn, subjected to contrapuntal treatment, and gradually built up into a complex form having somewhat distinct divisions or stages of development and a marked climax at the end."[58]

It is in the Newsreels that the themes are first stated contrapuntally by several voices, and it is in the Camera Eye, biography, and fictional narrative sections that the themes are contrapuntally developed. The fugue of *U.S.A.* has, most broadly speaking, two basic themes, whose interactions throughout the novel create the ironic juxtapositions which so dramatically characterize the work. The themes, as we will show, were first stated in "Facing the Chair."

Introduced and reiterated most clearly in the Newsreels, each theme might be identified most clearly by the timbre and tone of the voice that characteristically states it: theme A is a fanfare trumpted by a bugle-corps; theme B is the wail of a solitary blues-singer. The two themes are developed through a series of patterned oppositions: success and defeat, fulfillment and emptiness, prosperity and destitution, morality and depravity, freedom and repression.

Theme A, aligned with success, fulfillment, prosperity, morality, and freedom, is the rhetoric of dreams: an upbeat, proud, optimistic, confident, promising fanfare trumpeted by a bugle corps of headline writers, admen, bards of tinpan alley, revolutionaries, apostles of the gospel of wealth, dreamers of every stripe.

If theme A is the rhetoric of dreams, theme B is a recitative of facts, a solitary blues singer wailing a chronicle of individual hardship, deprivation, deadlock, defeat, and despair.

Throughout *U.S.A.* balloons of abstract rhetoric are constantly inflated, only to be brought down to earth by a statement of concrete fact which punctures with the inevitability of a bullet. The A theme always returns, and the B theme always follows shortly on its heels. As Dos Passos weaves these themes together in the Newsreels, Camera Eyes, biographies, and fictional narratives, the fugue that is America begins to take shape.

As the buglers proclaim America to be a land one can be proud of, a land one is glad to defend, a free and moral land in which all may share in the benefits of progress, the blues singer moans a soft refrain of lives lost in war, bodies mangled in factories, individuals lynched by mobs for their ideas. While the bard of tinpan alley sings a song of endless opportunity, the balladeer sings of dead ends and endless deadlock. As fanfares of exuberant rhetoric boast of a nation that respects life, liberty, and the pursuit of happiness, that holds out the promise of fulfillment and prosperity to all its citizens, solitary singers document facts of emptiness, destitution, and despair, of death and repression, ever present beneath the free and prosperous façade.[59]

All who assert that the "promised land" lives up to all of its promises, Dos Passos feels, are blinded to the ways in which the nation has compromised some of its most basic values. By artfully juxtaposing reality and rhetoric, Dos Passos forces his reader to confront the world of fact freshly. His goal is to help his reader strip away the blinders that constrict his vision and see, with his own eyes, what the U.S.A. is, as well as what it might be.

To assert that *U.S.A.* has a basically fugal structure is not to claim that the trilogy conforms to a fixed, tight, and rigid scheme. Any given Newsreel is likely to contain, in addition to instances of ironically juxtaposed rhetoric and reality, items existing primarily to fix the point in time, or to give a realistic sense of the absurd concatenation of headlines that bombard the individual every day. The Camera Eyes present occasional autobiographical fragments that resist being categorized in terms of the book's major themes, and the biographies often relate facts that are simply interesting in and of themselves. The fictional narratives sustain the reader's interest both as story and as an expansion of the themes stated in the Newsreels.

For Dos Passos is, in the end, a novelist and not a social scientist or propagandist. He is interested in telling the story of a nation and its people, not in constructing an abstract, schematized vision of their world. But the book is much more highly structured than is usually assumed, and these structures warrant examination.

Themes A and B are introduced in the first Newsreel of *U.S.A.* Theme

A enters first as a brazenly trumpeted vision of America as the land of
the free and the home of the brave:

It was that emancipated race
That was chargin' up the hill
Up to where them insurrectos
Was afightin' fit to kill[60]

The song evokes the image of a free people, an "emancipated race,"
fighting an unnamed but undoubtedly just cause. The headlines and
story fragments which follow this song reinforce images of confident
patriotism and pride, of a nation secure in its greatness and in its power,
a nation comfortable in its sense of its own superiority.

The year is 1900 ("CAPITAL CITY'S CENTURY CLOSED"), and America is a land where generals are composed and brave and proud, and
soldiers are fearless and bold: "General Miles with his gaudy uniform
and spirited charger" reviews the band and retains composure despite
the unfortunate accident which befalls him; the general "never permits a
flag to be carried past him without uncovering and remaining so until
the colors have passed,"

And the Captain bold of Company B
Was afightin' in the lead
Just like a trueborn soldier he
Of them bullets took no heed. (P. 28)

America, land of bold soldiers and respectful generals, has just acquired control of the Philippines ("CLAIMS ISLANDS FOR ALL TIME").
America is a great land ("we are now leading by the nose the original and
greatest of colonizing nations") (p. 29).

It is a land whose model of civilization and progress merits exporta-
tion across the globe:

In responding to the toast, "The Twentieth Century," Senator Albert
J. Beveridge said in part: *The twentieth century will be American.*
American thought will dominate it. American progress will give it
color and direction. American deeds will make it illustrious.
   Civilization will never lose its hold on Shanghai. Civilization will
never depart from Hongkong. The gates of Peking will never again be

closed to the methods of modern man. The regeneration of the world, physical as well as moral, has begun, and revolutions never move backwards. (P. 29)

Yet into the optimistic bustle of "NOISE GREETS NEW CENTURY," "LABOR GREETS NEW CENTURY," "CHURCHES GREET NEW CENTURY," "NATION GREETS CENTURY'S DAWN," a somber note is injected not once, but four separate times.

For there's many a man been murdered in Luzon.

And later,

For there's many a man been murdered in Luzon and Mindinao

And still,

For there's many a man been murdered in Luzon and Mindinao and in Samar

And finally (the concluding words of the Newsreel),

There's been many a good man murdered in the
Philippines
Lies sleeping in some lonesome grave. (Pp. 28-29)

Here, as throughout *U.S.A.*, Dos Passos draws no direct connection between the rather mournful song and any headline that may be linked with it. Rather, the effect of this grim refrain is a constant deflation of the rhetoric of confidence and success. The message that works its way into the reader's subconscious is that imperialism takes its human toll, that murder may be a handmaiden to "civilization," and that for every "Captain bold of Company B" immortalized in song, "There's been many a good man murdered . . . sleeping in some lonesome grave."

This B theme recurs in the following Camera Eye (1) (pp. 29-30), which documents Dos Passos's own first encounter with the human costs of imperialism. In the climate of hatred surrounding the Dutch and English colonial struggles in the Transvaal (1900) young Dos Passos finds himself and his mother being chased and stoned by a Dutch mob that thinks they are English. This Camera Eye lets the reader "in on" the process of creation, for in the following section this scene will be transported to America and transmuted into art. Here, as the reader sees Mac (Fainy McCreary) dodge the stone-hard, ice-covered snowballs of the "Bohunk and Polak" kids who shout "Scared cat . . . Shanty Irish . . . Bowlegged Murphy . . . Running home to tell the cop" (p. 32), he gains some insight into how the author may have restructured his own experiences into art.

The confident, prosperous, patriotic, idealistic A theme is picked up in Camera Eye (2) which follows the first installment of Mac's story. Here vast quantities of "brass tiny cannons just big enough to hold the smallest size red firecracker at the battle of Manila Bay" (p. 37) shower the passengers boarding the train Olympia, delighting, in particular, one increasingly familiar little boy who listens as a friend of the family

> was holding forth in the parlor car Why Lucy if it were necessary
> for the cause of humanity I would walk out and be shot any day you
> would Jack wouldn't you? wouldn't you porter? who was bringing
> apollinaris and he had a flask in the brown grip where the silk initialed
> handkerchief always smelt of bay rum. (P. 37)

The upbeat rhythms of Camera Eye (2) are quickly deflated by the first words spoken in the "Mac" narrative which follows it: "Well, Tim, I feel like a whipped cur . . ." (p. 37).

No less than four times does Pop repeat this refrain in this narrative segment. Jobless due to a strike he didn't want, pained by his wife's death, broken by doctors' bills, undertakers' bills, and rent, Pop is forced to leave town to avoid his creditors. His brother-in-law Tim tries to comfort him:

> it ain't your fault and it ain't my fault . . . it's the fault of poverty
> and poverty's the fault of the system . . . The only man that gets
> anything out of capitalism is a crook an' he gets to be a millionaire
> in short order . . . But an honest workin' man like John or myself
> we can work a hundred years and not leave enough to bury us decent
> with . . .
> "Tim, I tell yer I feel like a whipped cur."
> "It's the system, John, it's the goddam lousy system." (P. 38)

Tim's social analysis is consoling but not compelling; by presenting explanations for the way things are in the words of his characters

189

(rather than omnisciently as he did in "Facing the Chair"), Dos Passos is able to force his reader to evaluate each view of the social structure for himself, without the aid of an author's clear endorsement or condemnation.

Destitute, powerless, a broken man, Pop

> got pneumonia and died quietly at the Sacred Heart Hospital. It was about the same time that Uncle Tim bought a linotype machine. (P. 41)

The death and despair (B) of a broken man gives way to the hopes and promises (A) to be secured with the help of the new machine. The A theme returns as Tim sets in type his dream of a better world:

> The first print Uncle Tim set upon the new machine was the phrase: "Workers of the world unite; you have nothing to lose but your chains." (P. 42)

It is in his uncle's print shop that Mac, who will become one of the leading socialists in *U.S.A.*, first confronts the brazen and confident rhetoric of revolution. But for now at least, he finds the rhetoric of the "help wanted" section of the newspaper more exciting. As Mac composes letters of application in his head, drunk with the possibilities that await him, the A theme, trilling optimism and confidence, is continued in the opening lines of Newsreel II.

NEWSREEL II

Come on and hear
Come on and hear
Come on and hear

In his address to the Michigan state Legislature the retiring governor, Hazen S. Pingree, said in part: I make the prediction that unless those in charge and in whose hands legislation is reposed do not change the present system of inequality, there will be a bloody revolution in less than a quarter of a century in this great country of ours.

CARNEGIE TALKS OF HIS EPITAPH

Alexander's Ragtime Band
It is the best
It is the best

the luncheon which was served in the physical laboratory was replete with novel features. A miniature blastfurnace four feet high was on the banquet table and a narrow gauge railroad forty feet long ran round the edge of the table. Instead of molten metal the blastfurnace poured hot punch into small cars on the railroad. Ice cream was served in the shape of railroad ties and bread took the shape of locomotives.

Mr. Carnegie, while extolling the advantages of higher education in every branch of learning, came at last to this conclusion: Manual labor has been found to be the best foundation for the greatest work of the brain.

VICE PRESIDENT EMPTIES A BANK

Come on and hear
Alexander's Ragtime Band

It is the best
It is the best

brother of Jesse James declares play picturing him as bandit trainrobber and outlaw is demoralizing district battle ends with polygamy, according to an investigation by Salt Lake ministers, still practiced by Mormons clubwomen gasp

It is the best band in the land

say circus animals only eat Chicago horsemeat Taxsale of Indiana lost marks finale of World's Fair boom uses flag as ragbag killed on cannibal isle keeper falls into water and sealions attack him.

The launch then came alongside the half deflated balloon of the aerostat which threatened at any moment to smother Santos Dumont. The latter was half pulled and half clambered over the gunwale into the boat.

The prince of Monaco urged him to allow himself to be taken on board the yacht to dry himself and change his clothes. Santos Dumont would not leave the launch until everything that could be saved had been taken ashore, then, wet but smiling and unconcerned, he landed amid the frenzied cheers of the crowd. (Pp. 48–49)

The upbeat and secure fanfare with which Newsreel II opens (theme A) is interrupted by Governor Pingree's observations on the "present system of inequality" and the potential for "bloody revolution in America" (theme B). The B theme is then drowned out almost completely by three affirmative choruses of "Alexander's Ragtime Band," by the confident rhetoric of one of the main apostles of the American dream, by the moral righteousness manifested by Jesse James's brother, and by the clubwomen.

Like Santos Dumont's "half deflated balloon," the rhetoric of moral, peaceful, proud, confident, superior well-being is only partially deflated by the lingering memory of Pingree's words, and by mildly disturbing allusions to strife ("district battle"), immorality ("polygamy"), disrespect ("flag as ragbag"), and violence ("Keeper attacked by sealions"). The B theme will be voiced more strongly in the Camera Eye (3) and biography of the "Lover of Mankind" which follow.

In Camera Eye (3) the reader sees Dos Passos's first contact with the fact of inequality Pingree had voiced in Newsreel II. Here he finds out for the first time that the potteries whose chimneys blaze all night are run by "workingmen and people like that laborers travailleurs greasers," and his mother's story suggests that for some reason these men's lives are not as valuable as those of other people (p. 50). "Long ago Before theworldsfair Beforeyouwere born," his mother says, "one night Mother was so frightened on account of the rifleshots but it was allright turned out to be nothing but a little shooting they'd been only shooting a greaser that was all" (p. 50). (Her words echo in tone those of Huck Finn who, when asked if anyone had been killed during a steamboat accident, replied, "No'm, killed a nigger.")[61]

In the biography of Eugene Debs which follows, the B-theme reality of inequality and destitution is juxtaposed to Debs's A-theme dream of a society "where everybody would split even," where everyone would have enough (p. 51). His dream of a society of "free men" is undercut by the fact that "Woodrow Wilson had him locked up in Atlanta for speaking against the war."[62] His dreams are further deflated when the very people he would help, blinded to the realities of their world by Wilsonian rhetoric, reject Debs in the name of the very ideals—prosperity, democracy—that are closest to his heart.

Similar patterns may be seen in the section of *The 42nd Parallel* beginning with Newsreel VI.

NEWSREEL VI

(1) Paris Shocked At Last
(2) HARRIMAN SHOWN AS RAIL COLOSSUS
(3) noted swindler run to earth
(4) TEDDY WIELDS BIG STICK

(5)   straphangers demand relief.
(6)   *We were sailing along*
           On moonlight bay
       You can hear the voices ringing
       They seem to say
       You have stolen my heart, now don't go away
           Just as we sang
               love's
                   old
                       sweet
                           song
               On moonlight bay
(7)   MOB LYNCHES AFTER PRAYER
(8)   when the metal poured out of the furnace I saw
       the men running to a place of safety. To the right of the
       furnace I saw a party of ten men all of them running
       wildly and their clothes a mass of flames. Apparently some
       of them had been injured when the explosion occurred
       and several of them tripped and fell. The hot metal ran
       over the poor men in a moment.
(9)   PRAISE MONOPOLY AS BOON TO ALL
(10)   industrial foes work for peace at Mrs. Potter Palmer's
(11)   *love's*
                           old
                               sweet
                                   song
           We were sailing along
               on moonlight bay (Pp. 100–101)
                                   [item numbers added]

In this Newsreel while the A theme affirms the existence of moral rectitude, well-being, power, love, and peace, the B theme counters with instances of moral turpitude, ill-being, powerlessness, hate, and strife. The apparent triumph of moral responsiveness asserted in lines 1 and 3 is undercut by the depravity voiced in line 7. The images of prosperity and strength of lines 2, 4, and 9 are sharply contrasted with the images of discomfort and helplessness of lines 5 and 8. Visions of love and peace that emerge in items 6, 10, and 11 are exploded by the instances of hate and violence in lines 7 and 8. These ironic juxtapositions between A and B themes force the reader to experience the gaps between rhetoric and reality, between things "as we were told they ought to be" and "things as they are."

The counterpoint established in this Newsreel continues in the pages following it. In Camera Eye (7) (p. 101) (which follows immediately) the "all-American" children aligned with the A theme (Teddy and the "colossus"—the "big stick" wielded here is now a hockey stick) dodge the snowballs of the children of immigrants aligned with the B theme (workers drowned in molten metal) (p. 101).

> . . . look out for the muckers everybody said Bohunk and Polak kids put stones in their snowballs write dirty words up on the walls do dirty things up alleys their folks work in the mills
> we clean young American Rover Boys handy with tools Deer-slayers played hockey Boy Scouts and cut figure eights on the ice Achilles Ajax Agamemnon. . . . (P. 101)

The B-theme headline "MOB LYNCHES AFTER PRAYER" is figuratively reenacted in the biography of "The Plant Wizard" that follows Camera Eye (7). Here the "churches and congregations" (where the "clean young American Rover Boys" go when they grow up?) in effect "lynch" Luther Burbank after prayers; he dared to dream (A) the dirty heresy of "everyblooming everbearing hybrids" (pp. 101–2).

The A-theme dreams of "love's old sweet song" (p. 101) and of a better social order weave through the fictional narrative which follows, in which both the rhetoric of love and the rhetoric of revolution fail to describe the realities Mac encounters in San Francisco and in Mexico. [63] Instead of "sailing along on moonlight bay" singing "love's old sweet song," Mac finds himself out of a job, $500 in debt, supporting a child sick with measles and a wife concerned only with the "kind of clothes" and the "fine new victrola" her sister-in-law has bought. [64] Mac follows the slogans of revolution to Mexico, where, instead of hearing of a people devoted to establishing an order of peace and freedom, he hears of everyday happenings which make "the German atrocities" look like "a Sunday school picnic"; the realities underlying the rhetoric cause Mac to find himself, when the "Revolution" finally arrives in Mexico City, on a train to Vera Cruz, eating "chickenwings and almond paste" with his girlfriend and her mother (pp. 321, 330).

While in "Facing the Chair" Dos Passos tries to analyze the ways in which American morality has gone awry, in *The 42nd Parallel* he allows the reader to witness this process for himself by juxtaposing the rhetoric of moral outrage with the grim and genuinely outrageous facts which go ignored by that rhetoric. The rhetoric of morality, especially in the Newsreels, is most often associated with what Dos Passos elsewhere called a "decayed puritanism."[65]

Moral outrage is disproportionately focused on sexual prurience despite the many issues at which it might be more justly directed. In Newsreel VII, for example, one reads, "woman and children blotted out amidst he saw floggings and even mutilations but no frightful outrages."[66] Even more striking is the headline, "WHITES IN CONGO LOSE MORAL SENSE." The point Dos Passos wants to drive home is that nearly everybody seems to have lost his moral sense, that the rhetoric of morality in America is completely misdirected.

Headlines such as "Englewood clubwomen move to uplift drama," "COLLEGE HEAD DENIES KISSES,"[67] give the illusion of a nation of conscience, on its guard to defend against the onslaught of depravity. But the moral sense seems to atrophy when a genuine outrage is at hand. Untroubled by lynchings, mob violence, cheating, murder, corruption, inequality, and injustice, undisturbed by the brutal way in which America crushes its dreamers, the upholders of morality in America inveigh against kissing. The ironies of a morality gone awry are reiterated in the biographies, where, almost without exception, America punishes those who have manifested a genuine moral concern and rewards those who have successfully managed to avoid dealing with moral questions.

The second volume of *U.S.A.*, *Nineteen Nineteen*, published two years after *The 42nd Parallel*, continues the fugue the first book had begun, countering the confident rhetoric of patriotism with the somber realities of war. Some of the juxtapositions, such as the contrast within one Newsreel (XXIII) between the following two items, are almost too obvious:

(A) smiles of patriotic Essex County will be concentrated and recorded at Branch Brook Park, Newark, New Jersey, tomorrow afternoon. Bands will play while a vast throng marches happily to the rhythm of wartime anthems and airs. Mothers of the nation's sons will be there; wives, many of them carrying babes born after their fathers sailed for the front, will occupy a place in Essex County's graphic pageant; relatives and friends of the heroes who are carrying on the message of Freedom will file past a battery of cameras and all will smile a message recording installment number 7 of Smiles Across the Sea. The hour for these folks to start smiling is 2:30 . . .

(B) it was a pitiful sight at dusk every evening when the whole population evacuated the city, going to sleep in the fields until daylight. Old women and tiny children, cripples drawn in carts or wheeled in barrows, men carrying chairs bringing those too feeble and old to walk.[68]

But *Nineteen Nineteen* also contains some of the most trenchantly moving biographies in the trilogy, including the profiles of Joe Hill and Wesley Everest.

The juxtaposition of abstract rhetoric and concrete reality reaches a climax in the concluding section, "The Body of an American," which is one of the finest prose passages Dos Passos ever wrote:

"Whereasthe   Congressoftheunitedstatesbyaconcurrent resolutionadoptedon the4thdayof march lastauthorizedthe Secretaryofwar to cause to be brought to theunitedstatesthe body ofan   Americanwhowasamemberoftheamericanexpeditionary forceineuropewholosthislife duringtheworldwarandwhoseidentityhas notbeenestablished for burialinthememorialamphitheaterofthe nationalcemeteryatarlingtonvirginia"

In the tarpaper morgue at Chalons-sur-Marne in the reek of chloride of lime and the dead, they picked out the pine box that held all that was left of

enie menie minie moe plenty other pine boxes stacked up there containing what they'd scraped up of Richard Roe

and other person or persons unknown. Only one can go. How did they pick John Doe?

how can you tell a guy's a hundredpercent when all you've got's a gunnysack full of bones, bronze buttons stamped with the screaming eagle and a pair of roll puttees? . . . and the gagging chloride and the puky dirtstench of the yearold dead . . .

"The day withal was too meaningful and tragic for applause. Silence, tears, songs and prayer, muffled drums and soft music were the instrumentalities of today of national approbation."

John Doe was born (thudding din of blood in love into the shuddering soar of a man and a woman alone indeed together lurching into

and ninemonths sick drowse walkinginto scared agony and the pain and blood and mess of birth). John Doe was born and raised in Brooklyn, in Memphis, near the lakefront in Cleveland, Ohio, in the stench of the stockyards in Chi, on Beacon Hill, in an old brick house in Alexandria, Virginia, on Telegraph Hill, in a half-timbered Tudor cottege in Portland, . . .

—busboy harvestiff hogcaller boyscout champeen cornshucker of Western Kansas bellhop at the United States Hotel at Saratoga Springs officeboy callboy fruiter telephonelineman longshoreman lumberjack plumber's helper

worked for an exterminating company in Union City, filled pipes in an opium joint in Trenton, New Jersey.

Y.M.C.A. secretary, express agent, truckdriver, fordmechanic, sold books in Denver, Colorado: Madam would you be willing to help a young man work his way through college?

"President Harding, with a reverence seemingly
more significant because of his high temporal
station, concluded his speech:
'We are met today to pay the impersonal tribute;
the name of him whose body lies before us
took flight with his imperishable soul . . .
as a typical soldier of this representative
democracy he fought and died believing in the
indisputable justice of his country's cause. . . . (Pp. 462–64)

The fugue of *U.S.A.* culminates in the third volume of the trilogy, *The Big Money.* Dos Passos himself was aware of "a certain crystallization . . . of society" that existed in *The Big Money* "that didn't exist in the early part of *The 42nd Parallel.*"[69] *The Big Money* brings the story of the U.S.A. through 1929. It encompasses the Sacco-Vanzetti trial, the writing of "Facing the Chair," the beginnings of Dos Passos's work on *U.S.A.*, and his work on the report published as *Harlan Miners Speak.*

One senses a greater feeling of control, a greater mastery on Dos Passos's part, more confidence in his ability to structure his themes into a coherent and meaningful whole. The contrast between American ideals and American reality is expressed with greater grace and subtlety in *The Big Money.* Here Dos Passos relies less on mechanical juxtaposition of headlines than on artful exposition through symbol and story. Indicative of this change is the fact that *The Big Money* opens with fictional narrative, while the two earlier volumes both begin with Newsreels.

The themes of the fugue are introduced in *The Big Money* when Charley Anderson enters New York harbor on the boat taking him home from the war. " 'Do you see the Statue of Liberty, yet, Charley?' Joe Askew inquires, 'No . . . yes, there she is. I remember her lookin' bigger.' " [70] The gap Charley sees between fact and symbol will soon be echoed by the gap the reader sees between rhetoric and reality. Newsreel XLIV delineates a familiar contrast between upbeat, proud, prosperous rhetoric and troubling facts of deadlock and defeat (pp. 35-36).

But while the themes themselves may be familiar, the pace and intensity of their interactions are decidedly new. In this volume the fugue moves to a climax which illuminates and unifies its progress throughout the trilogy. For the first time in *U.S.A.*, the Newsreels, fictional narratives, and Camera Eyes all deal directly with the same set of events: those which destroyed the lives of Sacco and Vanzetti and changed Dos Passos's career as a writer. While the biographies do not deal with people who touched the lives of Sacco and Vanzetti (or Dos Passos) directly, they do profile people who, in various ways, shared their dreams. At the trilogy's close, the themes which have been woven together contrapuntally throughout the three books acquire a stunning compactness and coherence.

Headlines referring to the Sacco-Vanzetti case begin to appear as early as the second Newsreel, building to a climax in Newsreel LXVI (pp. 467-68), where the B theme is voiced by a headline expressing the inevitability of the prisoners' fate, and the A theme is represented by a phrase from the "International":

HOLMES   DENIES   STAY

A better world's in birth. (P. 467)

Mary French, Jerry Burnham, and assorted other fictional characters are involved in the Sacco-Vanzetti case, occasionally coming into contact with each other. Mary takes a job as press secretary for the Sacco-Vanzetti defense committee in Boston, and finds that "Although most of the newspapermen who had any connection with the case thought the two had been wrongly convicted, they tended to say that they were just two wop anarchists, so what the hell?" (p. 458).

One such newspaperman is Jerry Burnham, who deflates Mary French's idealism with his cynicism:

"But, Jerry, how can you stand it?" [Mary asks] "If the State of Massachusetts can kill those two innocent men in the face of the pro-

test of the whole world it'll mean that there never will be any justice
in America ever agan." "When was there any to begin with?" he
said with a mirthless giggle, leaning over to fill her glass . . . It was
Jerry Burnham who taught her to drink. (P. 458)

Mary French, one of the few genuinely attractive and admirable fictional characters in *U.S.A.*, works long and exhausting hours to counter
this sort of cynicism on the part of so many reporters; but she knows
that her job is "uphill work" (p. 457).

Through his pictures of Mary French's waking activities and nighttime
dreams, Dos Passos exercises his prerogative as a novelist to give his
reader an internal view of events externally documented in the Newsreels:

As courtdecision after courtdecision was lost and the rancid Boston
spring warmed into summer and the governor's commission reported adversely and no hope remained but a pardon from the governor himself, Mary worked more and more desperately hard. She
wrote articles, she talked to politicians and ministers and argued with
editors, she made speeches in unionhalls. . . . Hurrying along the
stonepaved streets she'd be whispering to herself, "They've got to be
saved, they've got to be saved." When at last she got to bed her
dreams were full of impossible tasks; she was trying to glue a broken
teapot together and as soon as she got one side of it mended the
other side would come to pieces again, she was trying to mend a rent
in her skirt and by the time the bottom was sewed up the top had
come undone; . . . she was climbing a shaky hillside among black
guttedlooking houses pitching at crazy angles where steelworkers lived,
at each step she slid back, it was too steep, she was crying for help,
yelling, sliding back. (P. 459)

Dos Passos captures vividly, in these expressionistic nightmares, the
anguish felt by everyone who recognized the insurmountable obstacles
that obstructed justice in Boston the summer of 1927.

The dreams of the doomed men are echoed in the dreams of other
Americans, such as Valentino, who wanted "to make good"; Thorstein
Veblen, who thought about "the new matter-of-fact commonsense
society dominated by the needs of men and women who did the work
and the incredibly vast possibilities for peace and plenty offered by the
progress of technology"; or even Frank Lloyd Wright, who dreamed of
a "Usonian city" that could be built "only in freedom."[71]

It is in the Camera Eyes, however, that Dos Passos best achieves a consciousness of the implications of the Sacco-Vanzetti trial and attains an awareness of his role as a writer. In the Camera Eyes of *The Big Money* Dos Passos manages, with enviable grace and artful self-consciousness, to share with the reader the processes by which the book was made.

In Camera Eye (46), the reader hears Dos Passos "ponder the course of history and what leverage might pry the owners loose from power and bring back (I too Walt Whitman) our story book democracy" (pp. 167–68). In Camera Eye (47) he watches Dos Passos "painstakingly . . . shape words . . . to rebuild yesterday":

> hock the old raincoat of incertitude (in which you hunch alone
> from the upsidedown image on the retina painstakingly out of color
> shape words remembered light and dark straining
> to rebuild yesterday to clip out paper figures to stimulate growth
> warm newsprint into faces smoothing and wrinkling in the various
> barelyfelt velocities of time)
> tonight now the room fills with the throb and hubbub of departure
> the explorer gets a few necessities together and coaches himself on
> a beginning
> better the streets first a stroll uptown downtown along the wharves
> under the el peering into faces in taxicabs at the drivers of trucks
> at old men chewing in lunchrooms at drunk bums drooling puke in
> alleys what's the newsvendor reading? what did the elderly wop
> selling chestnuts whisper to the fat woman behind the picklejars? . . .
> (P. 211)

The "beginning" on which the "explorer" has embarked in his passage is clearly the beginning of *U.S.A.*, which does, in fact, start out in the streets, with a stroll:

U.S.A.

> The young man walks fast by himself through the crowd that thins
> into the night streets; feet are tired from hours of walking. . . .
> (P. xviii)

In Camera Eye (49) the reader sees Dos Passos researching the book which began as "Facing the Chair":

walking from Plymouth to North Plymouth through the raw air of
Massachusetts Bay at each step in a cold squudge through the sole of
one shoe . . .

this is where the immigrants landed the roundheads the sackers of
castles the kingkillers haters of oppression this is where they stood
in a cluster after landing from the crowded ship that stank of bilge
on the beach that belonged to no one between the ocean that
belonged to no one and the enormous forest that belonged to no
one. . . .

for threehundred years the immigrants toiled into the west
and now today
walking from Plymouth to North Plymouth suddenly round a bend
in the road beyond a little pond and yellowtwigged willows hazy
with green you see the Cordage huge sheds and buildings company-
houses all the same size all grimed the same color a great square
chimney long roofs sharp ranked squares and oblongs cutting off the
sea the Plymouth Cordage this is where another immigrant worked
hater of oppression who wanted a world unfenced   when they fired
him from the cordage he peddled fish   the immigrants in the dark
framehouses knew him   bought his fish listened to his talk following
his cart around from door to door   you ask them   What was he
like? why are they scared to talk of Bart scared because they knew
him scared eyes narrowing black with fright?   a barber the man in the
little grocerystore the woman he boarded with in scared voices they
ask Why won't they believe? We knew him We seen him every day
Why won't they believe that day we buy eels? only the boy isn't scared
pencil scrawls in my notebook the scraps of recollection the broken
halfphrases the effort to intersect word with word to dovetail clause
with clause to rebuild out of mangled memories unshakably (Oh
Pontius Pilate) the truth. (Pp. 443-44)

He outlines with a radiant lucidity the role he is to play:

accustomed the smokingcar accustomed the jumble of faces rumble
cozily homelike toward Boston through the gathering dark how
can I make them feel how our fathers our uncles haters of oppression
came to this coast how say Don't let them scare you you make
them feel who are your oppressors America
rebuild the ruined words worn slimy in the mouths of lawyers

district-attorneys collegepresidents Judges without the old words the
immigrants haters of oppression brought to Plymouth how canyou
know who are your betrayers America
    or that this fishpeddler you have in Charlestown Jail is one of your
founders Massachusetts? (P. 444)

Here, and in Camera Eye (50) which follows, Dos Passos sums up the
goal that has animated *U.S.A.* from the start: his desire to shatter the
complacency of the "accustomed" by forcing them to think in fresh
and new patterns, his need to "rebuild the ruined words," to restore to
the "old words the immigrants haters of oppression brought to Plymouth" the meaning "worn slimy and foul" through generations of abuse:

... America our nation has been beaten by strangers who have turned
our language inside out who have taken the clean words our fathers
spoke and made them slimy and foul ...
    America our nation has been beaten by strangers who have bought
the laws and fenced off the meadows and cut down the wood for
pulp ... and when they want to hire the executioner to throw the
switch
    but do they know that the old words of the immigrants are being
renewed in blood and agony tonight do they know that the old
American speech of the haters of oppression is new tonight in the
mouth of an old woman from Pittsburgh of a husky boilermaker
from Frisco who hopped freights clear from the Coast to come here
in the mouth of a Back Bay socialworker in the mouth of an Italian printer of a hobo from Arkansas the language of the beaten nation
is not forgotten in our ears tonight
    the men in the deathhouse made the old words new before they
died. (Pp. 468–69)

While an occasional figure such as Thorstein Veblen (with the "sharp
clear prism of his mind") (p. 122) manages to transcend the limitations
of a culture that has turned the clean words "slimy and foul," each of
the fictional characters in *U.S.A.* suffers from a sharply constricted
vision of himself and of his world. In his artful juxtapositions of rhetoric
and reality (and his parallel juxtapositions of dream and fact, image and
actuality), Dos Passos forces the reader to achieve a vision larger than
that of any character in the book. He forces the reader to extricate him-

self from the patterns of thought with which he may have approached the book, and demands that he confront old facts in new ways. The final Camera Eye of *U.S.A.* follows Dos Passos to Harlan County, Kentucky, where he is documenting the conditions of the striking miners. In a last indulgence of the artfully ironic montage that he perfected in this work, Dos Passos allows Camera Eye (51) to flow into the biography of Samuel Insull ("Power Superpower") which succeeds it, as follows (p. 523):

THE CAMERA EYE (51)

... the law stares across the desk out of angry eyes his face reddens in splotches like a gobbler's neck with the strut of the power of submachineguns sawedoffshotguns teargas and vomitinggas the power that can feed you or leave you to starve

sits easy at his desk his back is covered he feels strong behind him he feels the prosecutingattorney the judge an owner himself the political boss the minesuperintendent the board of directors the president of the utility the manipulator of the holdingcompany

he lifts his hand towards the telephone

the deputies crowd in against the door

we have only words against

POWER SUPERPOWER

The admission of defeat is simultaneously a note of triumph; in the "dark strikesilent hills" there may be deadlock and defeat, but on the pages of *U.S.A.* there is victory. Samuel Insull, master of wartime propaganda and peacetime public relations,[72] may have pulled the strings of power so adeptly that he was beyond the reach of the law, but he was not beyond the reach of the artist's words. Dos Passos cuts through his carefully manipulated public image and incarcerates him, for generations to come, in his own amoral audacity.[73] As Dos Passos once said, the "writer who writes straight is the architect of history."[74]

U.S.A. culminates in a series of scenes of deadlock, death, and defeat. The nation portrayed in the book is one which destroys its dreamers, ignores its artists, and kills those who work for social change. It is a society in which nothing is born (of the two pregnancies in the final volume, one ends in abortion and the other in a blind child who dies after several days). It is a place filled with natural and man-made disasters (devastating hurricanes, dreadful industrial accidents, suicides, train wrecks, the stock-market crash). Alfred Kazin called it "one of the saddest books ever written by an American."[75] Yet there is a force which runs counter to all the grimness and despair: the energy of the narrative itself. While on the one hand the society in the book is one in which nothing gets born, on the other hand it is also a society that can give birth to a *U.S.A.*—a brilliantly fresh, irreverent, devastatingly clear-sighted book that is vibrantly alive, that reverberates with "the speech of the people," with concrete images of American life dizzying in their diversity. It is a book that leaves the reader not with the despair of defeat, but with the challenge to somehow "make the old words new" himself.

The book's epilogue, "Vag," intertwines the A and B themes of the fugue in a final chord:

> The young man waits at the edge of the concrete, with one hand he grips a rubbed suitcase of phony leather, the other hand almost making a fist, thumb up . . .
> went to school books said opportunity, ads promised speed, own your home shine bigger than your neighbor, the radiocrooner whispered girls, ghosts of platinum girls coaxed from the screen, . . .
> waits with swimming head, needs knot the belly, idle hands numb, beside the speeding traffic.
> A hundred miles down the road.[76]

Dos Passos wants to teach his reader how to challenge the authority of the many attractive but misleading "texts" that surround him. He wants him to learn how to see the gaps between the glowing rhetoric of school books and the shameful injustices they ignore; between the glossy promises of advertising and propaganda and the grim realities they mask; between the lyrics of popular songs or the scripts of Hollywood's films and the complexities of life and love that they deny. By constantly challenging the authority of these and other "texts," Dos Passos, like Whitman (whom he admired greatly), pushes each reader to become an active producer of the text on his own.

EPILOGUE

During the last two decades the line between fact and fiction has grown more and more blurred. Of course, this is not the first time this has happened. Lennard Davis, in *Factual Fictions: The Origins of the English Novel*, makes a convincing case for the idea that both newspapers and the novel share common origins in what he calls the "news/novel discourse" of the sixteenth and seventeenth centuries.[1] In eighteenth-century England, as the novel began to come into its own, the boundary between this new imaginative genre and journalism was still indistinct; novels by former journalist Daniel Defoe, for example, were often presented as factual accounts by their author.[2] In America, the Puritan hostility toward fiction led eighteenth- and early nineteenth-century sentimental novelists to claim that their books were "founded on fact."[3] While the rise of objectivity in American journalism in the nineteenth century generally defined the province of American newspapers as the world of fact,[4] newspapers still occasionally included within their columns fictions of various sorts (such as serialized novels, humor columns, or thinly disguised hoaxes). Whitman, Twain, and Dreiser all admit having invented stories on slow days (while usually providing their readers with clues that the story was not to be taken at face value). These inventions were the exception, however, and not the rule. Whitman, Twain, Dreiser, Hemingway, and Dos Passos all accepted the notion that the journalist should traffic in the world of fact, and that it was their job as journalists to cover that world as accurately as they could. They respected the role newspapers could play in a democracy by laying the facts before the public.

From the middle of the nineteenth century on, the journalist and the imaginative writer were generally held to different standards and were subject to different expectations on the part of the reader. The journalist's facts must be verifiable; the artist's truths must cohere into an aesthetically satisfying whole.[5] The decade during which those lines were drawn most clearly was probably the 1920s;[6] the decade during which they began to be most seriously blurred was the 1960s.[7] In the sixties, reporters, impatient with the rigid conventions the press had adopted in the name of facilitating the objective reporting of the news, started to borrow technical devices from the novel;[8] novelists, dissatisfied with the realm of the "sea bottom of the id" that fiction writers had claimed as their natural habitat, began to borrow research methods and subjects from journalism.[9] By the 1980s E. L. Doctorow was ready to assert: "There is no longer any such thing as fiction or nonfiction, there is only narrative."[10] Or is there?

Two polar positions in this controversy are exemplified by Norman Mailer and John Hersey, each of whom has distinguished himself as both journalist and novelist. Mailer, who has reported on a wide range of social, cultural, political, and technological subjects, and whose novels include *The Naked and the Dead* and *Ancient Evenings*, believes the realms of fact and fiction may be fruitfully mixed. To this end he subtitled his 1960s classic *Armies of the Night*, "history as the novel/ the novel as history."[11] Hersey, whose journalism includes his reporting on the bombing of Hiroshima (published first in the *New Yorker* and later as a separate book), and whose fiction includes *A Bell for Adano* and *The Wall*, believes—passionately—that "a great deal of harm has been done in recent years by the notion that something *can* be both a novel and journalism at the same time."[12]

These two positions came into direct conflict most recently with the 1979 publication of Mailer's stunningly powerful and eloquent novel, *The Executioner's Song*. Mailer's publisher (with Mailer's assent) promoted the book as both "a novel" and "a model of precise and accurate reporting."[13] In his afterword, Mailer himself claimed that the book was "a factual account" that was "as accurate as one can make it."[14] In an article in the *Yale Review*, John Hersey raised a number of specific challenges to the factual accuracy of the book.[15] When Mailer appeared as a guest at my seminar on "The Journalist as Novelist" at Yale, students confronted him with several of those charges. He refuted them, asserting that he had, in fact, been meticulously accurate on those points. (He had not added a single metaphor, for example, to any of Gilmore's letters.)[16] On the same occasion, however, he also confessed to having largely invented several other parts of the book ("The stuff on Gilmore's mother is probably two-thirds fanciful. The stuff on April, the sister of Nicole, is probably three-quarters fanciful . . . I'd say it was ninety-five percent fictional, in fact, with April . . . ").

What troubled Hersey in his piece in the *Yale Review* was the notion that a work that clearly manifested such impressive powers of invention might try to pass as "a model of precise and accurate reporting."

As to journalism, we may as well grant right away that there is no such thing as absolute objectivity. It is impossible to present in words "the truth" or "the whole story." The minute a writer offers nine hundred ninety-nine out of one thousand facts, the worm of bias has begun to wriggle. The vision of each witness is particular. Tolstoy pointed out that immediately after a battle there are as many remembered versions of it as there have been participants.

Still and all, I will assert that there is one sacred rule of journalism. The writer must not invent. The legend on the license must read: NONE OF THIS WAS MADE UP. The ethics of journalism, if we can be allowed such a boon, must be based on the simple truth that every journalist knows the difference between the distortion that comes from subtracting observed data and the distortion that comes from adding invented data.

The threat to journalism's life by the denial of this difference can be realized if we look at it from the reader's point of view. The reader assumes the subtraction as a given of journalism and instinctively hunts for bias; the moment the reader suspects additions, the earth begins to skid underfoot, for the idea that there is no way of knowing what is real and what is not real is terrifying.[17]

That which Hersey finds terrifying, Mailer finds intriguing. "One of the oddest aspects of twentieth-century life," he told my class,

is this business of not knowing which matrix we're in, what are our axes, what's our frame of reference, where are we? . . . The tension between the journalistic aspects of the book [*The Executioner's Song*] and the novelistic aspects of the book I thought were ideal for getting at a certain twentieth-century mood. Always, as one's reading that book, one's saying, how real is it? Is he telling the truth? . . . What is the space this book inhabits? Does it inhabit fiction or does it inhabit fact? I think there's something agreeable about that going back and forth.[18]

Mailer may well be right—there is something agreeable to "that going back and forth" in a work of fiction. Indeed, that kind of tension enlivens not only novels like *The Executioner's Song*, but also *An American Tragedy*, *U.S.A.*, and, more recently, E. L. Doctorow's *Ragtime* and Robert Coover's *A Public Burning*, in which real people—Henry Ford, Emma Goldman, Stanford White, Julius and Ethel Rosenberg, etc.— move in and out of the lives of fictional beings to create what Mailer calls a peculiarly "twentieth-century mood." But what may be healthy— even invigorating—for fiction, can be perilous for journalism.

In September 1980, the same month Hersey published his article in the *Yale Review,* a young reporter named Janet Cooke published a news story called "Jimmy's World" in the *Washington Post.* The story began,

> Jimmy is 8 years old and a third-generation heroin addict, a precocious little boy with sandy hair, velvety brown eyes and needle marks freckling the baby-smooth skin of his thin brown arms.
>
> He nestles in a large, beige reclining chair in the living room of his comfortably furnished home in Southeast Washington. There is an almost cherubic expression on his small, round face as he talks about life, clothes, money, the Baltimore Orioles, and heroin. He has been an addict since the age of 5.
>
> His hands are clasped behind his head, fancy running shoes adorn his feet and a striped Izod T-shirt hangs over his thin frame. "Bad, ain't it," he boasts to a reporter visiting recently. "I got me six of these."
>
> Jimmy's is a world of hard drugs, fast money and the good life he believes it can bring. Every day, junkies casually buy heroin from Ron, his mother's live-in lover, in the dining room of Jimmy's home. They "cook" it in the kitchen and "fire up" in the bedrooms. And every day, Ron or someone else fires up Jimmy, plunging a needle into his bony arm, sending the fourth grader into a hypnotic nod.[19]

The story, a detailed intimate profile of "Jimmy" and his family, described how "Jimmy" went to school only to learn math—a subject that would help him be a better drug dealer when he grew up. It ended with a vivid and shocking scene in which his mother's boyfriend injected him with a dose of heroin. The story was dramatic, powerful, and immediate. The *Los Angeles Times–Washington Post* news service distributed it to three-hundred clients, making "Jimmy" known nationally and internationally. Janet Cooke refused to divulge "Jimmy's" whereabouts to either her editors or the police, claiming that she had promised confidentiality to her sources (and that her life had been threatened as well). Her editors told her they would back her up completely if she were subpoenaed, and nominated the story for a Pulitzer Prize. Mayor Marion Barry and Chief of Police Burtell Jefferson launched an intensive city-wide search for "Jimmy," deploying a special task force of police and social workers, combing every neighborhood and school in Southeast Washington—to no avail. "Jimmy" could not be found.[20]

The mayor had expressed his own doubts about the piece after his investigation yielded no sign of the child: he said the article must have been "part myth, part reality." One of Cooke's colleagues began to have his doubts about the truth of the story when he accompanied Cooke to the area in which she had supposedly interviewed the boy and she didn't seem to know her way around. Other colleagues had their own suspicions—but they seem to have kept them largely to themselves. The truth came out only after Cooke was awarded a Pulitzer Prize that spring. As the national press reported biographies of the winners, the truth surfaced, and it became apparent that Cooke had invented phony degrees and accomplishments for herself in her official curriculum vitae. After a grueling interrogation by her editors, Cooke admitted to having invented "Jimmy" as well. [21]

Washington Post Executive Editor Ben Bradlee sent a telegram to the Pulitzer board members saying that Cooke's story "was in fact a composite, that the quotes attributed to a child were in fact fabricated and that certain events described as eyewitnessed did not in fact happen." [22] On the basis of material she had gathered from social workers and other sources, Cooke had written, basically, a work of fiction. The *Washington Post* returned the prize.

It was a dark day for American journalism, one that prompted extravagant metaphors and dire prophecies. "When blind Samson pulled down the central pillars of the temple at Gaza the entire structure fell," wrote journalist and novelist James Michener in *U.S. News and World Report*, "When Janet Cooke turned in a fake story, she knocked down the central pillar of her profession—integrity—and the reverberations went far." [23] Michener felt Cooke "would make a fine novelist" ("when I read her story I noticed how well she depicted the setting, the characters, the dialogue"), but bemoaned the fact that she had never learned "to distinguish between truth and fiction." Janet Cooke "had used charisma, unquestioned talent and a fierce ambition to attain a position sought after by thousands, but she reached it without two essential attributes: a deep commitment to the historical traditions of her profession and an understanding of what makes a newspaper acceptable to its community." Columnist Ellen Goodman felt Janet Cooke had "greased the chute of public disbelief," eroding the trust American journalists continually worked so hard to earn. [24] In a *Newsweek* poll, fully a third of those who knew about the scandal felt the Janet Cooke affair was not an isolated incident. Reporters, they felt, often make things up but don't always get caught. [25]

What, exactly, had Janet Cooke done? While persuading her editors that she was protecting the confidentiality of a source, she had created a composite, a fictional creation. She then proceeded to pass off her fictional being as a creature of fact. She was not the first American journalist to create a composite. Indeed, one of the earliest composites in American journalism was crafted by John Hersey in an article he published in *Life* magazine on July 3, 1944, "Joe Is Home Now." But Hersey's article, unlike Cooke's, "flagged" the strategy for the reader.[26] The article was accompanied by the following note:

> Like the best-selling novel *A Bell for Adano* by the same author, this story is in fiction form but is based on fact. It is distilled from the actual experiences of 43 different discharged soldiers. Joe Souczak does and says things which actually were done and said by various of those men. Only such changes of dialog and situation have been made as would give the story a consistent thread and the discharged man a consistent character. . . . There is no typical discharged soldier, but Joe Souczak's experiences may be taken as fairly representative. (P. 68)

In the 1960s unidentified composites began to populate magazines like *Esquire*, *New York*, and *Rolling Stone*. But while no formal "flag" may have been present, the reputation of the publication and the name of the writer attached to the piece (such as Tom Wolfe, Gail Sheehy, Hunter Thompson) served to alert the reader that the norms of conventional journalism would not be rigorously observed.[27] Janet Cooke, by way of contrast, presented a fabrication as fact within the format of conventional journalism. "The fabricated event, the made-up quote, the fictitious source . . . debases communication, and democracy," said the *New York Times*.[28] The *Washington Post* assured its readers in an eighteen-thousand-word *mea culpa* that all had been thoroughly investigated, that safeguards had been bolstered, and that a bizarre aberration like "Jimmy's World"—a fluke, really, they maintained—certainly would not recur.[29] But the "chute of public disbelief" was soon to receive another coat of grease.

It seems that while Janet Cooke was busy not interviewing "Jimmy" for the *Washington Post*, Michael Daly, a talented young columnist on the *New York Daily News*, was busy not interviewing a British army gunner in Belfast named "Christopher Spell."[30] Spell, like Jimmy, did not exist; Daly, like Cooke, was soon out of a job. The infection had spread north but the great Newspaper of Record was still untouched. Then Christopher Jones came along.

On December 20, 1981, the cover story in the *New York Times Magazine* was a dramatic firsthand account of life inside Cambodia titled "In the Land of the Khmer Rouge." The subhead proclaimed: "An American reporter takes a journey into the Cambodian jungle, where the shadowy Pol Pot leads his peasant army in savage guerilla warfare against the Vietnamese invaders."[31] Written by freelance reporter Christopher Jones, the article purported to document a month-long journey Jones had taken that summer with Cambodian guerillas, during which time he witnessed jungle battles with Vietnamese forces, interviewed the Cambodian premier and foreign minister, and even caught a glimpse of Pol Pot. It took several months for all the doubts to surface. Cambodia experts noted various factual errors ("Phnom Mali is a mountain range, not the capital city of Democratic Kampuchea; the Khmer Rouge do not put poison on their punji sticks; Comrade Kanika who is described by Jones as 'a man with short gray hair' is actually a woman—and has represented the Cambodians in Paris for several years").[32] The *Washington Post*, still smarting from the *Times*'s rather holier-than-thou castigations during the Janet Cooke affair, checked with Cambodian officials and concluded that Jones "neither visited the Cambodian rebels . . . nor interviewed people quoted in the piece."[33] But it was Alexander Cockburn of the *Village Voice* who dealt the most damaging blow: Jones had not only invented material himself, he had cribbed inventions from one of the twentieth century's greatest novelists and passed them off as his own reporting. Cockburn showed convincingly that Jones had plagiarized portions of his report from André Malraux's 1930 novel, *The Royal Way*.

The *New York Times*, the *Washington Post*, and the *New York Daily News* had all been caught passing off fabrications as fact. Was there no place one could safely turn without meeting what I would call a "fabrifact"? A likely candidate might be the *New Yorker*, a magazine with an eight-member fact-checking department "that combs every article, perusing reams of evidence—often delivered by the shopping bagful—to verify every fact."[34] The head of this department, Martin Baron, boasts, "if we say the paint on the wall of the hospital is yellow, it's yellow," and asserts that every detail "is absolutely correct down to whether or not there were coffee stains and tobacco ashes on the floor of the hospital" in a given piece. "We try to come as close as we possibly can to independently verifying every fact in the magazine."[35] The magazine's editor, William Shawn, asserts that "at the *New Yorker*, not only accuracy but truthfulness is sacred . . . I venture to say that the *New*

Yorker is the most accurate publication not only in this country, but in the entire world."[36] His view is echoed often by colleagues. However, in an article published in the *Wall Street Journal* on June 18, 1984, staff reporter Joanne Lipman revealed that Alastair Reid, "who has been appearing in the *New Yorker's* prestigious pages since 1951, says he has spent his career creating composite tales and scenes, fabricating personae, rearranging events and creating conversations in a plethora of pieces presented as nonfiction."[37] In a February 22, 1982, piece titled "Notes from a Spanish Village," for example, Reid describes riding " 'through the olive groves, the earth reddened by the evening sun,' " as he listened to Colonel Antonio Tejero Molina speak of the failed coup of 1981: " 'It's been good for us, I think, for we were getting too cocky, too pleased with ourselves . . . It has sobered us up. I don't think there will be another coup. . . . But I tell you, I was scared. I stayed up the whole night, and I won't forget it, ever.' "[38] Joanne Lipman quotes Mr. Reid as saying that the account is "not factually true, probably." In a December 2, 1961, "Letter from Barcelona," he described " 'a small, flyblown bar by the harbor, a favorite haunt of mine for some years because of its buoyant clientele,' " and described the reaction of the bar's patrons to a televised speech by Generalissimo Franco:

> . . . faces watched the set a bit sheepishly, finding it perhaps difficult to believe that the dapper little figure on the screen could have any connection with the sins committed in his name. But as the implacable bombast unrolled, they first began to gawk in disbelief and then to hoot with laughter . . . "For you, little Paco, I give up eating meat," muttered a small man beside me.
>
> "There is always room in prison, even for the fattest," growled another.[39]

An "enormous man" called El Cinico is quoted as telling the others,

> "You all make me sick. . . . If you don't like little Paco, why don't you turn him off? I'll tell you why—because then you'd have to think instead of just grumbling, and if this whole dust heap of a country depended on the fruits of your mosquito brains, we wouldn't even have sitdown toilets."

As Lipman notes, "The lively bar went over big with *New Yorker* readers: Mr. Reid says he received letters from people who insisted they had tracked it down. But, according to Mr. Reid, the bar by the harbor doesn't exist. The bar did once exist, Mr. Reid says, but had closed by the time he watched Franco on television—which he did, in reality, he says, at the home of a friend."[40] "Whether the bar existed or not was irrelevant to what I was after," says Reid, "If one wants to write about Spain, the facts won't get you anywhere."[41]

As Joanne Lipman reported, Reid "took disparate elements from different places—a bar here, a bartender or a television speech there—and 'moved them around and put them in a whole different place and made a poetic whole.' He says further that 'El Cinico' was a real character, a friend of his—but that the other two men were 'disembodied voices' asking 'the questions that a lot of people in Spain were asking at the time.' "[42] Reid "considers himself a poet"—indeed his first published work at the *New Yorker* was poetry. " 'There is a truth that is harder to get at and harder to get down towards than the truth yielded by a fact. . . . Readers who are factual-minded are the readers who are least important.' "

Once again the journalistic community was in an uproar. Reid's fabrications were front-page news in the *New York Times* and were the subject of a scathing editorial on "The Fiction of Truth."

The end of the world seems near now that our colleagues at the *New Yorker*, that fountainhead of unhurried fact, turn out to tolerate, even to justify fictions masquerading as facts. Quotes that weren't ever spoken, scenes that never existed, experiences that no one ever had—are all said to be permissible in journalism, provided they're composed by honest reporters to illustrate a deeper truth. . . . Why should not writers, like carnival barkers, pretend that fictions are facts? First, last and always, because the reader lured into the House of Facts, poor sap, has paid to experience facts . . .[43]

"Wrong truths are always correctable, with facts," the editorial concluded, "Fictional facts are forever counterfeit."[44] The *New Yorker*, self-proclaimed upholder of standards of accuracy for the world, was now tarred with the same brush that had tarred the *Times*, the *Post*, and the *News*. The story was picked up by other papers around the country. Reid, after all, was no novice. Unlike Cooke or Daly he was not starting out on a promising career, he had "arrived." He was not motivated, as *L.A. Times* media-critic David Shaw suggested Janet Cooke

215

had been, to break out of the pack by hitting "a grand slam home run."[45] He was simply, quietly, privately, fiddling with the facts in the interest of a larger truth.[46]

There is no reason why fine journalism cannot aspire to the level of art, why it can't strive to achieve a larger truth.[47] (Hemingway must have agreed with this notion, for on several occasions he reprinted—unchanged—as fiction, pieces which he wrote originally as journalism.)[48] Journalism can be enriched by the judicious use of the techniques of the fiction writer; it is when the journalist starts to borrow the *prerogatives* of the fiction writer that he gets into trouble.

As every journalist knows, it is not easy to get the perfect quote, or to witness the emblematic scene. Reporters constantly interview inarticulate people and then struggle to make their stories coherent without changing their words. They constantly follow leads that turn into nothing, wait for scenes that don't happen, hope for confidences that never come. It is hard, frustrating work, as all of the writers in this book found out. Janet Cooke, Michael Daly, Christopher Jones, Alastair Reid, and other protonovelists among them express their contempt for that hard work by replacing it with their own inventions. Why spend days interviewing more and more people to get a better quote when you can make one up that says it all? Why wait for the perfect scene to happen when you can invent it so plausibly, so beautifully, so poetically?

Unable or unwilling to write fiction, purveyors of "fabrifacts" try to pass off fiction as fact within the format of conventional journalism. Whereas great fiction enhances the reader's awareness and powers of discrimination, *their* confidence game dulls the reader's powers of discrimination and dims his sensitivity to deception. Fictions presented as fact (the "fabrifact" frauds of recent journalism) cloud the reader's vision with new illusions; facts presented as fiction (the journalistically rooted imaginative works of our five writers) enable the reader to see more clearly. Borrowings from fiction by writers of fact have produced some of journalism's most embarrassing moments. Borrowings from journalism by writers of fiction have produced a distinctively American pattern of literary creation—the journey traveled by Whitman, Twain, Dreiser, Hemingway, and Dos Passos.

These five writers understood that in a society as rife as any other with delusion, deception, hypocrisy, and fraud, the press played a special role in exposing the gaps between rhetoric and reality, between illusion and fact. As journalists they played that role to the best of their ability. They came to understand, firsthand, both the press's potential and its limitations. They came to realize that the misleading abstractions, misguided fictions, slippery rhetoric, limited perspectives, and reductive world views they challenged directly in their journalism could be more effectively questioned in their art. As artists they could rearrange familiar facts and visions, cast them in new lights, place them in larger contexts. They could challenge the reader's comfortable habits of thought and ways of understanding the world. They could move him to weigh society's laws against the laws of his own conscience. They could encourage him to try on unfamiliar perspectives. They could help him decipher the invisible codes that pervaded his culture and his language. Most importantly, they could help him acquire the skills he needed to question what he heard or read and construct new patterns of meaning on his own. "You shall no longer take things at second or third hand," the poet said, "You shall listen to all sides and filter them from yourself."[49]

NOTES

1. Introduction

1. Ralph Waldo Emerson, "Character," *The Complete Essays and Other Writings of Ralph Waldo Emerson*, ed. Brooks Atkinson (New York: Random House, 1940), p. 367.
2. Two biographical and critical studies which are exceptions to this rule are Charles Andrew Fenton, *The Apprenticeship of Ernest Hemingway: The Early Years* (New York: Farrar, Straus and Young, 1954), and Ellen Moers, *Two Dreisers* (New York: Viking Press, 1969). Larzer Ziff's chapters on magazines and newspapers in *The American 1890's* (New York: Viking Press, 1966), pp. 120-65, are very valuable as well.
3. Philip Rahv, "The Cult of Experience in American Writing," *Partisan Review*, 1940, reprinted in Philip Rahv, *Essays on Literature and Politics, 1932-1972*, (Boston: Houghton Mifflin, 1978), pp. 8-22.
4. F. O. Matthiessen, *Theodore Dreiser*, Men of Letters Series (Toronto: George J. McCleod, 1951), pp. 59-60.
5. Rahv, "Cult of Experience," pp. 14, 19.
6. "The Killers," by Cleanth Brooks and Robert Penn Warren, in *American Prefaces*, Spring 1942, cited in Rahv, ibid., p. 12. See also Rahv, p. 10, for contrasts between the "unifying principle" of American literature and that of German, French, and Russian literature.
7. Matthiessen, *Dreiser*, pp. 59-60.
8. R. W. B. Lewis, *The American Adam: Innocence, Tragedy and Tradition in the Nineteenth Century* (Chicago: University of Chicago Press, 1955), p. 9.
9. Stephen Crane to James Gibbons Huneker (December 1897), in *Stephen Crane: Letters*, ed. R. W. Stallman and Lillian Gilkes (New York: New York University Press, 1960), p. 160.
10. Mark Twain, "Spirit of the Local Press," *Territorial Enterprise*, December 23, 1865, reprinted in Bernard Taper, ed., *Mark Twain's San Francisco* (New York: McGraw-Hill, 1963), pp. 170-71.
11. Mark Twain, autobiographical dictation of June 13, 1906, in *Mark Twain in Eruption: Hitherto Unpublished Pages about Men and Events*, ed. Bernard DeVoto (New York: Harper Brothers, 1940), pp. 255-56.
12. Hemingway quoted in Fenton, *Apprenticeship of Hemingway*, p. 160.
13. Comments by these five authors on the limits of conventional journalism will

appear in the chapters that follow. For recent discussions of this subject by historians, sociologists, and journalists, see: Michael Schudson, *Discovering the News: A Social History of American Newspapers* (New York: Basic Books, 1978); Christopher P. Wilson, "Rhetoric of Consumption: Mass-Market Magazines and the Demise of the Gentle Reader, 1880–1920," in *The Culture of Consumption*, ed. Richard W. Fox and T. J. Jackson Lears (New York: Pantheon Books, 1983), pp. 39–64; Gaye Tuchman, *Making News: A Study in the Construction of Reality* (New York: Free Press, 1978); Hillier Krieghbaum, "Breaking Out of the Straitjackets of Journalistic Practices," in *Pressures on the Press* (New York: Thomas Y. Crowell, 1972), pp. 98–118; Tom Wolfe and E. W. Johnson, eds., *The New Journalism* (New York: Harper and Row, 1973); Edward Jay Epstein, *Between Fact and Fiction: The Problem of Journalism* (New York: Vintage Books, 1975); Herbert J. Gans, *Deciding What's News: A Study of CBS Evening News, NBC Nightly News, Newsweek and Time* (New York: Pantheon, 1979); *Making Sense of the News* (St. Petersburg, Fla.: Modern Media Institute, 1983); Lewis Lapham, Tom Wicker, et al., "Can the Press Tell the Truth?" *Harper's* 270, no. 1616 (January 1985): 37–51.

14. Walter Benjamin, "The Storyteller," *Illuminations* (New York: Schocken, 1969), p. 89.

15. In the language of contemporary critical theory, these writers produced "closed" texts as journalists and "open" texts as imaginative writers; their "closed" texts encouraged passivity on the part of the reader, while their "open" texts encouraged more active participation. For a fuller discussion of the theoretical implications of "closed" and "open" texts and of the role of the reader, see Umberto Eco, *The Role of the Reader: Explorations in the Semiotics of Texts* (Bloomington: Indiana University Press, 1979); Stanley E. Fish, *Self-Consuming Artifacts* (Berkeley and Los Angeles: University of California Press, 1972); Stanley E. Fish, *Is There a Text in This Class?* (Cambridge: Harvard University Press, 1980); Susan R. Suleiman and Inge Crosman, eds., *The Reader in the Text* (Princeton, N.J.: Princeton University Press, 1980); Jane Tompkins, ed., *Reader-Response Criticism* (Baltimore: Johns Hopkins University Press, 1980); and Steven Mailloux, *Interpretive Conventions: The Reader in the Study of American Fiction* (Ithaca: Cornell University Press, 1982).

16. Wolfe and Johnson, *The New Journalism*, p. 15.

17. Ibid. (Wolfe is speaking for himself, but he implies that the other writers featured in *The New Journalism* shared his goals.)

2. Walt Whitman

1. Michael Schudson, *Discovering the News: A Social History of American Newspapers*, p. 22.

2. Alexis de Tocqueville, *Democracy in America*, ed. Philips Bradley (New York: Random House, 1945), 2:59.

3. *New York Sun*, vol. 1, no. 1, 1833, quoted in Bernard A. Weisberger, *The American Newspaperman* (Chicago: University of Chicago Press, 1961), p. 94.

4. Benjamin Day in the *New York Sun*, quoted in Weisberger, ibid., p. 95.

5. James Gordon Bennett, in an early *New York Herald* editorial quoted in Weisberger, ibid., p. 98.

6. These pieces, not now identifiable, are referred to in Gay Wilson Allen, *The Solitary Singer: A Critical Biography of Walt Whitman* (New York: New York University Press, 1967), p. 18, and in Justin Kaplan, *Walt Whitman, A Life* (New York: Simon and Schuster, 1980), p. 79.

7. *New York Aurora*, March 28, 1842, quoted in *Walt Whitman of the New York Aurora: Editor at Twenty-Two, A Collection of Recently Discovered Writings*, ed. Joseph Jay Rubin and Charles H. Brown (State College: Pennsylvania State University Press, 1950), p. 2 (hereafter referred to as *Aurora*).

8. To the extent that they discuss Whitman's journalism at all, Kaplan and Zweig focus on what he wrote in the late 1840s for the *Brooklyn Eagle*, the *New Orleans Crescent*, and elsewhere, material which can, by and large (with the exception of the points raised here), be dismissed as having relatively little relation to the poetry that would follow. As Zweig notes, "However carefully we examine the writing Whitman published during these years, we find no sign of immature but struggling genius, no aborted trace of any literary adventure, however misguided. We find instead a drab, excitable journalist; a man so undistinguished from the swarm of his colleagues that it is almost impossible to tell how many of the newspaper articles attributed to him he actually wrote, they are so completely expressions of the age itself at its lowest and most ordinary." (Paul Zweig, *Walt Whitman: The Making of the Poet* [New York: Basic Books, 1984], pp. 3–4.) While Whitman's distinctive pieces in the *Aurora* were the exception rather than the rule, they should not be ignored; they yield special insight into the poet who would emerge in 1855.

9. Walt Whitman, "The New York Press," *New York Aurora*, March 29, 1842, in *Aurora*, p. 112.

10. Ibid.

11. Whitman, "Life in a New York Market," *New York Aurora*, March 16, 1842, in *Aurora*, pp. 20–22.

12. Whitman, "New York Boarding Houses," *New York Aurora*, March 18, 1842, in *Aurora*, pp. 22–24.

13. Whitman, ["Song of Myself"], in *Walt Whitman's Leaves of Grass: The First (1855) Edition*, ed. Malcolm Cowley (New York: Penguin Books, 1975), p. 28 (hereafter referred to as SOM).

14. Whitman, "Life in New York," *New York Aurora*, March 14, 1842, in *Aurora*, p. 19.

15. Whitman, " 'Marble Time' in the Park," *New York Aurora*, April 4, 1842, in *Aurora*, p. 42.

16. Although the practice was relatively rare, Whitman was not the only reporter in the penny press to experiment with these kinds of rhetorical devices. An article in the *New York Sun* that appeared April 14, 1834, began: "Reader, did you ever, just after nightfall, enter a pawnbroker's shop, and take note of the scenes that pass there? If you never did, step aside for a few minutes with us, and seat yourself here, in this obscure corner, behind the door, whence you can see what goes on without being yourself observed." Anon., quoted in Dan Schiller, *Objectivity and the News: The Public and the Rise of Commercial Journalism* (Philadelphia: University of Pennsylvania Press, 1981), pp. 69–70.

17. Whitman, ["How to Write a Leader"], *New York Aurora*, April, 19, 1842, in *Aurora*, p. 42. See also *Aurora*, pp. 119–21.

18. As Paul Zweig has commented, "There are flat programmatic poems in almost every edition of *Leaves of Grass*, where Whitman seems to be trying to complete a formula, to touch on all the issues, like an editor filling out his front page." *Walt Whitman*, p. 7.

19. The three articles are: (1) Anon., "City Intelligence," *New York Herald*, April 1, 1842; (2) Anon., "Destructive Fire," *New York Tribune*, April 1, 1842; and (3) Whitman, "Scenes of Last Night," *New York Aurora*, April 1, 1842.

20. "City Intelligence," *New York Herald*, April 1, 1842.

21. Whitman, "Scenes of Last Night," *New York Aurora*, April 1, 1842, in *Aurora*, pp. 36-38.

22. Whitman, "A City Fire," *Brooklyn Daily Eagle*, February 24, 1847, p. 2.

23. Whitman, "Dreams," *New York Aurora*, April 23, 1842, in *Aurora*, pp. 132-33; Whitman, "The Ocean," *New York Aurora*, April 21, 1842, in *Aurora*, pp. 130-31.

24. Whitman, "A Peep at the Israelites," *New York Aurora*, March 28, 1842, in *Aurora*, pp. 31-32; Whitman, "The Ocean," *New York Aurora*, April 21, 1842, in *Aurora*, pp. 130-31.

25. Whitman quoted in Emory Holloway, *Whitman: An Interpretation in Narrative* (New York: Alfred A. Knopf, 1926), p. 7.

26. Whitman, ["Preface"], *Leaves of Grass* (1855), in Whitman, *Leaves of Grass: The First (1855) Edition*, ed., Malcolm Cowley (New York: Penguin Books, 1976), p. 11.

27. Whitman, "Our City," *New York Aurora*, March 8, 1842, in *Aurora*, p. 98.

28. Whitman, "Old Landmarks," *New York Aurora*, April 18, 1842, in *Aurora*, p. 98.

29. Whitman, "More and Worse Suffering in Ireland—What Shall Be the Remedy?," *Brooklyn Daily Eagle*, December 27, 1847, reprinted in *The Gathering of the Forces: Editorials, Essays, Literary and Dramatic Reviews and Other Material Written by Walt Whitman as Editor of the Brooklyn Daily Eagle in 1846 and 1847*, ed. Cleveland Rodgers and John Black, 2 vols. (New York: G. P. Putnam's Sons, 1920), 1:169 (hereafter cited as *GF*).

30. Whitman quoted in Allen, *Solitary Singer*, pp. 92-93.

31. Whitman, *New York Evening Post*, June 27, 1851, quoted in Emory Holloway, ed., *The Uncollected Poetry and Prose of Walt Whitman* (Garden City, N.Y.: Doubleday, Page, 1921), p. 248 (hereafter cited as *UPP*).

32. Allen, *Solitary Singer*, p. 127.

33. Whitman to William Henry Seward (U.S. senator from New York and later Lincoln's secretary of state), December 7, 1855. "Could you do me the favor to put my address, as enclosed, on the list of those to whom it is convenient for you to send public documents, your speeches, and any government, congressional or other publications of general interest, especially census facts . . . I should be deeply obliged for a copy of the last census returns, reports of the Smithsonian Institution, and the like. I am a writer, for the press and otherwise. I too have at heart freedom and the amelioration of the people. Walt Whitman, Brooklyn, N.Y." *Walt Whitman: The Correspondence*, Vol. I: *1842-1867*, ed. Edwin Haviland Miller (New York: New York University Press, 1961), pp. 41-42.

34. Whitman, "Crossing Brooklyn Ferry," in Whitman, *Leaves of Grass*, Comprehensive Reader's Edition, ed. Harold W. Blodgett and Sculley Bradley (New York: W. W. Norton, 1965), p. 160; "Sparkles from the Wheel," pp. 389-90.
35. Whitman, "Song of the Exposition," in *Leaves of Grass*, Comprehensive Reader's Edition, p. 202.
36. Whitman, "Year of Meteors (1859-1860)," in *Leaves of Grass*, Comprehensive Reader's Edition, pp. 238-39.
37. Whitman, "A Backward Glance O'er Travel'd Roads," in *Leaves of Grass*, Comprehensive Reader's Edition, p. 564.
38. Whitman, "American Munificence and English Pomp," *Brooklyn Daily Eagle*, July 16, 1846, p. 2 (reprinted in *GF*, 1:38-40).
39. Schiller, *Objectivity and the News*, p. 51.
40. Whitman, "The Sewing-Women of Brooklyn and New York," *Brooklyn Daily Eagle*, January 29, 1847, p. 2 (reprinted in *GF*, 1:148-51).
41. Whitman, SOM, p. 48.
42. Whitman, "You Felons on Trial in Courts" and "To A Common Prostitute," *Leaves of Grass*, Comprehensive Reader's edition, pp. 385, 387.
43. Whitman quoted in *Aurora*, p. 140.
44 James Robinson Newhall quoted in Allen, *Solitary Singer*, p. 53.
45. For further details on Whitman's discharge from the *Aurora* see Joseph Jay Rubin, *The Historic Whitman* (University Park: Pennsylvania State University Press, 1973), pp. 80, 362, and Kaplan, *Walt Whitman: A Life*, pp. 103-4.
46. See Kaplan, ibid., p. 144, for details; and also *UPP*, 2:77-78.
47. See notes 43-46 above, and *Aurora*, p. 40.
48. The *Aurora*'s owners thought Whitman "lazy" (see Kaplan, *Whitman*, p. 104), presumably, in part, for indulging in so many strolls about the city on their time.
49. In his efforts to win and keep mass readership Whitman voluntarily honored a number of his readers' expectations regarding subject and length of stories even when his own views on the matter conflicted with theirs. "As our account has already stretched to the limits beyond which it is not judicious to go in a paper like ours," he wrote, "we shall give the remainder of what we saw during our stay at the synagogue in the *Aurora* tomorrow." Whitman, "A Peep at the Israelites," *New York Aurora*, March 28, 1842, in *Aurora*, p. 32. Years later, Whitman would comment on the ephemeralness at the core of newspaper work: "The newspaper is so fleeting," he would tell a friend, "is so like a thing gone as quick as come: has no life, so to speak: its birth and death almost coterminous." Horace Traubel, *With Walt Whitman in Camden*, 5 vols., (Philadelphia: University of Pennsylvania Press, 1906-64), 4: 2. (For additional comments by Whitman on the press, see "One of the Sacredest Rights of An American Citizen Outraged—Punishment of an Editor for Daring to Speak His Mind," *Brooklyn Daily Eagle*, February 15, 1847, and "Tone of the American Press—Personality," *Brooklyn Daily Eagle*, February 26, 1847" (*GF*, 2:248-55).
50. Horace Greeley, "Mr. Emerson's Second Lecture," *New York Tribune*, March 7, 1842, p. 4.
51. Whitman, "Mr. Emerson's Lecture," *New York Aurora*, March 7, 1842, in *Aurora*, p. 105.

52. Thomas L. Brasher, ed., *Walt Whitman: The Early Poems and the Fiction*, (New York: New York University Press, 1963), p. xv (hereafter cited as *EPF*).

53. Whitman, "Time to Come," *New York Aurora*, April 9, 1842, revised version of earlier poem, "Our Future Lot," printed in *Long Island Democrat*, October 31, 1838, and labeled "From the Long Islander," *EPF*, p. 27.

54. Ibid.

55. See Whitman, "Young Grimes" (1839); "The Inca's Daughter" (1840); "The Spanish Lady" (1840); "The Columbian's Song" (1840); "The Winding-Up" (1841); "Each Has His Grief" (1841); "The Punishment of Pride" (1839), in *EPF*, pp. 3–4, 6–7, 10–11, 12–13, 14–15, 16–17, 18–19.

56. Whitman, "The Love that is Hereafter" (1840), in *EPF*, pp. 8–9.

57. Whitman, "Death in the School-Room (A Fact)," *United States Magazine and Democratic Review*, August 1841, in *EPF*, pp. 55–60.

58. Whitman, "Bervance: or, Father and Son," *United States Magazine and Democratic Review*, December 1841, in *EPF*, pp. 80–87.

59. Whitman, *Franklin Evans or the Inebriate: A Tale of the Times*, "Introductory," *New World*, e.s., 10 (November 1842):1–31, in *EPF*, p. 126.

60. Whitman, "Some Fact-Romances," *The Aristidean*, n.v., n.n. (1845), in Thomas Ollive Mabbott, ed., *The Half-Breed and Other Stories by Walt Whitman* (New York: Columbia University Press, 1927), pp. 100–104.

61. *Charlotte Temple* (1794) was subtitled "A Tale of Truth," and *The Coquette* (1797) was subtitled "Founded on Fact." Such subtitles were still in fashion when Whitman wrote.

62. Whitman, ["Preface"], *Leaves of Grass* (1855), p. 9.

63. Benjamin Day quoted in Edwin Emery and Michael Emery, *The Press in America* (Englewood Cliffs, N.J.: Prentice-Hall, 1978), p. 120.

64. Whitman, ["Preface"], *Leaves of Grass* (1855), p. 5.

65. Whitman quoted in Emory Holloway, *Whitman: An Interpretation in Narrative* (New York: Alfred A. Knopf, 1926), p. 6.

66. Whitman, ["Preface"], *Leaves of Grass* (1855), pp. 7–8.

67. Whitman, "A Backward Glance O'er Travel'd Roads," *Leaves of Grass*, Comprehensive Reader's Edition, p. 564.

68. The image appeared in a circumscribed, purely political context on this occasion. "If there is a political blessing on earth that deserves to stand in the near neighborhood of the great common blessings vouchsafed us by God—life, light, freedom and the beautiful and useful ordinations of nature—that blessing is involved in the *union* of these United States together into an integral Republic, 'many in one.'" Whitman, "The Next Blessing to God's Blessing—Shall it be Jeopardized?," *Brooklyn Daily Eagle*, February 6, 1847, p. 2. (The phrase "many in one" echoes, of course, the motto printed on American coins, "e pluribus unum," or "out of many one.")

69. Whitman, "American Workingmen, Versus Slavery," *Brooklyn Daily Eagle*, September 1, 1847, p. 2 (reprinted in *GF*, pp. 208–21).

70. Whitman, ["Preface"], *Leaves of Grass* (1855), p. 10; SOM, pp. 31, 80.

71. SOM, p. 40.

72. Ralph Waldo Emerson, "The American Scholar" (1837), in *The Portable Emerson*, ed. Mark Van Doren (New York: Viking Press, 1946), p. 31.

73. Allen, *Solitary Singer*, p. 126.

74. Whitman quoted in Richard Chase, ed., *Walt Whitman Reconsidered* (Minneapolis: University of Minnesota Press, 1961), p. 91. See note 15 of Introduction on reader-response criticism.
75. Whitman, "The Mexican War Justified," *Brooklyn Daily Eagle*, May 11, 1846, p. 2 (reprinted in *GF*, 1:241).
76. Whitman, ["Who Learns My Lesson Complete"], *Leaves of Grass* (1855), p. 140.
77. Whitman, ["Specimen Days"], in Malcolm Cowley, ed., *The Complete Poetry and Prose of Walt Whitman*, Deathbed Edition (New York: Pellegrini and Cudahy, 1948), 2:197.
78. Whitman retreated from the "openness" of his text in later editions. Indeed, the "Song of Myself" that appears in all subsequent editions, from 1856 on, is much more conventional and less distinctive and unique.

    In the 1856 edition the author's name is no longer buried in a copyright notice; it is prominently displayed. Every poem is numbered and called, somewhat awkwardly, "poem." The infinitely open ending of the 1855 "Song of Myself" is replaced by the punctuation symbol with which poets customarily end their poems: a period. After 1855 Whitman became less willing to admit his reader as a cocreator of the text.
79. Whitman, ["Preface"], *Leaves of Grass* (1855), p. 22.

3. Mark Twain

*For ease of exposition Samuel L. Clemens will always be referred to as "Mark Twain." (Clemens first used the pen name on February 2, 1863.)

1. They were (listed in the order in which Twain worked for them) the *Hannibal Journal*, the *Keokuk Post*, the *St. Louis Evening News*, the *Virginia City Territorial Enterprise*, and the *San Francisco Alta California*.
2. Bernard A. Weisberger, *The American Newspaperman* (Chicago: University of Chicago Press, 1961), p. 112.
3. Ibid., p. 129.
4. Henry Nash Smith, ed., *Mark Twain of the Enterprise: Newspaper Articles and Other Documents 1862-1884* (Berkeley and Los Angeles: University of California Press, 1969), p. 7.
5. Mark Twain quoted in Edgar M. Branch, ed., *Clemens of the Call: Mark Twain in San Francisco* (Berkeley and Los Angeles: University of California Press, 1969), p. 7.
6. While stunts and hoaxes grew particularly frequent in the 1860s they were not unknown in earlier periods as well. For details on the famous "moon hoax" perpetrated by Benjamin Day's *New York Sun* in 1835, see Robert A. Rutland, *Newsmongers: Journalism in the Life of the Nation 1690-1972* (New York: Dial Press, 1972), pp. 140-41. See also Schiller, *Objectivity and the News*, pp. 76-80.
7. [Samuel Clemens], "Historical Exhibit A No. 1 Ruse," *Hannibal Daily Journal*, September 9, 1852. [Samuel Clemens], "Women's Rights and Man's Rights," *Hannibal Daily Journal*, May 23, 1853.
8. W. Epaminondas Adrastus Blab [Samuel Clemens], "Blabbing Government Secrets," *Hannibal Journal*, September 23, 1852.

9. Sergeant Fathom [Samuel Clemens], "River Intelligence," *New Orleans Daily Crescent*, May 17, 1859.

10. Here are some examples of Twain's parodies in each category: (1) Stock prospectus: "A Gorgeous Swindle," *Territorial Enterprise*, December 30, 1863, in Smith, ed., *Twain of the Enterprise*, pp. 119-21; (2) Political speeches: "Nevada State Constitutional Convention: Third House," *Territorial Enterprise*, December 13, 1863, in Smith, ed., *Twain of the Enterprise*, pp. 100–110; (3) Art criticism: "An Unbiased Criticism," *Californian*, March 18, 1865, reprinted in Alan Trachtenberg, ed., *Democratic Vistas: 1860-1880* (New York: George Braziller, 1970), pp. 314-19; (4) Romantic novels: (Letter dated Carson City, March 20, 1862), *Daily Gate City* (Keokuk, Iowa), June 25, 1862; (5) Travel guidebooks: (Letter dated October 25, 1867), *New York Daily Tribune;* (6) Sunday-school primers: "The Story of the Good Little Boy Who Did Not Prosper," *Galaxy*, March 1870; (7) History textbooks: "Biographical Sketch of George Washington, By Mark Twain," *Golden Era*, March 4, 1866.

11. Thomas Jefferson Snodgrass [Samuel Clemens], "Correspondence: St. Louis, October 18, 1856," *Keokuk Saturday Post*, November 1, 1856. The other letters are: "Snodgrass' Ride on the Railroad," *Keokuk Daily Post*, November 29, 1856, and "Correspondence," *Keokuk Daily Post*, April 10, 1857.

12. Twain's rendition of the vernacular speech of a stagecoach driver in a humorous squib for the *Enterprise*, for example, attests to his early sensitivity to the subtleties of regional dialect. His excellent account of a day at the San Francisco stock exchange shows his ear's alertness to vocational jargon, as well. Twain's reports on the Nevada legislature are filled with instances in which the pomposity of politicians' rhetoric is exposed and deflated. (See "Over the Mountains," *Territorial Enterprise*, September 13, 1863, in Smith, ed., *Twain of the Enterprise*, pp. 76-77; "Daniel in the Lion's Den—And Out Again," *Californian*, November 5, 1864, in Bernard Taper, ed., *Mark Twain's San Francisco* (New York: McGraw-Hill, 1963), pp. 66-74; and "Nevada State Constitutional Convention: Third House," *Territorial Enterprise*, December 13, 1863, in Smith, ed., *Twain of the Enterprise*, pp. 100-110.)

13. Examples of these achievements would include Twain's description of a landscaping project in connection with a local fair, his depiction of an awful emetic he took to cure a cold, and his account of the "horrible hole" called the San Francisco Police Court. ("A Hint to Carson," *Territorial Enterprise*, October 19, 1863, in Smith, ed., *Twain of the Enterprise*, pp. 83-85; "The Wake-Up Jake," *Territorial Enterprise*, August 23, 1863, idem, pp. 73-75; and "The Black Hole of San Francisco," *Territorial Enterprise*, December 23, 1865, in Taper, ed., *Mark Twain's San Francisco*, pp. 171-73.)

14. Twain quoted in Edgar M. Branch, ed., *Clemens of the Call: Mark Twain in San Francisco* (Berkeley and Los Angeles: University of California Press, 1969), p. 2.

15. Walt Whitman quoted in Holloway, *Whitman*, p. 7.

16. Arthur McEwen, *San Francisco Examiner*, January 22, 1893, quoted in Smith, ed., *Twain of the Enterprise*, p. 30.

17. Samuel L. Clemens [Mark Twain], "License of the Press" (speech before the Monday Evening Club, Hartford, 1873), in Charles Neider, ed., *The Complete Essays of Mark Twain* (Garden City, N.Y.: Doubleday, 1963), p. 12.

18. For early examples of tall tales in America, see Constance Rourke, *American*

Humor (New York: Harcourt, Brace, 1921), pp. 53–76. "Horseplay in print was a standard Nevada commodity," according to Henry Nash Smith, when Twain went to Nevada as a journalist (*Mark Twain of the Enterprise*, p. 21).

19. [Mark Twain], "Petrified Man," *Territorial Enterprise*, October 4, 1862.
20. Samuel L. Clemens [Mark Twain], "The Petrified Man," *Sketches New and Old* (New York: Harper and Brothers, 1929), p. 288.
21. Samuel L. Clemens [Mark Twain], "A Gorgeous Swindle," *Territorial Enterprise*, December 30, 1863, in Smith, ed., *Twain of the Enterprise*, p. 119.
22. Ibid., p. 120. Note Twain's analysis of the ways in which the document attempts to manipulate the reader's inferences. This is an early example of his sensitivity to the kinds of reader response elicited by different kinds of texts.
23. Walt Whitman, "The Sewing-Women of Brooklyn and New York," *Brooklyn Daily Eagle*, January 29, 1847, p. 2 (reprinted in *GF*, 1:151).
24. Samuel L. Clemens [Mark Twain], "A Gorgeous Swindle," in Smith, ed., *Twain of the Enterprise*, p. 121.
25. Samuel L. Clemens [Mark Twain], "The Carson Undertaker—Continued," *Territorial Enterprise*, February 13, 1864, in Smith, ed., *Twain of the Enterprise*, p. 160.
26. Twain, "Spirit of the Local Press," December 23, 1865, *Territorial Enterprise*, reprinted in Taper, ed., *Mark Twain's San Francisco*, pp. 170–71.
27. Twain, autobiographical dictation of June 13, 1906, in *Mark Twain in Eruption: Hitherto Unpublished Pages about Men and Events*, ed. Bernard DeVoto (New York: Harper Brothers, 1940), pp. 255–56.
28. Twain, *A Connecticut Yankee in King Arthur's Court* (New York: Penguin Books, 1971), p. 249 (originally published in 1889).
29. Ibid., For additional comments by Twain on journalism see "Journalism in Tennessee" and "How I Edited an Agricultural Paper," Twain, *Complete Short Stories*, ed. Charles Neider (Garden City, N.Y.: Hanover House, 1957), pp. 27–32, 46–50; also see "License of the Press," a talk by Twain before the Monday Evening Club in Hartford in 1873, in *Complete Essays of Mark Twain*, ed. Charles Neider (Garden City, N.Y.: Doubleday and Co., 1963), pp. 10–14.
30. Twain returned to the subject of the treatment of the Chinese in San Francisco in the marvelous ascerbic little satire, "Disgraceful Persecution of a Boy," which he published in his "Memoranda" column in the *Galaxy*, in May 1870, and in the bitingly caustic fictionalized correspondence between a Chinese immigrant and a relative in October and November of 1870 and in January 1871, titled, "Goldsmith's Friend Abroad Again." See pp. 69–71, below.
31. Bernard DeVoto, *Mark Twain's America* (Boston: Little, Brown, 1932). Books in this category included Samuel Fisk's *Dunn Browne Abroad* and Theodore Witmer's *Wild Oats Sown Abroad*, both well established by 1860. "Not novelty," DeVoto wrote of Twain's book, "but superiority gave the book its distinction," p. 245.
32. Twain, *The Innocents Abroad* (New York: New American Library, Signet Classic Edition, 1966), p. 369 (originally published in 1869).
33. Whitman, SOM, p. 26.
34. Twain, *Innocents Abroad*, pp. 368–70.
35. Tony Tanner, in *Reign of Wonder: Naiveté and Reality in American Literature* (Cambridge, Eng.: Cambridge University Press, 1965), offers some pertinent

examples of Twain's indulgence in "guidebook" rhetoric himself. "An insidious impulse to gravitate towards the sublime, generalized, or poetic phrase is everywhere in evidence [in *The Innocents Abroad*]. Examples could be proliferated: 'Many a strange clime'—'domed by the bending heavens'—'summits swathed in clouds'—'dancing wavelets'—'created mountains of water'—'It was the aurora borealis of the frozen pole exiled to a Summer Land'—'clothed in purple gloom'—'Finny armies'; or one could consult the dramatic gesturing over Damascus, or the pompous plangency of the description of the hermits, or the Sphinx: all these are examples of the debilitated rhetorical phrase-clusters which stray unchecked into his work." While Twain deplores the "'paint, ribbons, and flowers'" he finds in the writings of others, Tanner writes, "his own work is still heavy with the ballast of an older style . . . " (p. 109).

36. Twain, *Innocents Abroad*, pp. 111, 114, 230, 185.

37. Twain, Letter 4, *Alta California*, March 15, 1867.

38. Twain, "Disgraceful Persecution of a Boy," *Galaxy*, May 1870, pp. 717-18.

39. Twain, *Adventures of Huckleberry Finn*, ed. Leo Marx (Indianapolis: Bobbs-Merrill, 1967), p. 244.

40. Twain, "Goldsmith's Friend Abroad Again," Letter 1, Shanghai, 18——, *Galaxy*, November 1870. (Note: Twain's title alludes to Oliver Goldsmith's "Citizen of the World" journalism.)

41. Twain, "Goldsmith's Friend Abroad Again" (cont.), Letter 5, San Francisco, 18——," *Galaxy*, November 1870.

42. Twain, "Goldsmith's Friend Abroad Again" (cont.), Letter 6, San Francisco, 18——," *Galaxy*, January 1871.

43. John Dos Passos, *U.S.A.*, 3 vols., vol. 3: *The Big Money* (New York: New American Library Signet Classic reprint edition, 1969), p. 468.

44. Twain, "A True Story, Repeated Word for Word as I Heard It," *Atlantic Monthly: A Magazine of Literature, Science, Art and Politics* 34 (November 1874): 591-94.

45. For more on traditional box structure, see Leo Marx's introduction to *Adventures of Huckleberry Finn*, pp. xix-xx.

46. Twain, "A True Story," p. 592.

47. Twain quoted in Edward Wagenknecht, *Mark Twain: The Man and His Work* (New Haven: Yale University Press, 1935), p. 55.

48. William Dean Howells quoted in Philip Foner, *Mark Twain: Social Critic* (New York: International Publishers, 1958), p. 202.

49. Samuel L. Clemens [Mark Twain], "My Debut as a Literary Person," in *The Complete Essays of Mark Twain*, ed. Charles Neider (Garden City, N.Y.: Doubleday, 1963), p. 259.

50. Twain, "Forty-Three Days in an Open Boat—Compiled from Personal Diaries," *Harper's New Monthly Magazine* 34, no. 199 (December 1866):104-13.

51. Twain, Letter from Honolulu, "Burning of the Clipper Ship Hornet At Sea—Detailed Account of the Crew," *Sacramento Daily Union*, July 19, 1866.

52. Samuel L. Clemens [Mark Twain], "Old Times on the Mississippi," *Life on the Mississippi*, Author's National Edition, 25 vols. (New York: Harper and Brothers, 1883), 9:107.

53. Ibid., pp. 187, 187, 187, 219-22, 317, 317-22, 332-33, 225-30.
54. Ibid., p. 334 ("Extract from Prospectus of a Kentucky 'Female College' ").
55. Ibid., pp. 334-36 ("Extracts from the Public Journals").
56. Twain, "Fenimore Cooper's Literary Offenses" (1894), reprinted in Cleanth Brooks, R. W. B. Lewis, and Robert Penn Warren, eds., *American Literature: The Makers and the Making* (New York: St. Martin's Press, 1973), 2:1331, 1334.
57. Samuel L. Clemens [Mark Twain] and Charles Dudley Warner, *The Gilded Age*, (New York: Harper and Brothers, 1904), 2:34. Claims of veracity abound in *The Gilded Age*. For example, another footnote (1:54) states, "The incidents of the explosion are not invented. They happened just as they are told.—THE AUTHORS."
58. Samuel L. Clemens [Mark Twain], "Huck Finn and Tom Sawyer Among the Indians," *Life*, December 20, 1968 (special inset). Twain mentioned in a letter he wrote on July 15, 1884, that he was working on the manuscript published here for the first time; the fragment was written while Twain was at work on *Huckleberry Finn* (*Life*, December 20, 1968, p. 32).
59. [Twain], "Our Assistant's Column," *Hannibal Daily Journal*, May 23, 1853.
60. [Twain], "The Heart's Lament," *Hannibal Daily Journal*, May 5, 1853, p. 1.
61. Twain, "The Celebrated Jumping Frog of Calaveras County," reprinted in Samuel L. Clemens [Mark Twain], *Sketches: New and Old*, Author's National Edition, *The Writings of Mark Twain*, 25 vols. (New York: Harper and Brothers, 1899), 19:15-34.
62. Twain, *Innocents Abroad*, p. 5. Tony Tanner, in *City of Words: American Fiction 1950-1970* (London: Jonathan Cape, 1971), rightly and eloquently observes: "Since the time of the Puritans, there has been a strong tendency for Americans to regard the fictional as the false, the made thing as the mendacious thing, at least in the realm of art and when viewing the customs and manners of society (technological invention falls in another category)" (p. 29). While in *City of Words* Tanner uses this observation to explore postwar American fiction and does not relate it directly to any nineteenth-century works, his "made-mendacious" conception is useful in explaining the achievement of Mark Twain.
63. Twain, *Huckleberry Finn*, pp. 45, 62, 92, 9.
64. Ibid., pp. 60, 90, 91, 141, 144, 156.
65. Ibid., p. 79. Relevant here is Richard Bridgman's comment in *The Colloquial Style in America* (New York: Oxford University Press, 1966), p. 92, that the "steady, relentless hewing to a line of particulars" that characterizes Huck's language suggests "that material reality is all that is trusted, all that can be depended upon to convey meaning."
66. Noted in Leo Marx's introduction to *Adventures of Huckleberry Finn*, p. xxvii.
67. Twain also explores, in a related vein, the absurdities which result when characters allow their misreadings of various texts to determine their conduct and view of the world. Tom Sawyer, inspired by Sir Walter Scott, sends a boy running about town with a blazing stick to call his robber band together (p. 23). Miss Watson, misreading the Bible, never tires of pushing Huck into the closet to pray (p. 21). Aunt Sally, accepting without question the categories implied by the legal documents making slaves "property" and not human beings,

says, when she learns "a nigger" had been killed in the steamboat accident, "Well, it's lucky; because sometimes people do get hurt" (p. 252).

68. The Grangerford household greatly resembles the house described by Twain in *Life on the Mississippi* as the "residence of the principal citizen, all the way from the suburb of New Orleans to the edge of St. Louis" (p. 322). When Twain returned to the Mississippi Valley in 1882 to gather more material for his last chapters of *Life on the Mississippi* he had already completed much of *Huckleberry Finn*, including a version of chapter 7, in which Huck gave his description of the Grangerford house (Leo Marx, ed., *Huckleberry Finn*, Appendix C, p. 347). The fact that the journalism was written, in this case, after a version of the fiction had been written, does not invalidate a comparison of how the two modes treat the same material from different perspectives and in very different ways. For a detailed discussion of Twain's composition of *Life on the Mississippi* see Horst H. Kruse, *Mark Twain and "Life on the Mississippi"* (Amherst: University of Massachusetts Press, 1981).

69. Twain, *Huckleberry Finn*, p. 120.

70. As Laurence Holland has noted, "the text is haunted by the recognition of its status as fiction and of the moral hazards entailed in the enterprise of fiction. Indeed it is haunted by the implications of the particular narrative structure that Twain devised for his masterpiece." Laurence B. Holland, "A 'Raft of Trouble'—Word and Deed in *Huckleberry Finn*," reprinted from *Glyph 5: Johns Hopkins Textual Studies* (Baltimore, 1979), in *American Realism*, ed. Eric J. Sundquist (Baltimore: Johns Hopkins University Press, 1982), p. 76.

71. Twain, *Huckleberry Finn*, chaps. 23 and 24, pp. 178–91.

72. Twain, *Innocents Abroad*, p. 15.

73. Twain, *Innocents Abroad*, p. 5.

4. Theodore Dreiser

1. For statistics on changes in numbers of papers see Stanley Kobre, *The Development of American Journalism* (Dubuque: Wm. C. Brown, 1969), p. 350. "The Age of the Reporter" is a term used by writer Irwin Cobb (a friend of Dreiser's), in *Exit Laughing* (Indianapolis: Bobbs-Merrill, 1941), pp. 251–64, and by Michael Schudson, *Discovering the News: A Social History of American Newspapers*, p. 65. Increased use of the "by-line" and the signed column are discussed in Frank Luther Mott, *American Journalism: A History of Newspapers in the U.S. Through 250 Years, 1690–1940* (New York: Macmillan, 1941), p. 488; reporters' salaries are discusssed on p. 489. See also "Newspapers and the Bowery," chap. 1, in Ellen Moers, *Two Dreisers* (New York: Viking Press, 1969), pp. 15–31.

2. Theodore Dreiser, *Newspaper Days* (New York: Beekman Publishers, 1974), p. 4 (originally published as *A Book About Myself*).

3. Ibid., pp. 34–35.

4. Larzer Ziff, *The American 1890s* (New York: Viking Press, 1966), p. 120.

5. Frank Luther Mott, *A History of American Magazines, 1885–1905*, 4 vols. (Cambridge, Harvard University Press, 1957), 4:11.

6. Ibid.

7. For additional comments on *Ev'ry Month* see Ellen Moers, *Two Dreisers*, chap.

2, "Magazines and Pictures," pp. 32-42; and Donald Pizer, ed., *Theodore Dreiser: A Selection of Uncollected Prose* (Detroit: Wayne State University Press, 1977), pp. 15-16 (hereafter cited as *Dreiser: Uncollected Prose*).

8. Dreiser quoted in W. A. Swanberg, *Dreiser* (New York: Charles Scribner's Sons, 1965), p. 112, 115.

9. For an illuminating discussion of Dreiser's career at Butterick's, see Janice Radway, "Theodore Dreiser at *The Delineator:* Ideology, Readers, and Early Twentieth Century Magazines," December 1984 (unpublished paper).

10. Thomas P. Riggio, ed., *Theodore Dreiser: The American Diaries, 1902-1926* (Philadelphia: University of Pennsylvania Press, 1982), p. 15.

11. For a discussion of the new display of sensationalism see Schudson, *Discovering the News*, p. 95.

12. Murder-rate statistics from Stanley Kobre, *Development of American Journalism*, pp. 356-57.

13. Cartoon by R. F. Bunner, "In the Old Pit Shaft," *Life*, 29, no. 733 (January 7, 1897):32.

14. For atmosphere among Chicago journalists in the 1890s see John Tebbel, *The Compact History of the American Newspaper* (New York: Hawthorn Books, 1963), p. 156, as well as numerous other accounts of the period, including Kobre, *Development of American Journalism*, pp. 444-53. Dreiser comment from *Newspaper Days*, pp. 69-70.

15. Dreiser, *Newspaper Days*, p. 212.

16. [Dreiser], "A Negro Lynched. Taken from Jail at Rich Hill, Mo., and Hanged—His Crime the Usual One." *St. Louis Republic*, September 17, 1893, p. 2. For attribution of all unsigned pieces of Dreiser's journalism see Donald Pizer, Richard W. Dowell, and Frederic E. Rusch, *Theodore Dreiser: A Primary and Secondary Bibliography* (Boston: G. K. Hall, 1975).

17. Dreiser, "Nigger Jeff," in *The Best Short Stories of Theodore Dreiser*, introd. by James T. Farrell (Greenwich, Conn.: Fawcett Publications, 1961), p. 164.

18. Dreiser, *Newspaper Days*, p. 487.

19. [Dreiser], "Fever's Frenzy. John Finn Tries to Kill His Four Children." *St. Louis Republic*, August 9, 1893, p. 1; [Dreiser], "Brilliant Beyond Compare. The Annual Ball in Honor of the Veiled Prophet," *St. Louis Republic*, October 4, 1893, p. 1. (Artist's illustrations accompany both stories.)

20. For more on the changing role of advertising during this period, see Schudson, *Discovering the News*, pp. 93-101, and Daniel Pope, *The Making of Modern Advertising* (New York: Basic Books, 1983), pp. 4-6.

21. "Homestead Riot—5000 Men Attack the Pinkertons" and "The Important Message: 110,000 Yards of Best Quality Printed India Silk Offered at 68 cents," both in the *Chicago Tribune*, July 6, 1892.

22. A. Bishop and Co., "the Reliable Furriers," took out a large display advertisement for their featured "Large Assortment of Fur Capes," *Chicago Tribune*, December 2, 1891.

23. Siegel Cooper and Co. promoted toilette sets at various prices as a Christmas gift in a full-page illustrated advertisement showing varying degrees of elegance ("Three Piece Toilet Set, Oxidized, in Embossed Plush Case, $1.65, Plush Toilet Cases from 75 cents"). They were clearly expected to be a big gift item that year. *Chicago Tribune*, December 6, 1891.

24. *Newspaper Days*, p. 65. Others have commented on the ways in which the "padding" common among newspaper reporters in the 1890s was due not to a love of "long-winded yarns" but to the economic necessities of the space-rate system, in which reporters were paid by the word. "The general practice of paying space rates had the effect of causing reporters to 'pad' their writing . . . Reporters tended to write long rather than tightly and concisely." Ted Curtis Smythe, "The Reporter, 1880–1900. Working Conditions and Their Influence on the News," *Journalism History* 7, no. 1 (Spring 1980):6. The editor of the *Journalist* commented in 1887, "It is easy for a man with an ample salary to say that a newspaper writer should state facts just as they are, with no exaggeration, but when a reporter knows that the plain 'fire' is worth a dollar and the 'conflagration' will make him a possible ten, the fire is very apt to conflagrate if ingenuity can persuade the city editor to allow it to do so. It is the natural result of the space system where the worker is paid not for work but frequently for padding." "The Space System," *Journalist* 5 (August 6, 1887), quoted in ibid., p. 8. Dreiser was paid "on space" for a number of years.
25. Dreiser, *Newspaper Days*, p. 66.
26. Ibid., p. 415.
27. More than ninety clippings from Dreiser's "Heard in the Corridors" column are in the Dreiser clippings file at the University of Pennsylvania Library's Dreiser Collection.
28. Dreiser, "The Great Game To-Day," *St. Louis Republic*, July 17, 1893, p. 2.
29. Dreiser, *Newspaper Days*, p. 483.
30. Ibid., p. 485.
31. Ibid., p. 1.
32. Eugene Field, *Sharps and Flats* (a collection of Field's newspaper columns), 2 vols. (New York: Charles Scribner's Sons, 1900), collated by S. Thompson. For hoax stories see 1:108–11, 255–56.
33. Field, ibid., p. 90.
34. Ibid., p. 171.
35. Dreiser, *An American Tragedy* (New York: Horace Liveright, 1925), New American Library, Signet Classic reprint edition, p. 256 (this edition hereafter cited as *An American Tragedy*).
36. Schudson, *Discovering the News*, p. 71.
37. Ibid., pp. 72–77.
38. Dreiser, *Newspaper Days*, p. 78.
39. See David Brion Davis, "Dreiser and Naturalism Revisited," in Alfred Kazin, ed., *The Stature of Theodore Dreiser* (Bloomington: Indiana University Press, 1955), pp. 225–36.
40. Dreiser, *Newspaper Days*, p. 2.
41. H. L. Mencken in H. L. Mencken, ed., Theodore Dreiser, *An American Tragedy*, Memorial Edition (Cleveland: World Publishing Co., 1946), p. ix.
42. Ibid., p. xii.
43. Dreiser, *Newspaper Days*, p. 149.
44. Lincoln Steffens, *Autobiography* (New York: Harcourt, Brace, 1931), pp. 206–7 (cited in Ziff, *The American 1890s*, p. 152).
45. Ziff, ibid., p. 152.

46. Ibid., chap. 6, "The Tinkle of the Little Bell," pp. 120-45.
47. [Dreiser], "The Black Diva's Concert," *St. Louis Globe-Democrat*, April 1, 1893, p. 8.
48. Dreiser, *Newspaper Days*, pp. 184-88.
49. Ibid., p. 406.
50. The term "relative deprivation" was first coined by the authors of *The American Soldier*, ed. Samuel A. Stouffer et al. (Princeton, N.J.: Princeton University Press, 1949). See W. G. Runciman, *Relative Deprivation and Social Justice* (Berkeley and Los Angeles: University of California Press, 1966), for a fuller discussion of the concept.
51. [Dreiser], "Reflections," *Ev'ry Month* 2 (August 1896):6, signed, "The Prophet," reprinted in *Dreiser: Uncollected Prose*, "A New York City Tragedy," pp. 81-82.
52. [Dreiser], "Reflections," *Ev'ry Month* 2 (June 1896):5-6, signed, "The Prophet," reprinted in *Dreiser: Uncollected Prose*, "Suicide," pp. 68-69.
53. Dreiser, *An American Tragedy*, p. 220.
54. Dreiser, "The Loneliness of the City," *Tom Watson's Magazine* 2 (October 1905):474-75.
55. Dreiser, Editorial, *Delineator* 63, no. 2 (February 1909):n.p.
56. [Dreiser], "Reflections," *Ev'ry Month* 3 (October 1896): 6-7, signed, "The Prophet," reprinted in *Dreiser: Uncollected Prose*, "The City," pp. 95-99.
57. Dreiser, "Great American Caricaturist," *Ainslee's* 1, no. 4 (May 1898):336.
58. Dreiser, "A Master of Photography: Alfred Steiglitz [sic] Has Proven that a Great Photograph Is Worth Years of Labor to Make," *Success*, June 10, 1899, p. 471.
59. Dreiser, "The Runner," *Moods: Philosophical and Emotional, Cadenced and Declaimed* (New York: Simon and Schuster, 1935), p. 323.
60. Dreiser, "Life, Art and America," *Seven Arts*, February 1917 (offprint), p. 7.
61. Ibid., pp. 19, 10, 10.
62. Ibid. Original "Mirage" title noted in *Theodore Dreiser: The American Diaries 1902-1926*, ed. Thomas P. Riggio (Philadelphia: University of Pennsylvania Press, 1982), p. 351n.
63. Dreiser, "Life, Art and America," p. 23.
64. Dreiser, "Hey, Rub-a-Dub-Dub!," in *Hey, Rub-a-Dub-Dub: A Book of the Mystery and Wonder and Terror of Life* (New York: Boni and Liveright, 1920), pp. 1-18.
65. Dreiser, "The Scope of Fiction," in "The Novel of Tomorrow: The Scope of Fiction," pt. 2, *New Republic*, April 12, 1922, p. 8.
66. Charles Hanson Towne, *Adventures in Editing* (New York: Farrar and Rinehart, 1937), p. 13. (While he produced a fair amount of drivel at Butterick's, Dreiser also dealt with such serious issues as the need for all citizens to address the growing urban problem of tuberculosis and its causes. See Dreiser, "The Sin of the Cities," *Delineator*, March 1909, p. 392.)
67. Robert Elias, ed., Preface to *Letters of Theodore Dreiser*, 3 vols. (Philadelphia: University of Pennsylvania Press, 1959), 1:8.
68. Dreiser to Harold Hersey, December 19, 1915, in Elias, ed., *Letters*, 1:205.
69. Swanberg, *Dreiser*, p. 45; James Lundquist, *Theodore Dreiser*, Modern Literature Monographs (New York: Frederick Ungar, 1974), p. 7.

70. The story was "The Shining Slave Makers." Swanberg, *Dreiser*, p. 82. Dreiser to Robert Underwood Johnson, January 9, 1900, in Elias, ed., *Letters*, 1:45. The story was eventually published as "McEwen of the Shining Slave Makers," *The Best Short Stories of Theodore Dreiser*, pp. 90–104.

71. Dreiser, "Curious Shifts of the Poor," *Demorest's* 36 (November 1900): 22–26, and "Whence the Song," *Harper's Weekly*, December 8, 1899, pp. 1165–66A. See also Richard Lehan, *Theodore Dreiser: His World and His Novels* (Carbondale: Southern Illinois University Press, 1969), p. 55. There is some question (raised by the dates of publication of the articles) as to whether the articles were written with the novel in mind or whether they were written primarily as journalism.

72. W. A. Swanberg, *Dreiser* (New York: Charles Scribner's Sons, 1965), p. 87.

73. Dreiser, "A Lesson from the Aquarium," *Tom Watson's Magazine* 3 (January 1906): 306–8.

74. Robert Penn Warren, *Homage to Theodore Dreiser: August 27, 1871–December 28, 1945, On the Centennial of His Birth* (New York: Random House, 1971), p. 74.

75. The other books in the trilogy were *The Titan* (1914), and *The Stoic* (1947).

76. [Dreiser], "Pittsburgh" ("At the Sign of the Lead Pencil"), *Bohemian* 17 (December 1909): 712–14, reprinted in *Dreiser: Uncollected Prose*, pp. 171–74; [Dreiser], "The Factory," *1910* (n.d., n.p.), reprinted in *Dreiser: Uncollected Prose*, pp. 175–77; Dreiser, "The Man on the Bench," *New York Call*, November 16, 1913.

77. Dreiser to Jack Wilgus, April 20, 1927, in Elias, ed., *Letters*, 2:457–58.

78. Dreiser, "I Find the Real American Tragedy," *Mystery Magazine* 2 (February 1935):9–11, 88–90, reprinted in *Dreiser: Uncollected Prose*, p. 291.

79. Ibid., p. 293.

80. Ibid., p. 294.

81. Ibid., p. 293.

82. Ibid., p. 295.

83. Swanberg, *Dreiser*, p. 254.

84. Dreiser began one novel based on the 1899 case of a New York socialite named Roland Molineux, whose envy, ambition, and desire led him to commit murder. The novel was tentatively titled "The Rake," or "The Moron," and is considered by Moers and Lehan to be the first version of *An American Tragedy*. He began another novel based on the 1911 case of a young minister from Hyannis, Massachusetts, named Clarence Richesen, who murdered his pregnant sweetheart Avis Linnell when lured by marriage to a society girl and a prestigious post in a Cambridge church. A short story Dreiser wrote called "The Wages of Sin" may also have been based on a specific murder case. See Richard Lehan, *Theodore Dreiser* (Carbondale: Southern Illinois University Press, 1969), pp. 143–49; Ellen Moers, *Two Dreisers* (New York: Viking, 1969), pp. 197–99; and Robert Penn Warren, *Homage to Dreiser* (New York: Random House, 1971), pp. 97–98.

85. The dating of Dreiser's decision to base his novel on the Gillette case is that of Lehan, *Theodore Dreiser*, p. 143.

86. Dreiser, "I Find the Real American Tragedy," reprinted in *Dreiser: Uncollected Prose*, p. 294. Dreiser misremembered: the factory made skirts, not collars (nor shirts, as scholars have often wrongly noted).
87. For additional background, see Lehan, *Theodore Dreiser*, p. 147, on which much of this summary is based.
88. *New York World*, November 14, 1906, November 18, 1906, and November 29, 1906.
89. *New York World*, December 6, 1906, November 19, 1906, and November 19, 1906.
90. Swanberg (*Dreiser*, p. 254) states that in 1906 Dreiser saved clippings of the case and discussed it with Richard Duffy as a possible subject for a novel. Helen Dreiser, in a letter of February 15, 1945, to Robert H. Elias (in the Cornell University Library) enclosed a list of replies to a series of questions which Elias had asked Dreiser in a letter of February 4, 1945. In one such reply, Dreiser noted that he had been interested in the case in 1906 but that he did not think of it in connection with a novel "until four or five years" afterward. Dreiser's first recorded mention of the Gillette case occurs in his essay "Neurotic America and the Sex Impulse," written in 1918 and published in *Hey Rub-a-Dub-Dub*. Donald Pizer, *The Novels of Theodore Dreiser: A Critical Study* (Minneapolis: University of Minnesota Press, 1976), p. 364 (hereafter cited as *Novels*).
91. Dreiser "I Find the Real American Tragedy," reprinted in *Dreiser: Uncollected Prose*, p. 296.
92. Ibid., p. 297.
93. "Dreiser Bases New Novel on Famed Murder," *New York Herald Tribune*, January 3, 1926.
94. Ibid.
95. Ibid.
96. Ibid.
97. Both Moers (*Two Dreisers*, p. 44) and Pizer (*Novels*, pp. 215-17) acknowledge the difficulty of determining with precision the factual material on which Dreiser drew for the novel. Pizer makes a convincing case, however, for the idea that despite Dreiser's own reference to "testimony introduced at the trial," Dreiser in fact relied exclusively on the stories that appeared in the *New York World* "for his verbatim material and for almost all other explicit detail." The *World* presented paraphrased notes on the trial as verbatim transcript. The *New York Herald Tribune* article cited above simply cites newspaper files as *its* source, thus probably corroborating Pizer's hypothesis.
98. Pizer, *Novels*, p. 215.
99. Ibid., p. 365.
100. Helen Dreiser, *My Life with Dreiser* (Cleveland: World Publishing Co., 1951), p. 85. See also *Diaries*, pp. 400-402.
101. Dreiser to H. L. Mencken, December 3, 1925, in Dreiser, *Letters*, ed., Elias, 2:436. See also "Dreiser Interviews Pantano in Death House; Doomed Man Avows Faith in a Hereafter," *New York World*, November 30, 1935.
102. The one exception to this pattern is the Molineux case, in which the criminal intended to murder another man.

103. Dreiser to Jack Wilgus, April 20, 1927, in Elias, ed., *Letters*, 2:457-58.
104. Warren, *Homage to Dreiser*, p. 91.
105. The "collar" image suggests binding and confinement; Clyde will soon be bound and confined by the world he encounters in Lycurgus—by the social world to which he becomes attracted, by Roberta, and eventually, by the law. The camera is a more probable object to bring in a rowboat than a tennis racket was; it also reiterates the notion of fact as fate, since the pictures in the camera help make the case against Clyde. The addition of the local political battle to the trial makes Clyde once again seem something of a pawn in the hands of forces beyond his control and comprehension.

Donald Pizer comments on a number of additional changes in the Gillette story made by Dreiser in his novel: the casting of the major events of the novel in the 1920s, instead of the 1900s, making Lycurgus a more cosmopolitan city than Cortland had been, and making Cataraqui County more rural than Herkimer had been. Dreiser also revised the dates of the victim's pregnancy and of the trial. He compressed and condensed the court records in the novel, and rearranged the order in which the victim's letters were read to the court. All of these changes, Pizer notes, helped intensify the drama and immediacy of Clyde's story and helped render his fate more inevitable (Pizer, *Novels*, pp. 218-26).
106. Dreiser, "Life, Art and America," p. 7.
107. Dreiser, *Dawn: A History of Myself* (New York: Horace Liveright, 1931), p. 125. Titles specifically mentioned by Dreiser include: *Brave and Bold*, *Pluck and Luck*, and *Work and Win*.
108. Sam Barker, the hero of *The Young Outlaw* (1875) and *Sam's Chance* (1876), gambles, smokes, and steals. Only at the close of the second volume does his conscience become active. "When he realizes that he could carry the stigma of dishonor for the rest of his life, there is 'kindled in him a new and honorable ambition to attain a respectable position in society' " (*Sam's Chance*, p. 139). Gary Scharnhorst, *Horatio Alger, Jr.* (Boston: Twayne Publishers, 1980), p. 98. Sam regrets his past and resolves to turn over a new leaf. He is offered a respectable job and is on the mend when the novel closes.
109. Scharnhorst, *Horatio Alger, Jr.*, pp. 67-68. Other aspects of the standard Alger plot which Scharnhorst mentions have some bearing on Dreiser's plot as well. Scharnhorst refers to the hero's struggle to "clear his or another's name of false accusations." Clyde insists to his mother that he was not to blame for the accident. Scharnhorst refers to a foil that is frequently offered to Alger heroes, "usually a . . . snob, whose behavior is supremely selfish." Gilbert Griffiths has many of the "snob's" characteristics. The "trappings of respectability" with which the adult patron rewards the Alger hero are usually "a watch and a new suit." Clyde indicates that a new dress suit is one of the things he plans to buy with one of his first paychecks.
110. Dreiser, *An American Tragedy*, p. 169.
111. Moers, *Two Dreisers*, p. 201.
112. Ralph D. Gardner, *Horatio Alger, or The American Hero Era* (Mendota, Ill.: Wayside Press, 1964), p. 342.
113. Scharnhorst, *Horatio Alger, Jr.*, p. 92.

114. In addition to being able to dismiss the account as involving people very different from himself, the reader of a newspaper article is able to assume that he knows all he needs to know about the matter at hand. As Walter Benjamin has commented in *Illuminations*, a newspaper article gives the appearance of being "understandable in itself" (New York: Harcourt, Brace and World, 1968), pp. 88-90. Addressing this subject from a slightly different angle, Dreiser commented on the "mental pablum" newspapers normally fed their readers in an article entitled, "Our Greatest Writer Tells What Is Wrong with Our Newspapers," *Pep* 2, no. 7 (July 1917):9. The reader is presented with a set of tidy facts and explanations that reduce the complexity of events into a formulaic pyramid structure that suggests that anything that has been left out is of only minor importance. For additional comments on the press by Dreiser see "Reflections," *Ev'ry Month* 2 (May 1896): 2-3, signed "The Prophet," in Dreiser, *Uncollected Prose*, pp. 51-52, and "The Literary Shower," *Ev'ry Month* 2 (June 1896): 22, signed "Edward Al," in Dreiser, *Uncollected Prose*, p. 73.

115. Dreiser, *Newspaper Days*, p. 133.

116. Dreiser, *An American Tragedy*, p. 180.

117. Dreiser, "I Find the Real American Tragedy," reprinted in *Dreiser: Uncollected Prose*, p. 298.

118. James Lundquist makes this point in *Theodore Dreiser* (New York: Frederick Ungar, 1974), p. 98.

119. Ibid.

120. Lehan, *Theodore Dreiser*, p. 146.

121. Ibid., p. 149.

122. Another standard construction would allow Dreiser to insert "was" before plumbing, but this construction is more awkward and does not capture quite the same sense of the passage. I would suggest that what we have here is a fragment of the sort of sentence G. Scheurweghs cites in *Present-Day English Syntax: A Survey of Sentence Patterns* (London: Longmans, Green, 1959) as a participle "in a passive construction" (p. 167). His example of this pattern is: "The ship was found drifting in the North Sea" (p. 167). The complete sentence in *An American Tragedy*, revised according to this "passive construction" format, would read: "And suddenly becoming conscious that his courage . . . was leaving him, he found himself instantly and consciously plumbing the depths of his being."

123. Some early examples in the closing pages of book 2 of *An American Tragedy* are: (1) "And once on sure ground, actually pretending to be seeking out various special views here and there, while he fixed in his mind the exact tree at the base of which he might leave his bag against his return—which must be soon now—must be soon" (p. 490). (2) "And Clyde, assuring her that presently they would [be starting back]—after he had made one or two more pictures of her in the boat with those wonderful trees—that island and this dark water around and beneath her" (p. 491). (3) "And then, at this point and time looking fearfully about" (p. 491).

124. Some of these ambiguous constructions are oddly reminiscent of techniques Melville used in *The Confidence-Man*. For a lucid discussion of Melville's use

of "notations and counternotations, and . . . phrases that modify, hesitantly contradict, and then utterly cancel one another out, leaving not a rack of positive statement behind," see R. W. B. Lewis, *Trials of the Word: Essays in American Literature and the Humanistic Tradition* (New Haven: Yale University Press, 1965), pp. 64–66. Melville's self-negating sentences are indeed, as Lewis puts it, "mental and moral sabotage" (p. 65). While Dreiser's ambiguous constructions are not nearly as extreme as those of Melville, they serve a similar end, forcing the reader to wonder whether, in fact, he knows anything at all, with certainty, about the scene that has just been painted for him.

125. Vrest Orton, *Dreiserana: A Book About His Books* (New York: Stratford Press, The Corcorus Bibliographies, 1929), pp. 52–53.

126. Dreiser, *Moods*, p. 323.

127. Dreiser, *An American Tragedy*, pp. 7, 811. (A dash separates "Dusk" and "of" in chap. 1, and a comma in the closing chapter, "Souvenir.")

5. Ernest Hemingway

1. Hemingway quoted in George Plimpton, "An Interview with Ernest Hemingway" (1954), in *Hemingway and His Critics: An International Anthology*, ed. Carlos Heard Baker (New York: Hill and Wang, 1961), p. 37.

2. Ernest Hemingway, *Death in the Afternoon* (New York: Charles Scribner's Sons, 1932), p. 95.

3. Hemingway, *For Whom the Bell Tolls* (New York: Charles Scribner's Sons, 1940), p. 466.

4. Hemingway, *Death in the Afternoon*, p. 2.

5. "A family journal . . . strictly first-class," was how the *Kansas City Star* characterized itself in an early statement of purpose. *Kansas City Evening Star*, September 18, 1880, quoted in William G. Bleyer, *Main Currents in the History of American Journalism* (Cambridge, Mass.: Riverside Press, 1927; reprint edition, Da Capo Press, 1973), p. 315.

6. Icie F. Johnson, *William Rockhill Nelson and the Kansas City "Star,"* Introd. by William Allen White (Kansas City, Mo.: Burton Publishing Co., 1935), p. 152.

7. Ibid., p. 142.

8. Ibid., p. 127.

9. William Rockhill Nelson quoted in Bleyer, *Main Currents in American Journalism*, p. 316.

10. *The Kansas City Star* style sheet in use when Hemingway worked for the paper was graciously supplied by George R. Burg, executive assistant to the president of the *Kansas City Star* and the *Kansas City Times*. All references to the "style sheet" are to that version. According to Cruise Palmer, executive editor of the *Star* and the *Times* from 1967 to 1978, the style sheet was used as far back as the turn of the century, although there is no record of exactly when it was first assembled (personal communication). By the time Hemingway worked at the *Star* the style sheet was well established.

11. *Kansas City Star* "style sheet."

12. Hemingway quoted in Carlos Heard Baker, *Hemingway: The Writer as Artist* (Princeton, N.J.: Princeton University Press, 1973), p. 339.

13. Hemingway quoted in ibid., p. 179.

14. Hemingway, *Death in the Afternoon*, p. 191.

15. Ibid., p. 71.

16. Pete Wellington quoted in Charles Andrew Fenton, *The Apprenticeship of Ernest Hemingway: The Early Years* (New York: Farrar, Straus and Young, 1954), p. 42.

17. Hemingway quoted in ibid.

18. Ibid., pp. 42-43.

19. William Rockhill Nelson quoted in Icie Johnson, *Nelson and the Kansas City "Star,"* p. 89.

20. Fenton, *The Apprenticeship of Ernest Hemingway*, p. 35.

21. Ibid., p. 34.

22. Ernest Hemingway, "At the End of the Ambulance Run," *Kansas City Star,* January 20, 1919, reprinted in *Ernest Hemingway, Cub Reporter: Kansas City Star Stories,* ed. Matthew J. Bruccoli (Pittsburgh: University of Pittsburgh Press, 1970), pp. 27-33. (Hereafter cited as *Kansas City Star Stories.*)

23. Hemingway, "Would 'Treat 'Em Rough,'" *Kansas City Star,* n.d., reprinted in *Kansas City Star Stories,* pp. 50-55.

24. Hemingway, "Mix War, Art and Dancing," *Kansas City Star,* April 21, 1918, reprinted in *Kansas City Star Stories,* pp. 56-58.

25. Hemingway quoted in Fenton, *Apprenticeship of Hemingway,* p. 70.

26. Ibid., p. 76.

27. Hemingway, "The Best Rainbow Trout Fishing," *Toronto Star Weekly,* August 28, 1920, reprinted in *By-Line: Ernest Hemingway: Selected Articles and Dispatches of Four Decades,* ed. William White (New York: Charles Scribner's Sons, 1967), pp. 9-12.

28. Hemingway, "Plain and Fancy Killings, $400 Up," *Toronto Star Weekly,* December 11, 1920, reprinted in *By-Line,* pp. 13-15.

29. Hemingway, "Mussolini: Biggest Bluff in Europe," *Toronto Daily Star,* January 27, 1923, reprinted in *By-Line,* p. 63.

30. Hemingway, "King Business in Europe," *Toronto Star Weekly,* September 15, 1923, reprinted in *By-Line,* p. 77.

31. Hemingway, "Mussolini: Biggest Bluff in Europe," *Toronto Daily Star,* January 27, 1923, reprinted in *By-Line,* p. 69.

32. Hemingway, "The Best Rainbow Trout Fishing," *Toronto Star Weekly,* August 28, 1920, reprinted in *By-Line,* pp. 9-10.

33. Fenton, *Apprenticeship of Hemingway,* p. 172.

34. As Jeffrey Meyers has noted, Hemingway's experiences covering the aftermath of the Greco-Turkish war produced, in addition to fourteen articles for the *Toronto Star,* three vignettes in *in our time* (1924), "On the Quai at Smyrna," added to the 1930 edition of *In Our Time* (1925), two passages in *Death in the Afternoon* (1932), two flashbacks in "The Snows of Kilimanjaro" (1936), and other writings. Jeffrey Meyers, "Hemingway's Second War: The Greco-Turkish Conflict, 1920-1922," *Modern Fiction Studies* 30, no. 1 (Spring 1984): 25-36.

35. Fenton, *Apprenticeship of Hemingway*, p. 174.
36. Hemingway, "A Silent, Ghastly Procession," *Toronto Daily Star*, October 20, 1922, reprinted in *By-Line*, p. 51.
37. Hemingway quoted in Baker, *The Writer as Artist*, pp. 13-14.
38. Hemingway, "The Shelling of Madrid," NANA Dispatch, April 11, 1937, reprinted in *By-Line*, p. 259.
39. Hemingway to Gertrude Stein and Alice B. Toklas, November 9, 1923, in Carlos Baker, ed., *Ernest Hemingway: Selected Letters, 1917-1961* (London: Granada Publishing, 1981), p. 101. For additional comments by Hemingway on journalism, see "An Old Newsman Writes: Letter from Cuba," *Esquire*, December 1934, reprinted in *By-Line*, pp. 179-91, and "Monologue to the Maestro: A High Seas Letter," *Esquire*, October 1935, reprinted in *By-Line*, pp. 213-20.
40. Hemingway quoted in Fenton, *Apprenticeship of Hemingway*, p. 161.
41. Hemingway, *A Moveable Feast* (Harmondsworth, Eng.: Penguin Books, 1964), p. 16.
42. Ibid., p. 15.
43. Baker, *The Writer as Artist*, p. 8.
44. Ezra Pound, *Literary Essays of Ezra Pound*, ed. T. D. Eliot (Norfolk, Conn.: New Directions, 1954), pp. 43-44. (See also Richard K. Peterson, *Hemingway: Direct and Oblique* [The Hague: Mouton, 1969], p. 141.)
45. Hemingway, *A Moveable Feast*, p. 97.
46. Baker, *The Writer as Artist*, pp. 51-52.
47. Ernest Hemingway, *The Sun Also Rises* (New York: Charles Scribner's Sons, 1926), p. 245. As Harry Levin has observed, Wilsonian idealism and Wilsonian rhetoric had led a generation of writers to be suspicious of both ideals and rhetoric, mistrusting, indeed, words themselves. (Cited in Richard K. Peterson, *Hemingway: Direct and Oblique* [The Hague: Mouton, 1969], p. 121.) Richard Peterson has noted (p. 60) that a distrust of words runs like a refrain through the work of many of the expatriate writers who congregated in Paris after World War I. He sees it in

   E. E. Cummings's *The Enormous Room*, for instance, with its exposé of "those unspeakable foundations upon which are built with infinite care such at once ornate and comfortable structures as "La Gloire" and "Le Patriotisme," a book which Hemingway wrote Edmund Wilson in 1923 was the "best book published last year that I read." It appears in John Andrews' reflections after talking to the "Y" man in *Three Soldiers:* "Men were more humane when they were killing each other than when they were talking about it. So was civilization nothing but a vast edifice of sham, and the war, instead of its crumbling, was its fullest and most ultimate expression . . . Were they all shams, too, these gigantic phrases that floated like gaudy kites high above mankind? Kites, that was it, contraptions of tissue paper held at the end of a string, ornaments not to be taken seriously." Dos Passos' later hero Jimmy Herf echoes the distrust in the more "objective" manner of *Manhattan Transfer:* "His mind unreeling phrases, he walks on doggedly. . . . If only I still had faith in words."
48. Hemingway, *A Farewell to Arms* (New York: Bantam Books, 1949), p. 137.
49. For more on this point see also Peterson, *Hemingway: Direct and Oblique*, p. 20.

50. Ernest Hemingway, *in our time* (Paris: Bird and McAlmon, 1924). (*in our time* contained what would become the interchapters of *In Our Time*. None of the short stories was included in it.)
51. One recounts a robbery that Hemingway may have covered for the paper; it manifests the conciseness, precision, and freshness of perspective that was demanded of *Star* reporters, as well as the idiosyncrasies of spelling and terminology required by the style sheet (Fenton, *Apprenticeship of Hemingway*, p. 45). The second vignette, which describes the hanging of Sam Cardinella at the county jail, does not have a specific factual base in Hemingway's reporting; but the *Star*'s forty-year veteran police reporter William Moorhead has attested to the fact that in all aspects but the actual incident of the hanging, the narrative conforms to facts Hemingway had often recorded in his company on assignments in 1918 (p. 56). He found Hemingway's picture "an accurate description of the dismal, massive brick building" of the old Jackson County Jail at Missouri Avenue and Oak Street; he also mentioned a Kansas City criminal with the same name as the central figure in this vignette. See also Michael S. Reynolds, "Two Hemingway Sources for *In Our Time*," *Studies in Short Fiction*, Winter 1972, pp. 81–86.
52. Hemingway to Edmund Wilson, October 18, 1924, in *Letters*, p. 128.
53. Hemingway, "A Silent, Ghastly Procession," *Toronto Daily Star*, October 20, 1922, reprinted in *By-Line*, pp. 51–52.
54. Hemingway *In Our Time* (New York: Charles Scribner's Sons, 1925), p. 21.
55. Edmund Wilson, Introduction to *In Our Time: Stories by Ernest Hemingway* (New York: Charles Scribner and Sons, 1930), p. xv.
56. Some of the material that appears in an unpublished NANA cable Hemingway sent on May 2, 1937, in which he describes a trip he took to the Sierra de Guadarrama, prefigures material he would later use in *For Whom the Bell Tolls*. He comments on the difficulty of the climb to the high mountain positions and the intelligence and discipline of the people fighting in the mountains under the guidance of Loyalist army officers; he also describes the experience of riding along the mountain roads in an armored car under machine gunfire. The NANA cable was made available through the courtesy of the United Feature Syndicate Vice President and Executive Director Sidney Goldberg. (NANA was absorbed by United Feature.)
57. Hemingway, *For Whom the Bell Tolls*, p. 236.
58. Herbert L. Matthews, *The Yoke and the Arrows: A Report on Spain* (New York: George Braziller, 1957), p. 19.
59. See George Seldes, *Even the Gods Can't Change History: The Facts Speak for Themselves* (Secaucus, N.J.: Lyle Stuart, 1976), p. 57; and James Benet and Bruce Bliven, Jr., "Who Lied About Spain?," *New Republic*, June 28, 1939.
60. Benet and Bliven, "Who Lied About Spain?," pp. 211–12.
61. George Seldes, *Even the Gods Can't Change History*, p. 57.
62. Benet and Bliven, "Who Lied About Spain?," p. 212.
63. Hemingway to Hadley Mowrer, January 31, 1938, in *Letters*, p. 462. See also Herbert L. Matthews, *The Education of a Correspondent* (New York: Harcourt, Brace & Co., 1946), pp. 91–117.

64. Hemingway to Mrs. Paul Pfeiffer, Key West, February 6, 1939, in *Letters*, p. 476.

65. Jasper Wood, Introduction to *The Spanish Earth* (film script), by Ernest Hemingway (Cleveland: J. B. Savage Co., 1938), pp. 10–12.

66. Joris Ivens, *The Camera and I* (New York: International Publishers, 1969), p. 113–14.

67. Eric Barnouw, *Documentary: A History of the Non-Fiction Film* (New York: Oxford University Press, 1974), p. 136.

68. Reviews quoted in Ivens, *The Camera and I*, pp. 133–34.

69. Hemingway quoted in Baker, *A Life Story*, p. 308.

70. Hemingway quoted in ibid., p. 316.

71. Hemingway, *The Spanish Earth*, p. 23.

72. Ibid., p. 24.

73. When Hemingway read his own narration, Ivens recalls, "his commentary sounded like that of a sensitive reporter who has been on the spot and wants to tell you about it—a feeling that no other voice could communicate. The lack of a professional commentator's smoothness helped you to believe intensely in the experiences on the screen" (*The Camera and I*, p. 129). As Lillian Hellman, one of the "Contemporary Historians," has commented, Hemingway "felt deeply enough [about the cause the film hoped to further] not to care that he often sounded like a parody of himself." *An Unfinished Woman: A Memoir* (New York: Little, Brown and Co., 1969), p. 66.

74. Hemingway in Henry Hart, ed., *The Writer in a Changing World* (New York: Equinox Cooperative Press, 1937), p. 69.

75. Hemingway, *For Whom the Bell Tolls*, pp. 13, 439.

76. Ibid., p. 13. (Pablo, who could not read, appraises Jordan's claims to being the man he says he is by observing Jordan's knowledge of horses.)

77. Arturo Barea, "Not Spain But Hemingway," in *Hemingway and His Critics*, ed. Baker, pp. 202–12. "As a novel about Spaniards and their war," Barea writes, the book "is unreal and, in the last analysis, deeply untruthful." Critics who challenged Hemingway's political analysis often claimed, nevertheless, that "Hemingway knows his Spain profoundly," or commended Hemingway for having documented "astonishingly real Spanish conversation"; but Barea proves, with painstaking care, that Hemingway lacks in significant ways, a genuine understanding of both Spain and the Spanish language. Reading *For Whom the Bell Tolls*, Barea writes,

   you will indeed come to understand some aspects of Spanish character and life but you will misunderstand more, and more important ones at that. Ernest Hemingway does know "his Spain." But it is precisely his intimate knowledge of this narrow section of Spain which has blinded him to a wider and deeper understanding, and made it difficult for him to "write the war we have been fighting." Some of his Spanish conversations are perfect, but others, often of great significance for the structure of the book, are totally un-Spanish. He has not mastered the intricate "hierarchy of Spanish blasphemy" (anyhow the most difficult thing for a foreigner in any language, since it is based on ancient taboos and half-conscious superstitions). He commits a series of grave linguistic-psychological mistakes in this book—such, indeed, as I have heard him commit when he joked with the orderlies in my Madrid office. Then we grinned at his solecisms because we liked him. Hemingway has understood the emotions which our "people as a whole" felt in the bull ring, but not those which it felt in the collective action of war and revolution. . . . The strength of his artistry makes fiction sound like distilled reality. (Pp. 202-3)

78. John Darnton, "On the Hemingway Literary Trail Through Spain," *New York Times*, July 3, 1984. John Darnton cites a paper given by Professor Ramon Buckley at the Madrid meeting of the Hemingway Society, in which Buckley noted that "the terrain [of the Guadarrama mountains where *For Whom the Bell Tolls* is set] did not have caves for Pablo's band of fighters to live in. Nor was it likely, as Mr. Buckley noted, that any single mountain band of Republican guerillas included such an odd-lot assortment of peasants, gypsies, Basques and Castillians."

6. John Dos Passos

1. Oscar Wilde, *The Decay of Lying* (1889), excerpted in *The Modern Tradition*, ed. Richard Ellmann and Charles Feidelson (New York: Oxford University Press, 1965), p. 19. Reference to "rimeless sonnets," Dos Passos to Rumsey Marvin (Spring 1916), in Townsend Ludington, ed., *The Fourteenth Chronicle: Letters and Diaries of John Dos Passos* (Boston: Gambit, 1973), pp. 32-33.

2. John Dos Passos, *The Best Times: An Informal Memoir* (New York: New American Library, 1966), p. 23.

3. Ibid.

4. Ibid., p. 24. For more on Dos Passos's Harvard years see Charles Bernardin, "John Dos Passos' Harvard Years," *New England Quarterly* 27, no. 1 (March 1954): 3-26. See also Malcolm Cowley, *A Second Flowering* (New York: Viking Press, 1972), pp. 74-89; Townsend Ludington, *John Dos Passos: A Twentieth Century Odyssey* (New York: E. P. Dutton, 1980), pp. 50-94, and Virginia Spencer Carr, *Dos Passos* (Garden City, N.Y.: Doubleday, 1984), pp. 48-93.

5. Dos Passos, "The Unemployment Report," *New Masses*, February 13, 1934, pp. 11-12.

6. Dos Passos, *U.S.A.*, 3 vols., vol. 3: *The Big Money* (New York: New American Library Signet Classic reprint edition, 1969), pp. 52-53, 553-56 (originally published in 1936).

7. Dos Passos, "Back to Red Hysteria," *New Republic* 66 (April 1, 1931): 168-69.

8. Dos Passos, *The Big Money*, pp. 441-556.

9. Dos Passos, "300 N.Y. Agitators Reach Passaic," *New Masses* 1 (June 1926): 8.

10. Dos Passos, "Paint the Revolution," *New Masses* 2 (March 1927): 150; "Relief Map of Mexico," *New Masses* 2 (April 1927): 24; "Zapata's Ghost Walks," *New Masses* 3 (September 1927): 11-12.

11. Dos Passos, "Detroit: City of Leisure," *New Republic* 71 (July 13, 1932): 280-82.

12. Dos Passos, *The Big Money*, Newsreel LIX, p. 299.

13. Dos Passos, "An Appeal for Aid," *New Republic* 67 (August 5, 1931): 318;

"Harlan: Working Under the Gun," *New Republic* 69 (December 2, 1931):62–67; "In Defense of Kentucky," *New Republic* 69 (December 16, 1931): 137.

14. Dos Passos, *The Big Money*, Newsreel LXVIII, pp. 519–21.

15. Dos Passos, *The Big Money*, Camera Eye #51, pp. 522–23.

16. For a good example of a *New Masses* biography in this style *not* written by Dos Passos, see Michael Gold, "The Loves of Isadora," *New Masses* 4 (March 1929): 20–21. Dos Passos was undoubtedly familiar with this piece and probably had it in mind when he wrote the "Art and Isadora" biography that appeared in *The Big Money* in 1936 (pp. 170–76). The analogy Dos Passos draws on p. 173 between Isadora and Walt Whitman was first drawn by Gold in this article with a slightly different slant ("The Loves of Isadora," p. 20). See Dos Passos, "American Portraits," *New Masses* 5 (January 1930): 3–5; "Two Portraits," *New Masses* 5 (February 1930): 8–9; "Lover of Mankind," *New Masses* 5 (March 1930): 8; "Jack Reed," *New Masses* 6 (October 1930): 13–14, etc.

17. Dos Passos, "Edison and Steinmetz: Medicine Men," *New Republic* 61 (December 18, 1929): 103–4.

18. Dos Passos, "Wanted: An Ivy Lee for Liberals," *New Republic* 63 (August 13, 1930): 371–72.

19. John Dewey, *Individualism Old and New* (New York: Minton, Balch, 1930), p. 44 (cited in Schudson, *Discovering the News*, p. 141).

20. Bureau of the Census, *Historical Statistics*, 2: 855 (cited in Ben H. Bagdikian, *The Media Monopoly* [Boston: Beacon Press, 1983], p. 151).

21. Coolidge speech quoted in Frank Spencer Presbrey, *The History and Development of Advertising* (New York: Doubleday, Doran, 1929), p. 619.

22. See Schudson, *Discovering the News*, pp. 138–44.

23. Dos Passos, "Wanted: An Ivy Lee for Liberals," p. 372. In this article Dos Passos discussed—half fancifully, half seriously—the idea of applying the talents of one of the rising stars of American public relations to persuade people that "the bitter sadism with which judges impose maximum sentences for political offenses are [*sic*] crimes against civilization and against the integrity of their own lives. The thought of what Eddie Bernays or Ivy Lee would do in the inconceivable possibility that enough money could be collected to hire one of these super-public-relations counsels and put him on the job is not entirely futile. After all, if by propaganda you can make women wear corsets and everybody believe cigarettes are good for the voice, it's conceivable that by propaganda you can make them hate cruelty or tolerate the idea of change" (p. 372).

24. Dos Passos, *The Big Money*, pp. 43, 69, 169, 178, 251, 269, 292, 300, 337, 338, 352, 353, 386, 442, 445, 471, etc.

25. Dos Passos, "Against American Literature," *New Republic* 7 (October 14, 1916): 269–71.

26. Dos Passos, *Rosinante to the Road Again* (reprinted from periodical contributions), (New York: George H. Doran Co., 1922), p. 131.

27. Dos Passos, "The World We Live In," *New Republic* 79 (May 16, 1934): 25.

28. Dos Passos, "Young Spain," *Seven Arts* (August 1917): 473–88.

29. Dos Passos's journalism on Spain, much but not all of which is reprinted in *Rosinante to the Road Again*, includes: "Antonio Machado: Poet of Castile,"

Dial 68 (June 1920): 734-43; "Farmer Strikers in Spain" *Liberator* 3 (October 20, 1920): 28-30; "A Novelist of Disintegration," *Freeman* 2 (October 20, 1920): 132-34; "An Inverted Midas," *Freeman* 2 (November 10, 1920): 203-5; "A Catalan Poet," *Freeman* 2 (February 2, 1921): 489-90; "A Gesture of Castile," *Freeman* 2 (March 2, 1921): 586-88; "Benavente's Madrid," *Bookman* 53 (May 1921): 226-30; "The Gesture of Castile," pts. 1-2, *Freeman* 4 (December 21, 1921): 348-89; "The Gesture of Castile," pts. 3-4, *Freeman* 4 (December 28, 1921): 372-73; "The Gesture of Castile," pts. 5-6, *Freeman* 4 (January 4, 1922): 396-97; "The Gesture of Castile," pts. 7-8, *Freeman* 4 (January 11, 1922): 420-22; "Andalusian Ethics," pt. 1, *Freeman* 4 (February 1, 1922): 491-93; "Andalusian Ethics," pt. 2, *Freeman* 4 (February 8, 1922): 517-18; "Two Professors," *Broom* 2 (April 1922): 59-71; "Spirit of Spain," *Mentor* 10 (August 1922): 13-28, and of course, "Young Spain," as noted above, n. 28.

30. John Dos Passos, "The Pit and the Pendulum," *New Masses* 1 (August 1926): 10, 11, 30.

31. Ibid., p. 11. The press, as well as the law, played its role in letting the guilty verdict stand. As Ben Bagdikian has noted,

At the time of the arrests, most newspapers supported the Palmer Raids and, despite the overwhelming evidence of gross improprieties of justice, were enthusiastic about convicting Sacco and Vanzetti. . . . But in its great numbers and variety, it [the press] is also supposed to be a kind of balance wheel, bringing reason and diversity of opinion to its reporting and commentary. The balance wheel had failed. By the time Sacco and Vanzetti were to be electrocuted in 1927, most of the serious press had changed its mind. Reporters confirmed the state had been dishonest and suppressed evidence. Editors had become convinced that there had been a grave miscarriage of justice. It was too late. By that time the pride of the Commonwealth of Massachusetts had become attached to the need to electrocute the two defendants. The state, frozen in its attitude, resisted a commutation because, in the words of Herbert Ehrmann, an admirable lawyer in the case, it would have "signaled a weakness in our social order." In the United States we depend on our mass media to signal, among other things, "weakness within our social order." In 1921, when Sacco and Vanzetti were tried, newspapers failed to send that signal, though there was ample evidence to support one. (*The Media Monopoly* [Boston: Beacon Press, 1983], pp. viii-ix)

The press's role in shaping public opinion would become a central concern of Dos Passos's in *U.S.A.*

32. Dos Passos, *Facing the Chair: Story of the Americanization of Two Foreignborn Workmen* (Boston: Sacco-Vanzetti Defense Committee, 1927; New York: Da Capo Press, 1970).

33. For other accounts of the trial which appeared within a few years of Dos Passos's volume, see Felix Frankfurter, *The Case of Sacco and Vanzetti: A Critical Analysis for Lawyers and Laymen* (Boston: Little, Brown, 1927); Osmond K. Frankel, *The Sacco-Vanzetti Case* (New York: Alfred A. Knopf, 1931); and Herbert Brutus Ehrmann, *The Untried Case: The Sacco-Vanzetti Case and the Morelli Gang* (New York: Vanguard Press, 1933). It is not within

the scope of this book to pass judgment on Dos Passos's evaluation of the facts he collected. It may be of interest to note, however, that in the summer of 1977 the governor of Massachusetts issued a proclamation stating that there was good reason to doubt whether the Sacco-Vanzetti trial had been conducted "fairly and impartially" due to the atmosphere of "prejudice against foreigners and hostility towards unorthodox political views" that surrounded it. "A Proclamation by His Excellency Michael S. Dukakis, Governor" Commonwealth of Massachusetts, July 19, 1977.

34. Dos Passos, "Facing the Chair," pp. 56-57.
35. Walt Whitman, "The Sewing-Women of Brooklyn and New York," *Brooklyn Daily Eagle*, January 29, 1847, p. 2.
36. Dos Passos, "Facing the Chair," p. 126.
37. It is not clear to what extent the daily dispatches he sent to the *Daily Worker* match the articles datelined "Boston" which appeared in the newspaper that month. The articles are unsigned and may represent a fair amount of editing; they may also be composite pieces drawn from the reports of Dos Passos and others. It is likely, however, that Dos Passos contributed to the following unsigned articles that appeared in the *Daily Worker:* "Boston Tense as Sacco-Vanzetti Doom Hour Nears; International Strikes and Meetings Continue," *Daily Worker*, August 3, 1927, p. 1; "Sacco, Vanzetti Expected Decision," *Daily Worker*, August 5, 1927, pp. 1-2; "Boston Will Hold Big Sacco and Vanzetti Demonstration Sunday," *Daily Worker*, August 6, 1927, p. 1.
38. Dos Passos, "An Open Letter to President Lowell," *Nation* 125 (August 1927): 176. For additional details on Dos Passos's efforts on behalf of Sacco and Vanzetti see Carr, *Dos Passos*, pp. 222-23, 225-29; Ludington, *John Dos Passos*, pp. 246-48, 260-63; and Daniel Aaron, *Writers on the Left* (New York: Avon Books, Discus Edition, 1969), pp. 186-91.
39. Dos Passos, "Sacco and Vanzetti," *New Masses* 3 (November 1927): 25.
40. Dos Passos quoted in Ludington, *John Dos Passos*, p. 256.
41. Dos Passos quoted in ibid. Dos Passos respected history intensely and even went so far as to claim, in 1927, that "history is always more alive and more interesting than fiction. I suppose that is because a story is the daydream of a single man, while history is mass-invention, the daydream of a race." Dos Passos, quoted in John Wrenn, *John Dos Passos* (New York: Twayne Publishers, 1961), p. 149.
42. Dos Passos, "Sacco and Vanzetti," *New Masses* 3 (November 1928): 25; *The Big Money*, p. 462.
43. Dos Passos to Rumsey Marvin (Spring 1916), in Ludington, ed., *Letters*, pp. 32-33.
44. Dos Passos, *One Man's Initiation: 1917* (Ithaca, N.Y.: Cornell University Press, 1969), pp. 159-60.
45. Dos Passos, "The Use of the Past," from *The Ground We Stand On* (New York: Harcourt, Brace and World, 1941), reprinted in John Dos Passos, *Occasions and Protests* (Chicago: Henry Regnery, 1964), p. 36.
46. The *Times* is quoted in Ray Eldon Hiebert, *Courtier to the Crowd: The Story of Ivy Lee and the Development of Public Relations* (Ames: Iowa State University Press, 1966), p. 243. The historian quoted is Jack J. Roth, *World War I:*

A *Turning Point in Modern History* (New York: Alfred A. Knopf, 1967), p. 109. Both are cited in Schudson, *Discovering the News*, pp. 142, 212.

47. Edward L. Bernays, *Propaganda* (New York: Horace Liveright, 1928), p. 27. Cited in Schudson, *Discovering the News*, pp. 141, 212.

48. Dos Passos, *One Man's Initiation: 1917*, pp. 159-60.

49. Dos Passos, "The New Masses I'd Like," *New Masses* 1 (June 1926): 20. Dos Passos refers to "the great semi-parasitic class that includes all the trades that deal with words from advertising and the Christian ministry to song writing. Whether his aims are KKK or Communist he takes on the mind and functional deformities of his trade. The word-slinging organism is substantially the same whether it sucks its blood from Park Avenue or from Flatbush. At this moment it seems to me that the word-slinging classes, radical and fundamentalist, are further away from any reality than they've ever been."

50. Dos Passos, "The Use of the Past," p. 40.

51. Ludington, ed., *Letters* (connecting biographical narrative), p. 377.

52. William Stott comments on Dos Passos's "pastiche of actual headlines, dispatches, song lyrics, leaflets, stump speeches, and slogans" that "Though these documents were authentic, to make them carry his meaning Dos Passos had to submerge their original values—a task at which he proved himself a master." (*Documentary Expression and Thirties America* [New York: Oxford University Press, 1973], p. 120.)

53. Dos Passos, *U.S.A.*, 3 vols., vol. 1: *The Forty-Second Parallel* (New York: New American Library Signet Classic reprint edition, 1969), p. 168 (originally published in 1930). Dos Passos refers to the minister as "Richardson" and not "Richeson," but many newspapers and critics have made the same error; the case is clearly the same one Dreiser followed. (See above, chap. 4, n. 84.)

54. See note 16 above.

55. Dos Passos quoted in Ludington, *John Dos Passos*, p. 256.

56. Dos Passos quoted in Wrenn, *John Dos Passos*, p. 147. For Eisenstein's theory of "montage," see "Sergei Eisenstein: Collision of Ideas," in *Film: A Montage of Theories*, by Richard Dyer MacCann (New York: E. P. Dutton, 1966). For more on Dos Passos's interest in "montage," see Dos Passos, "What Makes a Novelist," *National Review* 20 (January 16, 1968): 31.

57. Before starting *U.S.A.*, Dos Passos also experimented in very limited ways with a montage of narratives (if not of narrative modes) in his 1925 novel *Manhattan Transfer*, in which fictional narratives dealing with characters from different strata of American life are skillfully interwoven. Dos Passos's experiments in this novel foreshadowed the "city symphonies" which French, German, and Dutch filmmakers would begin to produce a few years later. The most notable of these "city symphonies"—"rhythmic and kaleidoscopic . . . realistic, nonfiction views of brief episodes of city life, united within a larger structure . . . by the recurrence of images, motifs and themes that provides continuity and progression of ideas" (Richard Meran Barsam, *Nonfiction Film: A Critical History* [New York: E. P. Dutton, 1973], p. 29)—are: Alberto Cavalcanti's "Rien que les Heures" (1926), Walther Ruttman's "Berlin: The Symphony of a Great City" (1927), and (although more limited than these others) Joris Ivens's "The Bridge" (1927) and "Rain" (1929).

58. *American Heritage Dictionary of the English Language*, ed. William Morris (Boston: Houghton Mifflin, 1969), s.v. "Fugue."

59. As Stuart Ewen has commented, by the 1920s

industry was aware that the austerity of factory life which most workers experienced undermined the attempt to create a widespread consciousness of industrial commodities as forming an affirmative and indulgent culture. Within business thinking, then, it appeared necessary to eradicate the productive process from the ideology that surrounded the products. In ads, the commodities of industrial society were presented as means of circumventing the ills of industrial life. The reality of life within the factory only tended to cast aspersions on the visions of happiness projected in consumer ideology, and it was an essential principle of commercial propaganda that depiction of this reality be avoided at all costs. (*Captains of Consciousness: Advertising and the Social Roots of Consumer Culture* [New York: McGraw Hill, 1976], p. 78.)

Dos Passos's ironic juxtapositions between advertising copy for consumer goods and reports of industrial hazards and accidents force the reader to reconnect products with the conditions of their production. For a fuller discussion of how copywriters of the period consciously accentuated the positive aspects of modern industrial life and avoided any hint of factors that marred the roseate pictures they were painting, see Daniel Pope, *The Making of Modern Advertising* (New York: Basic Books, 1983), p. 243.

60. Dos Passos, *U.S.A.*, vol. 1: *The 42nd Parallel*, "Newsreel I," p. 27.

61. Mark Twain, *Adventures of Huckleberry Finn*, ed. Leo Marx (Indianapolis: Bobbs-Merrill, 1967), p. 252.

62. Dos Passos, *U.S.A.*, vol. 1: *The 42nd Parallel*, "Lover of Mankind": p. 51: "but on account of the flag / and prosperity / and making the world safe for democracy, / they were afraid to be with him. / or to think much about him for fear they might believe him . . ." Ibid., p. 52.

63. Ibid., "Mac," pp. 104-11, 115-24, 129-47, 314-33.

64. Ibid., "Newsreel VI," p. 81; ibid., "Mac," p. 120.

65. Dos Passos, *Rosinante to the Road Again*, p. 131.

66. Dos Passos, *U.S.A.*, vol. 1: *The 42nd Parallel*, "Newsreel VII," p. 103.

67. Ibid., "Newsreel VIII," p. 126; ibid., "Newsreel IX," p. 128.

68. Dos Passos, *U.S.A.*, vol. 2 (New York: New American Library Signet Classic reprint edition, 1969), *Nineteen Nineteen*, "Newsreel XXIII," p. 122 (identifying letters added) (originally published in 1932).

69. Dos Passos to Malcolm Cowley, February 1932, in Ludington, ed., *Letters*, p. 404.

70. Dos Passos, *U.S.A.*, vol. 3: *The Big Money*, "Charley Anderson," p. 31.

71. Ibid., "Adagio Dancer," p. 206; ibid., "The Bitter Drink," p. 119; ibid., "Architect," p. 440.

72. Schudson, *Discovering the News*, p. 143, writes:

Insull, Chicago's electric power baron, had begun advising the American branch of the British propaganda office in 1914. . . . Insull contributed a quarter million dollars of his own to help distribute highly colored war information to American newspapers which had no wire service affiliations. . . . After the war, in 1919, Insull organized the Illinois Public Utility Information

Committee, borrowing the propaganda machinery he had used during the war. Insull's biographer writes that by 1923 the utilities in many other states had followed suit and "were turning out a stream of utility publicity that almost matched the volume of patriotic publicity during the war." The public relations of the public utilities in the twenties was the most prominent campaign of any industry.

73. Dos Passos, *U.S.A.*, vol. 1: *The Big Money*, "POWER SUPERPOWER," pp. 523-28.

74. Dos Passos, Preface to *Three Soldiers* (New York: Random House, Modern Library, 1932), p. viii.

75. Alfred Kazin, *On Native Grounds: An Interpretation of Modern American Prose Literature* (New York: Harcourt Brace Jovanovich, 1982), p. 352 (originally published 1942). Kazin's readings of *U.S.A.* in *On Native Grounds* and elsewhere remain some of the finest discussions of Dos Passos that have appeared. In particular, his recognition of the importance of viewing the book itself as "another American invention—an American *thing* peculiar to the opportunity and stress of American life, like the Wright Brothers' airplane, Edison's phonograph, Luther Burbank's hybrids, Thorstein Veblen's social analysis, Frank Lloyd Wright's first office buildings" has added immeasurably to our critical perspective on Dos Passos. See *On Native Grounds*, pp. 240-359; Kazin's Introduction to the New American Library edition of *The Big Money* (pp. v-xvii); and Alfred Kazin, *An American Procession* (New York: Alfred A. Knopf, 1984), pp. 374-97.

76. Dos Passos, *U.S.A.*, vol. 3: *The Big Money*, "Vag," pp. 553-56.

Epilogue

1. Lennard Davis, *Factual Fictions: The Origins of the English Novel* (New York: Columbia University Press, 1983), pp. 51, 56, 58, 61, 66-70.

2. See ibid., pp. 155-56; see also Ian Watt, *The Rise of the Novel* (Berkeley and Los Angeles: University of California Press, 1971), pp. 103-4.

3. Popular novels in America from at least 1789 often claimed to be "Founded in Truth" or "Founded in Fact" in their subtitles. As Terrence Martin observes in *The Instructed Vision: Scottish Common Sense Philosophy and the Origins of American Fiction* (Bloomington: Indiana University Press, 1967), "*The Power of Sympathy* (1789)—claims to be 'Founded in Truth'; *The Hapless Orphan* (1794) is 'A Tale of Truth'; *The Coquette* (1797) is 'Founded on Fact'; both *Amelia, or the Faithless Briton* (1798) and *Julia and the Illuminated Baron* (1800) are 'Founded on Recent Facts'; while *The Last Resource, or Female Fortitude* (1809) is 'Founded on Recent Facts in the Western Parts of Pennsylvania' " (pp. 80-81). See also pp. 60-76, "The Case Against Fiction."

4. See Michael Schudson, *Discovering the News* (New York: Basic Books, 1978), for a perceptive discussion of attitudes toward facts in American journalism in the late nineteenth and early twentieth century (pp. 71-72, 75-81, 88-90, 121-22). See also Dan Schiller, *Objectivity and the News: The Public and the Rise of Commercial Journalism* (Philadelphia: University of Pennsylvania Press, 1981), pp. 76-124.

5. This distinction applies primarily to the "information model" of journalism,

which has traditionally been accorded greater respect among journalists and others than the "story model." See Schudson, *Discovering the News*, "Two Journalisms in the 1890's," pp. 88-120.

6. During the 1920s the reporter's domain was defined by journalists like Walter Lippmann as the realm of objectively reported fact, while the artist's domain was defined by various disciples of the "gospel of style" as the realm of the autonomous imagination. (See Edmund Wilson, *Axel's Castle: A Study in the Imaginative Literature of 1870–1930* [New York: Charles Scribner's Sons, 1931], for a discussion of the goals of artists including Gertrude Stein, T. S. Eliot, and others. See Walter Lippmann, *Liberty and the News* [New York: Harcourt, Brace and Howe, 1920], and *Public Opinion* [New York: Macmillan, 1922], for a prescription of the ideals Lippmann felt should animate journalism.)

7. For a discussion of how the lines between journalism and fiction blurred in the 1960s see John Hersey, "The Legend on the License," *Yale Review* 70, no. 1 (Autumn 1980): 1-25; Michael Schudson, "Objectivity, News Management, and the Critical Culture," in Schudson, *Discovering the News*, pp. 160-94; David Eason, "The New Journalism and the Image-World: Two Modes of Organizing Experience," *Critical Studies in Mass Communication* 1 (1984): 51-65; and articles and books cited below.

8. See Tom Wolfe and E. W. Johnson, eds., *The New Journalism* (New York: Harper and Row, 1973); Ronald Weber, ed., *The Reporter as Artist: A Look at the New Journalism Controversy* (New York: Hastings House, 1974); Everette Dennis and William L. Rivers, *Other Voices: The New Journalism in America* (San Francisco: Canfield Press, 1974); John Hollowell, *Fact and Fiction: The New Journalism and the Nonfiction Novel* (Chapel Hill: University of North Carolina Press, 1977); Michael Johnson, *The New Journalism* (Lawrence: University of Kansas Press, 1971); Ronald Weber, *The Literature of Fact* (Athens: Ohio University Press, 1980); John Hellman, *Fables of Fact* (Urbana: University of Illinois Press, 1981); David Eason, "Telling Stories and Making Sense," *Journal of Popular Culture* 15, no. 2 (Fall 1981): 125-29; David Eason, "New Journalism, Metaphor and Culture," *Journal of Popular Culture* 15, no. 4 (Spring 1982): 142-49; Lewis H. Lapham, "Gilding the News," *Harper's*, July 1981, pp. 31-39; and the bibliography in Mas'ud Zavarzadeh, *The Mythopoeic Reality: The Postwar American Nonfiction Novel* (Urbana: University of Illinois Press, 1976), pp. 229-58. E. L. Doctorow has noted that not only journalists but social scientists have been blurring the line between their disciplines and that of the novelist since the 1960s, adopting such "fictional modes of discourse for their presentation [as] group portraiture, [and] writing character, which is what novelists do" (comments at the Poynter Fellowship symposium on "Artist/Critic: The Relation Between the Artistic and Critical Communities," April 7, 1981, Berkeley College, Yale University). For further discussion of the adoption of techniques of fiction by social scientists, see Mas'ud Zavarzadeh's discussion of Oscar Lewis's *La Vida* in *The Mythopoeic Reality*, pp. 209-21. For a discussion of how contemporary literary critics are grappling with the problem of distinguishing the realms of fiction and nonfiction, see Jonathan Culler, "Problems in the Theory of Fiction," *Diacritics* 14, no. 1 (Spring 1984): 2-11.

9. The phrase "the sea bottom of the id" is John Hersey's (personal communication). E. L. Doctorow has referred to this phenomenon as "the personalist novel, the novel of private life, of psychological reportage." He has characterized the move by novelists to incorporate into their works subjects and techniques usually considered within the domain of nonfiction as "an attempt to break out of the increasingly narrow constriction of our reservation, attempting to break out of the personalist novel, the novel of private life, of internal psychological reportage, an attempt to resume our role as larger social artists, by, on our side of the fence, blurring those distinctions that have already been blurred by the pseudo-novelists who call themselves anthropologists, or sociologists, or journalists" (comments at the Poynter Fellowship symposium, April 7, 1981, Berkeley College, Yale University). For further discussion of this theme see "Truman Capote: An Interview" (conducted by George Plimpton), in Ronald Weber, ed., *The Reporter as Artist*, pp. 188-206.

10. Doctorow quoted in John Hersey, "The Legend on the License," *Yale Review* 70, no. 1 (Autumn 1980): 2. (Doctorow confirmed the accuracy of this comment attributed to him at the Poynter Fellowship symposium cited above.)

11. Norman Mailer, *The Armies of the Night* (New York: New American Library, 1968).

12. John Hersey, comment at Poynter Fellowship symposium at Yale, April 1981.

13. Norman Mailer, *The Executioner's Song* (New York: Little Brown, 1979), dust jacket. Mailer voiced his agreement with the publisher's dust-jacket blurb when he attended my seminar on November 9, 1982, at Yale.

14. Mailer, *The Executioner's Song*, p. 1053.

15. Hersey, "The Legend on the License," pp. 1-25.

16. Comments made by Mailer at seminar on "The Journalist as Novelist" taught by Shelley Fisher Fishkin, Yale University, November 9, 1982.

17. Hersey, "The Legend on the License," p. 2.

18. Mailer, at Fishkin seminar.

19. Janet Cooke, "Jimmy's World," *Washington Post*, September 28, 1980.

20. Bill Green, "Janet's World: The Story of a Child Who Never Existed—How and Why It Came to be Published" [The Ombudsman Report], *Washington Post*, April 19, 1981, and David A. Maraniss, "Post Reporter's Pulitzer Prize Is Withdrawn," *Washington Post*, April 16, 1981. See also *After "Jimmy's World": Tightening Up in Editing* (New York: National News Council, 1981).

21. Bill Green, "Janet's World."

22. Lewis Grossberger and Lucy Howard, "The Pulitzer Prize Hoax," *Newsweek*, April 27, 1981, p. 63.

23. James A. Michener, "James A. Michener on Integrity in Journalism," *U.S. News and World Report*, May 4, 1981, pp. 78-79.

24. Ellen Goodman, "Credibility Our Only Credential," *Washington Post*, April 19, 1981.

25. "A Newsweek Poll: How The News Media Rate," *Newsweek*, May 4, 1981, p. 51; and Rebecca Pratt and Robert George, "A Searching of Conscience," *Newsweek*, May 4, 1981, pp. 50-55.

26. John Hersey, "Joe Is Home Now," *Life*, July 3, 1944, pp. 66-80. The regular section in which the story appeared, "Close-Up," always profiled real people.

Hersey's acknowledged fictional composite thus took its place alongside profiles of Senator Byrd of Virginia, novelist John P. Marquand, impressario Sol Hurok, and others, which appeared that summer.

27. See Wolfe, *The New Journalism*, for examples of such articles. (One of the most famous composites of the sixties was a prostitute named "Red Pants" who was profiled by Gail Sheehy. It is interesting to note that Janet Cooke, too, wrote an intimate portrait of a young prostitute after she wrote her "Jimmy" piece, but before her fabrication was exposed. Her editors—a bit wary for reasons they couldn't quite explain—asked her to produce the girl. When she couldn't they killed the story.)

28. "The Pulitzer Lie" (Editorial), The New York *Times*, April 17, 1981.

29. Bill Green, "Janet's World."

30. Thomas Griffith ("Newswatch"), "Fact, Fiction and Fakery," *Time*, June 8, 1981, p. 53; Daniel Seligman ("Keeping Up"), "Front Page Fakery," *Fortune*, June 15, 1981, p. 63.

31. Christopher Jones, "In the Land of the Khmer Rouge," *New York Times Magazine*, December 20, 1981, pp. 70-80, 86-87 (subtitle, p. 70).

32. "Hoax Hunt: A Story Too Good to Be True" ("Press"), *Time*, March 1, 1982, pp. 88-89.

33. "Once Again, a Case of New Journalism?" ("News Media"), *Newsweek*, March 1, 1982, p. 78.

34. Joanne Lipman, "At the New Yorker, Editor and a Writer Differ on the 'Facts,'" *Wall Street Journal*, June 18, 1984, p. 1.

35. Martin Baron quoted in Mark Feeney, "New Yorker Responds to Accuracy Issue," *Boston Globe*, June 20, 1984, p. 44.

36. William Shawn quoted in Lipman, "At the New Yorker," p. 1.

37. Lipman, ibid., p. 1.

38. Alastair Reid, "Notes from a Spanish Village," *New Yorker*, February 22, 1982, quoted in Lipman, ibid., p. 1.

39. Alastair Reid, "Letter from Barcelona," *New Yorker*, December 2, 1961, quoted in Lipman, ibid., pp. 1, 18.

40. Lipman, ibid., p. 18.

41. Ibid. Interestingly, Dos Passos reached much the same conclusion in 1922 but opted for a different solution. He knew that the articles he was writing about Spain and publishing in such magazines as *The Seven Arts* and *Bookman* were missing some essential aspects of Spanish culture—something that couldn't be satisfactorily addressed by straightforward, objective accounts of recent events in Spain, by essays on Spanish literature and art, or even by *New Yorker*-style profiles of individual Spaniards. Dos Passos began writing fictional dialogues between two young men, "Telemachus" and "Lyaeus," each embodying a particular element of the Spanish character; they had affinities with Don Quixote and Sancho Panza, but also with Dos Passos and his young friends. Their conversations were lively, philosophical, and highly imaginative. Dos Passos published most of the dialogues separately; there was no question that they were fiction. Then Dos Passos realized that by putting together a montage of the different kinds of writing about Spain he had done—the nonfiction narratives, the profiles of people, the essays on culture, and the fictional dialogues—

one might have a fuller, richer perspective on Spain and Spanish culture than any of the articles or stories alone might yield. An interesting little book, in which fictional chapters alternated with journalistic ones, *Rosinante to the Road Again*, was the result of that insight. His exploration of Spanish culture in *Rosinante to the Road Again* would prove to be a rehearsal for his exploration of American culture in *U.S.A.* See John Dos Passos, *Rosinante to the Road Again* (New York: George H. Doran, 1922). See also pp. 172–74, above.

42. Lipman, "At the New Yorker," p. 18.

43. "The Fiction of Truth," *New York Times* (Editorial), June 20, 1984. And Maureen Dowd, "A Writer for The New Yorker Says He Created Composites in Reports," *New York Times*, June 19, 1984, p. 1.

44. "The Fiction of Truth," *New York Times*.

45. David Shaw quoted in *Newsweek*, May 4, 1981, p. 55. ("A Searching of Conscience," by Rebecca Pratt and Robert George.)

46. Two weeks after Joanne Lipman's article about Alastair Reid appeared in the *Wall Street Journal*, a memorandum was distributed to the *New Yorker* staff which stated that "one veteran writer" (it did not mention Reid by name) had "made a journalistic mistake." The memo said, "He was wrong. The editors of the *New Yorker* do not condone what he did." It also stated, unequivocally, "We do not permit composites. We do not rearrange events. We do not create conversations." It also condemned the practice of inventing characters (except in the "Talk of the Town" section of the magazine, which has traditionally invented fictitious "friends" and "correspondents" and where the practice is "well understood by our readers"). In the memo, sent by Peter F. Fleischmann, the chairman of the magazine, *New Yorker* editor William Shawn, stated, "The New Yorker has devoted itself for fifty-nine years not only to facts and literal accuracy but to truth. And truth begins, journalistically, with the facts." *New Yorker* staff memo quoted by Edwin McDowell, "New Yorker Editor Now Terms Journalistic Technique Wrong," *New York Times*, July 3, 1984.

47. The vicissitudes of what one might call "literary nonfiction" in America—a rich and varied body of book-length narratives including essays, histories, autobiographies, documentary narratives, etc.—is a subject worthy of several books in itself. Works like Hemingway's *Green Hills of Africa*, in which the author aspired, as he noted in his foreword, "to write an absolutely true book to see whether the shape of a country and the pattern of a month's action can, if truly presented, compete with a work of the imagination," occupy this middle ground between journalism and imaginative writing (Hemingway, *Green Hills of Africa* [New York: Charles Scribner's Sons, 1935], p. iii). Histories by Francis Parkman (*France and England in North America*), essays by James Baldwin (*Notes of a Native Son, The Fire Next Time*), and documentary narratives by John Hersey (*Hiroshima, The Algiers Motel Incident*), for example, would warrant attention as "literary nonfiction" in such a study. Autobiographical narratives that would deserve consideration include Thoreau's *Walden*, Twain's *Roughing It*, Henry Adams's *The Education of Henry Adams*, James Agee's *Let Us Now Praise Famous Men*, Zora Neale Hurston's *Dust Tracks on a Road*, Richard Wright's *Black Boy, The Autobiography of Malcolm X*, Mailer's *Armies of the Night*, John Edgar Wideman's *Brothers and Keepers*, recent per-

sonal histories by Lillian Hellman, Alfred Kazin, and Alice Koller, and journalism by writers such as John McPhee and Joan Didion. (See the anthology *The Literary Journalists*, edited by Norman Sims [New York: Ballantine, 1984], for excerpts from works of literary nonfiction published between 1973 and 1984.) Also relevant are works of anthropology like Oscar Lewis's *Children of Sanchez* and *La Vida*. This tremendously diverse list of books embraces widely divergent attitudes toward the subjects and methods of journalism and fiction. Some attempt to be as objectively accurate as possible; others address themselves directly to the impossibility of objectivity. Some represent scrupulously careful reporting; others include unabashed invention. It is beyond the scope of this book to examine these texts and the attitudes they embody. They are, however, close first cousins of the kinds of journalism and imaginative writing that we have considered here. For further discussion of some of these forms see criticism by David Eason, John Hersey, Lewis Lapham, Mas'ud Zavarzadeh, and Jonathan Culler cited above, as well as essays by Ronald Weber and Donald Pizer in Weber, *The Reporter as Artist*; William Stott, *Documentary Expression and Thirties America* (New York: Oxford University Press, 1973); and James E. Young, "Documentary Literature and the Rhetoric of Fact" (unpublished paper).

48. As William White notes in *By-Line* (pp. xi–xii), some striking examples are: "Italy, 1927," a factual account of a motor trip through Spezia, Genoa, and Fascist Italy, first published in the *New Republic* (May 18, 1927), as journalism, then used as a short story in *Men Without Women* (1927) with a new title, "Che Ti Dice La Patria," and in *The Fifth Column and the First Forty-Nine Stories* (1938); "Old Man at the Bridge," cabled as a news dispatch from Barcelona and published in *Ken* (May 19, 1938) and also put into *The First Forty-Nine Stories* without even a new title; and "The Chauffeurs of Madrid," originally sent on May 22, 1937, by the North American Newspaper Alliance (NANA) to subscribers of its foreign service as part of Hemingway's coverage of the Spanish Civil War, and which was included by Hemingway in *Men at War* (1942), which he edited and subtitled "The Best War Stories of all Time."

49. Walt Whitman, "Song of Myself," *Leaves of Grass* (1855 Edition) (New York: Penguin Books, 1976), p. 26.

INDEX

Aaron, Daniel, 246n.
Adams, Henry, 253n.
Adventures of Huckleberry Finn
(Twain), 5, 7, 61, 63, 66, 69, 184,
228n., 248n.; deflation of fictions
in, 79–80; discussed, 78–84; influ-
ence of journalism on, 58–59, 61,
65, 69, 70, 74; use of facts in, and
importance of accuracy in, 78–80,
229n., 230n.; view of racism and
slavery in, 71–72, 83
Advertising, 93–95, 169–71, 244n.,
248n.
"Against American Literature" (Dos
Passos), 170
Agee, James, 3, 253n.
Ainslee's, 89, 108, 233n.
Ainsworth, William Harrison, 79
Alger, Horatio: influence on Dreiser,
122; typical novel of, compared
with *An American Tragedy*, 122–25,
236n.
Allen, Gay Wilson, 221n., 222n., 224n.
"American Munificence and English
Pomp" (Whitman), 25, 223n.
"American Portraits" (Dos Passos),
244n.
"American Scholar, The" (Emerson),
224n.
American Tragedy, An (Dreiser), 7, 92,
98, 99, 100, 105, 107, 110, 209,
232n., 233n., 237n., 238n.; ambigu-
ity in, 129–34, 237n.; and the
American dream, 126; choice of case
for, 115, 234n.; departures of, from
Gillette case, 112–34; incorporation
of journalism into, 112–13; influence of consumerism on, 94; original

title of, 109, 233n.; reasons for merg-
ing Alger romance and daily news-
paper in, 124–26; role of fact in, 120–
21; similarities to Alger novel, 122–
25; similarities to Gillette case, 117–
22, 236n.
American Whig Review, 43
"American Workingmen, Versus Slav-
ery" (Whitman), 36, 224n.
"Andalusian Ethics" (Dos Passos),
245n.
"Antonio Machado: Poet of Castile"
(Dos Passos), 244n.
"Appeal for Aid, An" (Dos Passos),
243n.
Arabian Nights, 82, 83
Armies of the Night, The (Mailer),
208, 251n., 253n.
Arts, 167
Asia, 167
"As I Ebb'd with the Ocean of Life"
(Whitman), 22
Atlantic Monthly, 69, 72–73, 74,
89, 228n.
"At the End of the Ambulance Run"
(Hemingway), 239n.
"At the Sign of the Lead Pencil"
(Dreiser), 234n.

"Back to Red Hysteria" (Dos Passos),
168
"Backward Glance O'er Travel'd Roads,
A" (Whitman), 25, 223n., 224n.
Bagdikian, Ben H., 244n., 245n.
Baker, Carlos Heard, 147, 238n., 239n.,
240n., 242n.
"Baker of Almorox, The" (Dos Passos),
172

255